BLACK THEOLOGY TODAY
LIBERATION AND CONTEXTUALIZATION

JAMES DEOTIS ROBERTS

Toronto Studies in Theology
Volume 12

The Edwin Mellen Press
New York and Toronto

Library of Congress Cataloging in Publication Data

Roberts, J. Deotis (James Deotis), 1927-
    Black theology today.

    (Toronto studies in theology ; v. 12)
    Includes bibliographical references. 1. Black
theology.   I. Title.   II. Series.
BT82.7.R58   1983   230'.08996073   83-17246
ISBN 0-88946-755-2

Toronto Studies in Theology ISBN 0-88946-975-X

Copyright © 1983, James Deotis Roberts

All rights reserved. For more information contact:

    The Edwin Mellen Press
    P.O. Box 450
    Lewiston, New York 14092

            Printed in the United States of America

PREFACE

These several chapters represent a pattern of thought which has developed over several years. Many of these essays have been examined in the context of intense dialogue. As a collection, they represent how my thoughts on the subject of "black theology" have moved forward into the present. They reflect not only what has been the past of black theology; they also point to the challenge for the future.

Many persons have participated in the bringing forth of this manuscript. Professor Herbert Richardson encouraged me to initiate a series of my collected works, and urged me to submit these essays for publication. As editor of The Edwin Mellen Press, Dr. Richardson procured the services of Dr. Frank Flinn to edit this collection. Dr. Flinn has accomplished an unusual task. He has taken essays which were researched, written and delivered at sundry times and on different occasions and given them a meaningful order. Mrs. Marcia Moldowan completed this difficult task as the person at The Edwin Mellen Press assigned the final editing task. Mrs. Minnie J. Wright, my personal secretary, has participated in the typing related to the various editorial inquiries and responses. My sincere gratitude goes out to all these helpful associates.

Through many years, my wife, Elizabeth and my three daughters have allowed me the freedom associated with these writings. Their inspiration has made the task enjoyable and possible.

If you, the readers of this provisional volume of reflections on the manner in which the Christian Faith impacts upon the liberation and reconciliation of human life, are moved to a quest for social justice, my efforts will be duly rewarded.

J. Deotis Roberts
July 7, 1982

TABLE OF CONTENTS

PART I
HERMENEUTICS AND METHOD

1. The Hermeneutic Circle of Black Theology — 3
2. The Methodological Crisis in Black Theology: Major Jones, William Jones and James Cone — 34
3. Black Liberation Theism — 48
4. Black Theology in Faith and Ethics — 58

PART II
LIBERATION AND CONTEXTUALIZATION

5. Oppression and Liberation in World History — 71
6. The Roots of Black Theology: An Historic Perspective — 83
7. The Future is Now: Conservatism, Liberalism, and Liberation — 95
8. Contextual Theology: Liberation and Indigenization — 106
9. Christian Liberation Ethics: The Black Experience — 115

PART III
BLACK POLITICAL AND SOCIAL THEOLOGY

10. The Impact of the Black Church — 127
11. The Black Caucus and the Failure of Christian Theology — 140
12. A Black Theologian Looks at Black Power — 151
13. Civil Rights: The Unfinished Agenda — 162

PART IV
BLACK MINISTRY: SPIRITUALITY AND LIBERATION

14. The Priestly and Prophetic Dimensions of Black Spirituality — 179
15. The Black Church's Ministry to Families: Priestly Ministry — 188
16. The Black Church/Family and the Power Structure — 201

PART I

HERMENEUTICS AND METHOD

THE HERMENEUTIC CIRCLE OF BLACK THEOLOGY

The idea of "a hermeneutic circle" is well known in Western theology. Rudolph Bultmann made good use of this concept. The New Testament faith was filtered through the historical-critical method and existential philosophy. After "de-mythologizing" faith and subjecting it to the fundamental ontology of Heideggerian existentialism, Bultmann calls our attention back to the New Testament. Juan Luis Segundo, a South American liberation theologian, looks upon Bultmann's "hermeneutic circle" with suspicion. He, like other Latin American theologians, would filter the biblical faith through the experiences of the poor by means of a Marxist analysis.

Segundo appropriately refers to his work as *The Liberation of Theology*.[1] So much of the history of Christianity has been in favor of the rich and powerful. Theology itself has been the preoccupation of the privileged classes. Indeed, theology needs to be liberated from its "Constantinian captivity." While I view Segundo's re-constituted hermeneutic circle as a decided gain, I do not find it adequate either. His circle is not holistic -- it falters on the side of personal spirituality. In several ways it does not reach out to the entire human family. Segundo notes that black theologian James Cone, among several candidates (e.g. M. Weber, H. Cox, et al), completes the hermeneutic circle. But in my view, if Cone accepts the limits prescribed in Segundo's hermeneutic circle, he will not be true to the African roots of black theology. We will return to this matter later in our discussion.

Jack B. Rogers has shared some preliminary results of some research he did at the Institute for Ecumenical and Cultural Research, Collegeville, Minnesota.[2] Rogers is Professor of Philosophical Theology at Fuller Theological Seminary in Pasadena, California. An avowed Evangelical, he, nevertheless, did a very careful objective study of theological literature during the academic year 1977-1978. He desired to update the theme of the book, *What Present-Day Theologians Are Thinking*, by Daniel Day Williams.

Rogers was in search of theological trends and would like to somewhat forecast what theology will be about in the 80's. He quotes approvingly from David Tracy who indicates that theology develops according to a model suitable for the community being addressed. Rogers notes that from the 30's to the 50's, theologians addressed the churches. In the 60's they spoke to the culture. In the 70's they focus in on the classroom.

The writer points to the 80's and predicts five factors that will influence theology during that period. First, theology will be "participatory." It will represent collaboration of several co-workers. Second, it will be more concerned with decribing relationships, operations and processes, than defining concrete facts. Third, theology will be "public." There will be an acceptance of secularity. Thought forms of theology will be those known in the general community. Political and social concerns of the 60's will again be raised. Fourth, theology in the 80's will be "pluralistic." It will be contextualized in various cultures. The meaning of the gospel will be particularized. This would included dialogue between Christianity and other religions. And fifth, "philosophy" will help shape theology in the 80's. Theologians will try to see things as a whole. Metaphysics will be returning to theology. The neo-classical metaphysics of process theology is an example.

Rogers then takes up four models of contemporary theology which he views as representative of the present situation and pointing to the future. These are process theology, theology of liberation, theology of story and conservative evangelical theology. The program of John B. Cobb, Jr. represents the first model. Gustavo Guitierrez is cited for the second. Sallie TeSelle is mentioned in relation to the third. Carl Henry is representative of the fourth and final position. It is refreshing to note that Rogers does not push Wolfhart Pannenberg and Jürgen Moltmann to center stage and Hans Küng is not mentioned. I take this to be an oversight. His point speaks to the desirability of the contextualization of theology in the United States. Furthermore, he perceives theological leadership will now be taken from Europe and emerge in the Third World.

Rogers is on a "quest." He accepts the limitations of his own range of vision. He is mainly concerned with what white-straight-male theologians are about now and what they will be doing in the next decade. But why does he omit both black theology and feminist theology? Assuredly, these belong under the category of liberation theologies. But liberation theology, when unspecified, refers to Latin American liberation theology. On the other hand, black and feminist theologies have their orientation in the United States.

Black theology has an affinity with both Latin American liberation theology as well as the theology of story, but it is distinctive and sufficiently developed to be treated separately in any discussion on theology in this country. It has a future as long as racism continues. On the positive side, black theology is a contextualized theology which calls for a long future task. I cannot see how feminist theology could be omitted either since the battle in the churches and the larger society over sexism has just begun. Theologies arising out of racism and sexism will be around for a long time; there are too many unsolved problems on these issues.

Finally, if Rogers really believes that theology is going to find its initiative in the Third World, how could he overlook black theology? Black theology is the one vital link American theology has with Third World theologies. On the whole, Rogers seems to be open to the kinds of questions I have raised. This is the reason why he granted me the privilege of reviewing this preliminary paper. My reason for referring to his paper here is that I found it to be an excellent basis for generating my own reflections. I take this to be an important part of the author's intention.

I. ENTERING THE HERMENEUTIC CIRCLE

Juan Luis Segundo's "hermeneutic suspicion" provides a convenient context for our entry into the hermeneutic circle of black theology. We are able to use his concept as a receptacle but we intend to pour new content and meaning into it. Segundo takes up Karl Mannheim on the sociology of knowledge as a framework for his discussion. Mannheim says:

> An increasing number of concrete cases makes it evident that (a) every formulation of a problem is made possible only by a *previous actual human experience* which involves such a problem; (b) in selection from the multiplicity of data there is involved an *act of will* on the part of the knower; and (c) forces arising out of living experiences are significant in the direction on which the treatment of the problem follows.[3]

Most theologies, according to Segundo, take the past seriously, but they neglect the present as if

> the Word of God is applied to human realities inside some antiseptic laboratory that is totally immune to the ideological tendencies and struggles of the present day.[4]

Liberation theology starts, however from the present realities and looks backwards. Since the Christian religion is biblical, theology must, therefore, begin and end with the *Book*. Theology must keep going back to the *Book* and re-interpret it. He writes:

> . . . It is the continuing change in our interpretation of the Bible which is dictated by the continuing change in our present-day reality, both individual and societal . . . .The circular nature of this interpretation stems from the fact that each new reality obliges us to interpret the word of God afresh, to change reality accordingly, and then to go back and reinterpret the word of God again and again. [5]

Next we must consider the preconditions for completing the hermeneutic circle. First, there must be a precondition that the questions rising out of the present be rich enough to force us to change our customary conceptions of life, death, knowledge, society, politics and the world in general. Second, there must be a theological assumption that a response to new questions is possible and that scriptures are to be re-examined in light of this new situation.

Against this background Segundo outlines his methodological perspectives: First, there is our way of experiencing reality, which leads us to ideological suspicion. Secondly, there is the whole ideological superstructure in general and the theological structure in particular. Thirdly, there comes a new way of experiencing theological reality that leads us to exegetical suspicion, that is, to the suspicion that the prevailing interpretation of the Bible has not taken important pieces of the data into account. Fourthly, we have our new hermeneutic, that is, our way of interpreting the fountainhead of our faith (i.e. scripture) with the new elements at our disposal.

Segundo runs the thought of Harvey Cox, Karl Marx, Max Weber and James Cone through his hermeneutic circle. Only the thought of Cone completes the circle as he draws it. Segundo bases his discussion on James Cone's *A Black Theology of Liberation*. Cone's *God of the Oppressed* was probably not available to the author. But the latter work is a more mature study and it is based upon a serious encounter with works dealing with the sociology of knowledge.

Segundo summarizes Cone's view as follows: First, Cone's position begins in personal experience and in an act of will. Second, Cone targets racial oppression as the next stage of analysis. Here he finds a general theory which enables him to unmask the reality of oppression. The general theory is expressed in theological discourse. Third, Cone seizes upon sources and norms that determine the questions asked and the answers given. Black theology is rooted, according to Cone, in the experience, history and culture of black people. Not scripture, but black experience is the source of black theology. Jesus Christ is the norm, but even Christology is determined by the black community's experience of Jesus Christ. Fourth, Cone offers a new interpretation of scripture based upon new and decisive questions. Jesus Christ and God's revelation, are seen as participating in the struggle for liberation. According to Segundo, this is how Cone completes the hermeneutic circle.

Segundo's criticisms of Cone are severe. He does, however, take Cone's program to be a serious effort and indicates a profound appreciation for his contribution. Segundo's treatment is methodological and his purpose in using Cone's theology is an objectivist one. He merely wants to illustrate that it is possible to apply his proposed methodology to an existent program in theology. He desires to overcome a devastating criticism by Western theologians that liberation theology cannot withstand the methodological test.[6] The fact is, however, black theology poses a similar challenge. It is being challenged from the West and from the Third World, especially from Africa. Cone is caught in the crossfire. By both lifting up Cone's program and exposing its weakenesses, Segundo may unwittingly have done a disservice to Cone. It would have been better if he had selected the writings of some other Latin American liberation theologian to illustrate his point. They would have shared a common set of problems and a common mission.

In my judgment, Segundo's circle does not meet the needs of black theology. It does not meet the challenge of the African and Afro-American religious experience. It does not pass the holistic test of persons-in-community. It emphasizes the "political" dimensions of the life of faith, but it does not do justice to the "healing" aspects of faith. Its focus is upon biblical texts, but it does not allow for a rich oral tradition. Segundo's circle would place an undue restriction on the dialogue between African and black theologians. This dialogue has already reached into the Caribbean and will surely involve people of African descent in Latin America. Thus it turns out to be a disservice to Cone, a key representative black theologian, that he has been used to demonstrate a hermeneutic circle that is inadequate for a *Theologica Africana*.

II. THE PLACE OF THE BIBLE

A serious theological project requires careful biblical study. During my recent dialogue with political theologians in West Germany, I was deeply impressed by the important place held by scripture in systematic theology. For instance, Gerhard Von Rad and Ernst Käsemann were mentioned as mentors together with Karl Barth and Frederick Schleiermacher. History of doctrine or philosophical schools did not eclipse the place of the Bible. One might almost contrast this with the de-emphasis upon the Bible among most process theologians who have pushed the Bible to the background and shoved Whiteheadian metaphysics to the foreground. During the spring term of 1978 I served as Visiting Professor of Theology at the School of Theology at Claremont. I gleaned the distinct impression that among notable biblical scholars like James Sanders, Dieter Betz and James Robinson on the faculty, process thought clearly held the dominant place. On the other hand, there are instances where Bible study clearly overshadows systematic theology. Southern Baptist Theological Seminary at Louisville is a case in point. Without being judgmental, I wish only to suggest the need for balance and interaction between the Bible and systematic theology.

This seems to be a place where black theology has a special mission. The black experience of the Christian faith is centered in the Bible. African church theologians have also taken a fresh look at the Bible. As we study African traditional religions, we readily understand why black slaves embraced the Bible almost spontaneously.

Aylward Shorter writes about the "content" of African traditional religions.[7] I mention his brief summary here because it enlarges our understanding of the black slave's response to scripture. Shorter outlines five characteristics in African religious experience: (1) The vision of wholeness or integration of life -- "sacred" and "profane" are relative terms; (2) conscious symbolism through which Africans bridge the sacred and the secular speak of the sacred in secular terms, making an integrated and balanced view of reality possible; (3) affirmation of the "fecundity"of life which places a great value upon physical generation, upon life and the sharing of life, upon interpersonal relationships and the value of the human person; (4) an emphasis placed upon humans-in-community, as in the writings of Senghor, Nyerere and Kaunda, which include the nature of community, the freedom of the individual within community and the responsibilitly of the individual for community; and (5) the relationships between human and spiritual beings and between the living and the dead.

Shorter does not mention the concept of God. The belief in a Supreme Being, with similar attributes, is almost universal in black Africa. In spite of the writings of European and American scholars, African theologians do not hesitate to assert that the traditional understanding of God is similar to the God of the Bible. This is especially true of creation and providence as activities of the Supreme Being. The traditional African conception of God is also monotheistic. The lesser spirits are ministers of God in relation to humans. Ancestors are revered but are not worshipped. In many ways this God resembles most the God portrayed in the Old Testament. But since the biblical revelation is unitary, Christians view the Old Testament God as true to the revelation of God in Jesus Christ.

When African slaves were introduced to the Bible, they were able to derive meanings from it that were hidden to their oppressors. They understood God against the background of traditional beliefs in a Supreme God. They were aware of the power and moral integrity of God. Jehovah, as described in the Old Testament, was a close facsimile of the African Supreme Being they had known. Facing a situation of great hardship, the liberation of the Hebrews from Egyptian bondage caught their fancy. As the black oppressed facing daily the white oppressors, the Exodus took on a political as well as a religious meaning. Black slaves believed that something would happen in heaven *and* on earth, when they sang:

> Go down Moses, way down in
> Egypt's land,
> Tell O'le Pharoah
> Let my people go!

Because of their understanding of life as sacred, life as whole, life as community, black slaves were drawn to the Bible. But their understanding of the Bible differed from that of those who held them in bondage. A careful study of a version of the "Ham Myth" by Thomas Virgil Peterson, has made this clear to me.[8] It was not possible for slaves to be of a common mind with their oppressors due to the beliefs they had as well as the oppressed conditions under which they lived.

There are an increasing number of black scholars specializing in the Bible. But some of these are reluctant writers. Others refuse the challenge which black theology presents. The Bible, however, is so central to the black experience that a "blackenization" of biblical exegesis would be the most rewarding and important contribution that they could possibly make in a lifetime. When one rereads the Bible in the light of the black religious experience, one is confronted by truths from these sacred texts often missed by the most careful exegetical scholars in the West. Exegesis from below, seen in solidarity with the oppressed, yields insights overlooked by those who read the Bible from the perch of privilege.

The work being done by Christian Marxist scholars in Europe as well as in Latin America opens a new window but it is a one-sided view. The Bible is personal-spiritual as well as social-political. It is at once priestly and prophetic. To juxtapose one aspect of religious experience to the other is to miss the holistic character of biblical faith. José Miranda, a Latin American biblical exegete, helps us to understand the biblical grounding for social justice in *Marx and the Bible*.[9] But this Marxist entré into biblical exegesis is incomplete. While it contributes much to an interpretation of scripture which lays bare the gospel of liberation from economic, social and political injustices, it does not handle with equal facility the spiritual dimensions of personal existence.

A more balanced view of biblical interpretation seems to flow from the understanding of black preachers and scholars. One gets the feel for the holistic message of the Bible in the sermons of Martin Luther King, Jr., and the meditations of Howard Thurman. Joseph A. Johnson, a bishop and New Testament scholar carries on this tradition in his most recent work, *Proclamation Theology*.[10] Robert Bennett and Charles Copher are among Old Testament scholars who have begun serious study, relating their knowledge of Old Testament language and literature to an examination of sources in the light of the black religious experience. Both writers have considered Africa in the biblical period.[11] Bennett has done work with black theologians in view. His writings have been well researched, critical and informative. Carl H. Marbury and Thomas A. Hoyt, Jr., have done similar work as New testament specialists. Both Marbury and Hoyt have examined Martin Luther King's use of scripture in separate projects.[12] Marbury has looked at Haley's *Roots* with biblical interpretation in view while Hoyt has completed doctoral research on the poor in Luke-Acts.[13] The findings of these and other black scholars in the biblical field are invaluable supports for a viable black theology.

Among black theologians, James Cone has treated scriptural interpretation more completely than anyone else. But since his hermeneutical perspective is western, perhaps even Teutonic, he operates in a one-sided manner. No committed black churchman or scholar would wish to tone down his liberation motif. Our people have suffered and are suffering too much for that. But the oppression-liberation formula does not adequately unlock the biblical understanding which flows from the black Christian experience. Neither does it adequately inform black believers.

This discussion on the place of the Bible suggests that much hard work is yet to be done. It should be obvious that I see this as a team effort resulting from the cooperation between blacks in the biblical field and those in theology. Bultmann's "hermeneutic circle" is centered in personal existence. Segundo moves to the opposite extreme of collective existence. It seems to me that black religious experience has the possibility of bringing these extremes together. A return to the Bible is a resource to that end. The figure of a hermeneutical circle is useful provided the circle is sufficiently inclusive to treat the revelation of God to all humans.

III. THE SYMBOL OF BLACKNESS

No black theologian has yet treated the symbol of "blackness" with the depth of meaning that the Filipino scholar Eulalio P. Balthazar has brought to his discussion. Balthazar begins with the important assertion that when Christians begin to accept blackness as the unique symbol of the Christian life, then they will assume the vocation of peacemakers in the world. Without the acceptance of "positive darkness" there is self-alienation and the projection of this alienation on the world.[14]

The black-white color symbolism in white theology touches the very depth and meaning of the Christian life. Black or darkness represents all that is opposed to Christ. Darkness, blackness, night are used to express negative values. The light-darkness antithesis is used in a metaphysical sense to symbolize being and existence, on the one hand, and nonbeing or chaos on the other.[15] At the moral level, light is associated with what is morally good and darkness is associated with what is morally evil. Light is also associated with love, while darkness is associated with hate. Light is a sign of moral conversion or illumination, while darkness is a sign of reprobation.

It is Balthazar's contention that the economic dominance of the European over the black African is not a sufficient explanation for the origin of white racism. He argues, correctly, that the concept of black and white was well established before the birth of colonialism. He offers the interesting thesis that the transference of symbolism to skin color was due to a metaphysical shift up through the medieval age, when theology and philosophy were dominated by Plato and Aristotle. In Plato, man was his soul. The body was a prison. Aristotle modified this somewhat. The body was, for Aristotle, a consubstantial principle. The theological anthropology of the medieval age was metaphysical. Plato influenced Augustine and Aristotle influenced Aquinas. Man was primarily soul, a spiritual being. Preachers spoke of the salvation of the soul. The soul was the form of the body, superior to the body, its essence or meaning. Balthazar concludes, therefore, that transference to skin color could not have been possible without also a metaphysical shift.

According to Balthazar the change began when nominalism emerged under William of Occam. But it was Descartes who, divorcing philosophy from its ancillary status to theology, gave the final impetus for change in philosophy in the direction of empiricism. Empiricism reached its full expression in Locke, Hume and Berkeley. Now phenomena, images and sense impressions became the objects of knowledge, rather than substances, universals and essences. Kant, influenced by Hume, accepted the view that all that the human mind can know are phenomena. When Hume asserts that man is a bundle of perceptions, we are close to the notion that man is his appearance or he is as he appears. This new philosophical perspective, according to Balthazar facilitated the transference of the color symbolism from the soul to the body.[16]

Balthazar relates this empirical outlook in philosophy and its influence on theology to the dominance of Europeans over Africans in the economic field. There is a relationship of reinforcement:

> . . . The economic superiority and dominance of Europeans confirmed their belief in the negative theological values attached to peoples with dark skins. The color symbolism which was previously applied to the condition of man's soul now came to be applied to man's skin and this latter symbolism was reinforced by the economic difference between whites and blacks.[17]

This metaphysical shift was the precondition of the theology which entered history after English voyagers touched upon the shores of Africa in 1550. Color symbolism was first made to justify economic domination and then slavery.[18]

Consistent with this new focus on skin color, Jesus Christ was bleached. He was transformed from a Semite to an Aryan person as Western painting demonstrates. The Jewish body of Jesus was no longer white enough. His hair was painted light and his dark eyes became blue. Balthazar refers to this as the "aryanization of Christ." He writes:

> The bleaching process in which Christ's hair and beard assumed the color of sunshine, symbolizing the brightness of the light above, and his eyes the color of the sky from which he descended and to which he returned, marked the entire history of Western painting.[19]

The logical result of the theological endorsement of this color symbolism was the establishment of segregation. Segregation was legally established in public places, in churches, in eating places, in trains and streetcars, in theaters, and in schools. It is a fact that churches, seminaries and church-related private schools are even now the most segregated institutions in this country. Balthazar argues that this is due largely to the fact that sin was viewed as a stain which was embodied in black persons. Any close association with black persons, therefore, would contaminate the white person. He reasons that over above any historical and economic factors, the causes of segregation are to be found in religious ideas of white being a symbol of purity and black a symbol of sin.

Thus Balthazar has presented a convincing argument to substantiate his claims that theology has contributed to racism in the West through its use of color symbolism. The antidote to this is to provide a positive symbol of blackness in theological terms. To pursue his constructive contribution would go beyond our purpose here. In a few words, he asserts that Western Apollonian theology has majored in reason. On the other hand, mystical theology or the Dionysian tradition portrays God as sumpremely positive as the Divine Darkness. This darkness is not the absence of light -- it is the excess of light. This also symbolizes a transcendent "Unknowing" -- a super knowledge not obtained by means of the discursive reason. Balthazar also insists that the Bible portrays blackness as a positive symbol of divine goodness which he calls the "Dark Center."[20]

This work should be studied carefully for it deals with the issues which cause a negative self-image on the part of blacks and an inflated self-image on the part of whites. This one-sided color consciousness must be eliminated. Balthazar's position is balanced -- he does not advocate a symbolism which would lead to racism in reverse. Western theology, he insists, has proclaimed light, clarity, rationalism and conceptualization. He would construct a theology of process, imagination, mystery, mythology and darkness. He writes:

> Darkness is the source of life and energy at all levels of being. As the source of green life is dark soil and as the source of light energy is the dark center of the sun, so the source of life for theology is the darkness of the mystery and myth and the source of the life of grace for the Christian is the saving darkness of faith which hides the Divine darkness.[21]

I applaud Balthazar's use of symbolic and intuitive ways of thinking. This can be useful in developing a constructive program in black theology. His distinctive contribution, however, is the manner in which he explains the transference of metaphysical symbolism to skin color and the racist effects this has had upon Christian thought and life. I am able to accept his corrective in part. But I wonder if his approach isn't too metaphysical. My suspicion is increased when he turns to process theology for a framework. This is a theology from "above." Black theology, as all liberation theologies, must seek to be a theology from "below." Feminist theology may be an exception. It, too, will not represent the cause of poor, black, minority women, unless it also becomes a theology from "below." Balthazar's position has profound metaphysical significance. My concern is that this be translated into a political perspective for social transformation.

IV. BLACK HERMENEUTICS DEFINED

Aristotle defined *hermeneia* as the operation of the mind in making statements which have to do with the truth or falsity of a thing. The intellect perceives meaning as a statement. Interpretations are, therefore, statements of that which is true or false. In his treatise *Peri hermeneias,* Aristotle defines them as "speech in which there is truth and falsity" (17 a 2).

Interpretation (enunciation) is not to be confused with logic, for logic proceeds from comparing enunciated statements. Enunciation deals only with the constructive and divisive operation of making statements in which there is truth or falsity. Enunciation is more fundamental than logic, rhetoric, or poetics; it is the enunciation of the truth or falsity of a thing or statement: The *telos* of the process is not to move emotions (poetics) or to bring about political action (rhetoric) but to bring understanding to statements. For Aristotle, then, interpretation precedes logical analysis, scientific analysis or literary criticism. It belongs to the higher and purer operations of the mind. Interpretation, in this sense, has to do with the way one turns to an object in speech. Analysis is a form of interpretation, but a derivative form. The tools of analysis will be determined by the manner one perceives an object.[22]

Only within a certain context is an event meaningful. An object does not have significance outside of a relationship of someone, and that relationship determines the significance. Explanatory interpretation makes us aware that explanation is contextual or "horizontal." It must be made within a horizon of already granted meanings or intentions. In hermeneutics, this area of assumed understanding is called pre-understanding. One must pre-understand a situation before one can enter the horizon of meaning. Without this pre-understanding, one cannot step into the "hermeneutical circle."

The modern development of hermeneutics is associated with the names of Schleiermacher, Dilthey, Heidegger, Ricouer, and Gadamer. The oldest and probably still the most widespread understanding of the word "hermeneutics" refers to the principles of biblical interpretation. The word came to modern use in relation to the proper exegesis of scripture. It occurs in the title of a book by J.C. Dannhauer in 1654. But even here it is distinguished from exegesis as actual commentary. It referred to the rules, methods or other fields and dates back to ancient times.

Schleiermacher reconceived hermeneutics as a "science" or "art" of understanding. He cuts hermeneutics loose from its dependency upon philology. He points beyond the concept of hermeneutics as an aggregate of rules and makes hermeneutics systematically coherent -- a science which describes the conditions of understanding in all dialogue. The result is a "general hermeneutics" (*allegemeine Hermeneutik*) whose principles can serve as the foundation for all kinds of text interpretation.

Wilhelm Dilthey was inspired by Schleiermacher and was in his own right one of the most outstanding philosophical thinkers of the late nineteenth century. Dilthey saw in hermeneutics the core discipline which could serve as the foundation for all *Geistes-Wissenschaften* -- all disciplines focused on understanding man's actions, art and writings. He emphasizes hermeneutics as an act of historical understanding. It calls into play a personal knowledge of what being human means. He called for a critique of the human sciences similar to Kant's critique of pure reason.

In approaching the ontological problem, Martin Heidegger turned to the phenomenological method of Edmund Husserl, his mentor. Heidegger undertook a phenomenological study of man's every day being in the world. He undertook to study the "hermeneutic of *Dasein*."[23] In order to proceed we need to digress and understand what Husserl meant by "phenomena." He attempts an analysis of consciousness. It is not psychological analysis because it aims essentially at answering the epistemological problem of the absolute foundation of the logic of science. Phenomenological analysis resembles the mathematical mind more than that of the logician. The mathematician manipulates ideal values or essences without having to inquire whether or not they correspond to a factual reality. Phenomenology silences experience provisionally (the *époche*), leaves the question of objective reality aside in order to turn its attention soley and simply on "the reality in consciousness" -- on what Husserl calls, "ideal essences." A phenomenon is that which manifests itself immediately in consciousness; it is grasped in an intuition that precedes any reflection or any judgment. It has only to be allowed to show itself, to manifest itself; the phenomenon is that which gives itself (*Selbstgebung*). The aim was to lay a foundation for the entire enterprise of philosophical reason.[24]

Heidegger's analysis indicated that hermeneutics are foundational modes of man's being. His writing developed the field and the meaning of the word hermeneutics. Hermeneutics is connected with the ontological dimensions of understanding and at the same time is related to Heidegger's special kind of phenomenology.

The Heideggerian tradition of hermeneutics is carried on by Hans-Georg Godamer, who in *Wahrheit und Methode* provides a history of hermeneutical development in Schleiermacher, Dilthey and Heidegger. Gadamer does more than provide this history; he relates it to aesthetics and to the philosophy of historical understanding. Gadamer goes further and introduces a "linguistic phase" in which he asserts that hermeneutics is "an encounter with Being through language." He goes on to assert the linguistic character of human reality itself and raises the philosophical questions of relation of language to being. Hermeneutics has now to deal with epistemological and ontological questions at the same time.[25]

Paul Ricoeur, in *De L'interpretation* (1965) adopts a meaning of hermeneutics which focuses upon textual exegesis as the distinctive and centrally defining element in hermeneutics. But "text" is not limited to documents. The psychoanalytic interpretation of dreams is for him a form of hermeneutics. The dream is the "text" filled with symbolic *meaning* images. It is the responsibility of the psychoanalyst to bring to the surface the hidden meaning of a dream. Hermeneutics is the process of deciphering from manifest content and meaning the latent or hidden meaning. The purpose of interpretation (of texts in the broad sense) may be the symbols of society or literature. Hermeneutics is the system by which the deeper signficance is revealed beneath the manifest content. Ricoeur seeks a philosophy that takes up the hermeneutical challenge in myths and symbols and breaks through to the reality behind language, symbol and myth.[26]

It is at this juncture of our discussion on hermeneutics that we can begin to make some direct contact with the symbol of "blackness." Charles H. Long, a black historian of religion, sees in what he calls "opaqueness" of this symbol "that unity that gives catholicity to the situation of Africans and their progeny all over the world."[27] Long juxtaposes "opaqueness" to Tillich's notion of "transparency." Tillich speaks out of Western enlightenment. The possession of power is a given. The colonized peoples, on the other hand, were stripped of their capacities to be foci of finite historical power. Long speaks of "the relegation of the non-enlightened peoples to the obscurity of reality "as that which defined them in western perspectives as the bearers of stain, pollution, and guilt." Colonized peoples have fought these stereotypes -- they have attempted to prove that they were enlightened as their oppressors. But in spite of their efforts, fundamental transformations are not forthcoming.

We must, according to Long, take a radical hermeneutical stance. We as blacks must decipher the "otherness" of our experience over the last three hundred years. We must move from a religion of black folks to an understanding of the primary symbol of opacity, of blackness. By understanding our discontinuity with the West we blacks will discover the meaning of our past, present and future. Blacks in America as well as

Hermeneutics and Method 17

all colonized peoples bear a double consciousness. Blackness is a source of otherness unknown by the colonizers. We have lived on both sides of this consciousness. The world now is to explore the other side of our being. Long celebrates this otherness, the discovery of the symbol of blackness, as "a strength and beauty we can affirm" -- "a form of holiness." "This confrontation," Long writes,[28]

> will be awesome and ecstatic. The significance of this confrontation should force us into the deeper historical and present experiences of opacity. It is ultimately from these black depths . . . that we may affirm a new humanity and a new orientation in this world.[29]

Long describes the opacity of blackness in its historical setting. We experience it as a new beginning, but we must also come to terms with our past. We must have a right relationship with our ancestors. Our present and future depends upon our past. Ricoeur, according to Long, points to a primary symbol. But because of Ricoeur's dependency upon biblical and Greek myths together with his Western outlook, he considers the initial response to the opacity of a primary symbol as sin and guilt. Long wonders why Ricoeur did not bypass the myth of the fall with its guilt, stain and sin and analyze the cosmogenic myth, the myth of creation. For Long, the hierophany of blackness expresses a critique of civilization in the Western sense. Ricoeur expresses a will to power. Long, on the other hand, urges a response to a reality which is prior to man's doing and action.[30] Ricoeur's program is one of recovery, not one of undergoing the opacity of the creative symbol.

The black community, Long concludes, has its own task -- an intellectual and cultural work:

> We must return and redirect a great deal of our time and energy to those strange, profound, comical and sober deposits of our past, not so that we might in any literal manner imitate them again, but to understand how they signify, how their very vagueness calls for interpretation. We must try to understand the intentionalities of the old preacher and his sermon, the minstrel, Simple, that great character of Langston Hughes; we must undertake to understand, decipher, criticize and place within a primodial context these our ancestors, for they were *already* human . . . they must be vindicated or we shall never be free . . . .[31]

Long reminds us that it is consistent with Ricoeur's understanding that symbol, the originative source of all human meaning and expression is not transparent but opaque. One cannot see through it; one could almost say that the symbol is black. We have seen, however, that Long differs from Ricoeur in the content to be poured into symbol as receptacle. Long wants to say that the symbol of our existence is not invisible, it is opaque, black.[32]

V. A MYTHO-POETIC AND POLITICAL HERMENEUTIC

A. A Theological Response to *Roots*

We will carry our discussion forward by looking now at two statements by Professor Carl Marbury.[33] As a specialist on the New Testament, Marbury is working at a reflection on this material from the perspective of the black religious experience. He has been greatly influenced by Amos Wilder and his writings on "theopoetics." But Marbury is doing excellent creative work in his own right. Marbury recalls that the publication of Haley's *Roots* was a great achievement in black self-understanding, as persons and as a people. Haley drew upon oral historics, both Afro-American and African. His work with old records and other research rewarded him with a discovery of his ancestral roots in the African village of Juffure in Gambia. Haley reconstructed the early life of Kunta Kinte, his abduction and the succeeding generations in the United States. Marbury observes:

> With the publication of his historical novel, Alex Haley has given black people for the *first* time a history and *transformed reality* that we thought never could be known. . . . There are certain ontological dimensions to his search, which makes it possible now to delineate more precisely a new hermeneutic and theological underpinning, which are grounded in a more *humanistic* and less idealogical *Weltanschauung*.[34]

A new sense of community and continuity has now dawned upon black Americans so that each generation does not have to grow up alone. Formerly our past had been erased from memory -- denied us. A black man had in fact become an incomplete white man. Other ethnic groups have their unique history, tradition and mythology -- a mythological mainstream. The black person was not a full citizen, had no recognized tradition and nowhere else to go either. Was James Baldwin correct when he referred to himself as a "bastard of the West?"[35] Haley, in *Roots* has made it possible, according to Marbury, for blacks to be authentic as a people -- to find their identity in a real historical tradition which is not part and parcel of the dominant culture in the West.

It is a mythic component of Haley's story which has deep implications for theology. Marbury is correct when he asserts that black theology has thus far been tied to the ideological and apologetic traditions of Western theology. Haley's epic

> places the black search and struggle within a mythological and typological stream of consciousness -- it is universal, but Judeo-Christian and/or biblical as well.[36]

Marbury points up the importance of myth in all cultures. Reference is made to the Hebrew myth of the trials of Job and the Greek myth of Prometheus. Mythology is said to express a people's attitude toward life, death and the universe. Thus the two myths, the Hebrew and the Greek, reveal the philosophies of two divergent cultures:

> The Greek stresses man's heroic striving for human values and societal order: The Hebrew emphasizes, rather, man's humble spiritual surrender to God's will. Abraham's willingness to sacrifice Isaac is the supreme symbol of this attitude in the Old Testament. The death of Christ is the symbol *par excellence* in the New Testament.[37]

We are told that both the telling and the response to the telling of a myth has great psychological importance. In a real sense *Roots* is the proper undergirding for an authentic black theology which is grounded in an *ethos* that is philosophical, psychological and historical:

> We might even say ontological because the missing element has been the black's disjunction from his cultural ground of being as epitomized by the destruction of the *mythic consciousness*, which gives human groupings" a sense of "belongingness."[38]

We now see the crucial importance Marbury assigns mythical thought in developing biblical hermeneutics. People understand themselves and their place in the world through myth. Myths operate on both the conscious and unconscious levels. They involve the interrelationship between myth and history. Haley's *Roots* represents a tangible, an integral and an intellectual opportunity for us to reexamine once again the mythology in the Bible as a basis for a black theology. Marbury concludes:

> A serious attempt at developing black theologies will of necessity place special use on myths, folklore, folk music, oral traditions, literature, cultural

linguistics with the African languages tradition, social anthropology, African religions, the family structures and value systems.[39]

Blacks have needs for roots as all humans do. The reality of having roots provides a sense of drawing power from some depth which enables the oppressed "to sail against the winds." The discovery of our past prepares us to face the future with courage. The value of Marbury's discussion on *Roots* for black theology is priceless. He has provided an entré into constructive biblical and theological interpretation.

B. The Biblical and Theological Rhetoric of M.L. King, Jr.

Beyond his work on *Roots*, Marbury examines the use which King made of the Bible, especially in his sermons. This discussion leads us forward in our quest for a black hermeneutic. Marbury launches his discussion with Krister Stendahl's reference to the preacher as a "bi-lingual translator." Thinking in two languages refers more to modes and patterns of thought than it does to Greek and Hebrew. He notes that King used another "bi-construct." He spoke "bi-ethically" in terms of white Christian and black Christian. His ministry was based, in the southern "Bible belt." King desired to prick the conscience of white racists so as to redeem and save them as well as to encourage black Christians to struggle for their freedom.[40]

According to Marbury, King was biblical interpreter -- his rhetorical style fits into the pattern of early Christian rhetoric. King knew biblical criticism well, but these methods were seldom useful for his intention. King did not let these get in the way of authentic preaching. His concern was the Word of God for black people in their *Sitz im Leben*. Marbury suggests that the scholarly method is often

> . . . inconsistent as it relates to the descriptive approach to the Scriptures which enables the church, its teaching and preaching ministry, to be exposed to the Bible in its original intention and intensity as an ever new challenge to thought, faith, and response.[41]

King's guiding concept, according to Marbury, was that scripture should be interpreted in such a way that the past becomes alive and illumines our present with new possibilities for personal and social transformation. One should not become preoccupied with past meanings. Obsession with technique, with the historical critical method may reduce the text to dead letters. The interpreter is the medium and the message for the contemporary era.

Marbury turns to Amos Wilder as one who brings a corrective to biblical study, especially New Testament scholarship. New Testament scholarship has made major advances in *form criticism* -- the identification of various literary and pre-literary or oral elements in these writings with their special features of style and language patterns. King, Marbury observes, combines these insights with contemporary literary criticism and new explorations in language and hermeneutics. There is the need to add to this literary study the textual and philosophical detail necessary -- the reconstruction of the background and all other disciplines which may prove useful. The purpose would be to understand scriptures and how they developed. Central to all these efforts is the desire to make Jesus become our contemporary. The writers of the New Testament bore witness to events which *led them to faith*.

Marbury argues that blacks are closer to the consciousness of the *Weltanschauung* of the scriptures than most people realize. *Oral tradition* is prior to written tradition in both cases. The scriptures constitute an historical and spiritual deposit of reality passed down through various literary forms, e.g. myths, parables, stories, poetry, proverbs, prophecies, oracles, and picturesque speech. Blacks and Africans had a long oral tradition. Slavery prolonged this oral tradition in that blacks were forbidden to read or write. Many blacks, especially preachers, received their education from reading the Bible. Dr. King inherited this tradition. Marbury asserts that there is no disjunction between this oral tradition, its picturesque speech forms, language constructs, myths, moral concerns, its folklore and that of the early church.

One line of tradition of literary criticism, which has influenced New Testament studies, traces to Aristotle's *Rhetoric* rather than to his *Poetics*. This tradition treats form as a vehicle for content which can stand in its own right, apart from form. Form, in this instance, becomes a means for effectively communicating the content. Persuasion was the aim of ancient rhetoric including the New Testament and its interpreters. This type of analysis fits the early Christian tradition and it carries over into the black Christian tradition."[2] Marbury writes:

> . . . The form and modes of the early Christian rhetoric is that of Afro-American preaching tradition. The form and the modes are inseparable from the substance of the Gospel in both cultural traditions. It is quite evident that *how* Jesus and his followers spoke and wrote could not be separated from what they communicated. New fruits of the lips, new tongues and new speech, and new rhetorical patterns emerged out of the natural human situation of the early Christian community."[3]

The gospel was creative in all that has to do with image, symbol and myth. The New Testament faith led to a liberation of speech. The prominence of story, parable and vision in the New Testament point to the dramatic character of the early Christian witness. Thus Marbury sums up Amos Wilder's observations on this matter.

We are told that the New Testament was written and handed down to us by imaginative persons who employed the world pictures and salvation pictures of their own time. It was a case of the *Word of God* speaking with the words of persons and with the everyday language of persons. These were image words. The gospel went forth clothed with familiar imagery and myth indispensable for evoking the cosmic and cultural significance of the claims put forward.⁴⁴

As a result of this excellent contribution of Marbury to black theology as a biblical scholar, I make two crucial observations. One is that the biblical message is to be made relevant to our present situation. The second is that it conveys a socio-political as well as a spiritual message. Discussions by other black biblical scholars sound the same note. An example would be Robert Bennett's comments:

> The black theologian will also be touched by biblical theology because his special constituency, the black church has a unique relationship to holy scripture. Like the biblical community, this community of faith met its lord in a very long moment of crisis. A very special link was forged during bondage between the God and scripture and the African slave bereft of every form of identity -- homeland, language, religion, kinship. His new life became marked by hope and a profound trust that the God of his enslaver would bring deliverance. The Bible for the slave ancestors was both holy book and primer. . . The new religion was a way both to salvation and a new socio-political existence.⁴⁵

Bennett's observation concerning the relationship between biblical and black theology is basically sound. He notes that biblical theologians and black theologians have parallel tasks -- one moving from the past to the present meaning of scripture and the other moving between that word and the realities of the modern situation. In other words black cultural awareness and perceptions pose vital questions to scripture and at the same time bring new insights in this encounter. In the use of language, knowledge of biblical history and texts and methods of exegesis, biblical experts help black theologians forge the necessary hermeneutic circle to unlock the meaning of the black religious experience.

VI. DOES BLACK THEOLOGY NEED A METAPHYSIC?

There are those who would answer this question in the negative. If I read him correctly, this is James Cone's conclusion. On the other hand, there are those who would seek a metaphysical foundation for black theology. William Jones represents this latter quest. Neither position appears tenable. Cone's argument rests upon his reasoning that white theology depends upon the culture of the oppressor while black theology is concerned with God's revelation to the oppressed.[46] But in our pluralistic context there is no way to be a purist as far as our cultural mix is concerned. Cone himself is greatly influenced by teutonic thought and has spent his career in a white theological setting. William Jones does not take the Christian revelation seriously and therefore he is not in a position to provide a methodological norm for black apologetics. Jones is more affirmative toward the humanistic existentialists than he is toward the black experience of the Christian revelation.[47] I do not gainsay the profound contribution of these two coworkers, but I would contend that their guidance is not helpful on the metaphysical question of black theology.

Roman Catholic African and Afro-American theologians are forced to take this question with great seriousness.[48] A look at African theological writers in Francophone Africa will confirm this. But their efforts to find a philosophical basis for theology similar to Aristotelian philosophy or Thomism has not been crowned with success.[49] The Africanization of Christian theology will not be done by those who impose an alien metaphysic upon African traditional beliefs and culture. Not only is this effort fruitless; it is deceptive. It is incapable of appropriating the unique manner of *thinking* and *believing* in the African setting. On the other hand, the Roman Catholic tradition is more tolerant of the varieties of cultural expressions than most Protestant communions. Its rich liturgical and sacramental emphasis allows for greater contextualization in worship than the churches of the Reformation do. Africanization in worship means little, however, when Africans and Afro-Americans face colonialism and/or racism in the larger society and even in the Body of Christ. The acceptance of African music and dance in liturgy does not necessarily "decolonize the mind." Black Catholics, for instance, have made great strides in developing "a black rite," but they have little power in a powerful church. The number of blacks who have been developed as theologians and bishops should be an embarrassment to the Roman Catholic Church in general and the American hierarchy in particular.

The suspicion that a colonial mentality and racist overtones still linger in the Roman Catholic Church is confirmed by an attack on American black theology by Father Gianpattisa Mondin in Rome. Mondin, Dean of the Philosophy Department of Rome's Pontifical Urban University, made the attack in *L'Osservatore Romano.* This same account was most affirmative of African theology. Apparently Mondin's knowledge of African theology is limited to those African theologians who are mainly imitators of theological initiatives in the West. Other African theologians are in substantial agreement with black theologians on cultural and political matters and would be highly insulted by Mondin's praise. This article has been rejected outright by leaders among black Catholics.[50]

Black theologians must have a cultural and political hermeneutic. Roman Catholics provide a concern for metaphysics and some freedom of cultural expression, but they do not provide the "political" component necessary for a viable black theology. They are part of a superchurch which is pro-Western. I will illustrate this by reference to the writings of the black theologian priest, Edward K. Braxton. He has made an attempt to outline a black Catholic theology.[51] His preoccupation is with the "classic" expression of theology: foundational theology, systematic theology and pastoral theology -- basic Roman Catholic classifications. According to Braxton's reading of the situation, black theology would fall mainly in the latter category, pastoral theology. This is exactly the basis of a controversy I have had with some of my Roman Catholic peers who wanted to list black theology as well as liberation theology as pastoral theology. My contention is that black theology and liberation theology are forms of systematic theology. Braxton enlists, however, Cone's tirade against western classical theology as bearing out his conclusions. The fact that Cone has been affirmed by German theologians more than any other black theologian indicates that Cone may have deceived Braxton. At any rate, Cone is not a proper guide on this point and he is not the sole spokesperson for black theology. Cone's position in print gives a shaky basis upon which to discern the philosophical basis of black theology.

Braxton's goal, nevertheless, is to establish black theology in the Catholic tradition as a "new classic" -- both particular and universal. This obsession leads him to make certain judgments about black theology which are different, if not unique among black theological observers. He exalts the work of William R. Jones above all other black theologians as being the most profound. Jones' philosophical bent appeals to Braxton. He is not concerned about the absence of a confessional component in Jones. Braxton does not ask if Jones has considered the black folk religious tradition or whether Jones has concerned himself adequately with the manner in which blacks have experienced the Christian faith. Braxton writes:

> William Jones' book is clear evidence that James Cone is overstating his case when he proposes that

speculative and philosophical issues are meaningless to *all* interpreters of "the Black experience."[52]

It is unfortunate that Braxton, with all the credentials to be a powerful theological spokesman for black Catholics is so obsessed with justifying black theology by Western classical standards to the neglect of cultural and political issues. His use of one of Cone's weakest points, even from the viewpoint of other black theologians, plays in the hands of those who would undermine the power of the movement. Braxton does not seem to share the cultural interests of many black Catholics as represented by the National Office for Black Catholics with whom I have been long associated.[53] It is not surprising that many black Catholics have more in common with the Protestant black theology movements which has been informed by the black consciousness/power movement. Braxton's search for a metaphysic for black theology may turn out to be a vital intellectual contribution. But the neglect of cultural and socio-political matters of black liberation is too great a price to pay for that. Only if there is a possibility for metaphysics to touch upon these more important matters is it worth the effort for the black theologian. In my judgment, serious and profound intellectual reflection does not need to overlook a confession of faith or the cultural and ethical questions of black existence.

Profound critical thought is essential to black theology. We must forge creative language and thought forms to capture the riches of the African/Afro-American religious and cultural tradition. This will be brought into contact with biblical faith and the history of doctrine. But it will be *transforming* as well as *transformed* by that encounter. Any purely metaphysical thought will not stand alone. There must be a wedding of thought and life. To this end disciplines other than pure philosophy may be the proper instruments for theological interpretation. We cannot ignore the classic tradition and neither may we depend upon it. The black theologian is called to a creative and constructive task in this and in all other matters of theological reflection.

VII. TOWARD A BLACK HERMENEUTIC

This discussion has taken us into many byways. We have looked at Segundo's critique of Western theology and his revision of liberation hermeneutics. We have used Rogers' forecast of theological trends to chart our future course. The entrance to the hermeneutic circle, once again, has been provided by Segundo, who takes Cone into his own perception of an adequate hermeneutic circle for liberation theology. We found Segundo's circle too small for a *theologia Africana* and continued our quest. We then tried to find the place for the Bible in black theology, noting the close relationship of the Bible to the black experience of the Christian faith in America. The symbol of blackness was then brought into our discussion. Balthazar's treatment of black-white symbolism in the history of western thought led us to a positive understanding of blackness.⁵ "After affirming blackness as an appropriate theological symbol, we sought a definition of hermeneutics in the black religious tradition. After looking at several interpretations of hermeneutics from Aristotle to Ricoeur, we explored the reflections of Charles Long and found his perspectives useful. This was followed by a look at what black biblical scholars have contributed to a mytho-poetic and political hermeneutic for black theology. And, finally, we raised the question: Does black theology need a metaphysic? My answer to this is affirmative if it contains cultural and political components related to black liberation. This last section will be a constructive section. It, too, is exploratory rather than conclusive.

Black theologians have been frequently criticized for relying upon Western intellectual tools. I make no apology for this for many reasons: (1) Some three-quarters of my life was spent in the study of Euro-American scholarship in a pluralistic context. History of religions led me to non-Western religions and this opened up knowledge and experience in the East. Racism dictated the rules of the game, however. Africa was virtually ignored even in non-Western study and travel. (2) Since we live in the West, we must keep abreast with all that goes on in our chosen field. Therefore, the examination of black sources is a *plus* and not a *minus*. (3) One does not become an "instant expert" in mid-career. Getting thoroughly acquainted with African black materials could consume a lifetime. One must function as a theologian proper and still work as a black theologian. It may well be that the next generation will need to finish the task begun by my generation of black theologians. It will likewise need to be a team effort. The foundation for this future task is, I believe, being laid deeply and profoundly. Already the process for the future has been set in motion.

If indeed a hermeneutic circle begins with the Bible and ends with the Bible, black theology can live with that. The Bible is central to the black experience of the Christian faith. There is, however, a remarkable affinity between the biblical revelation and traditional African experience. This does not mean, however, that any black church theologians or an African can "holify" *everything* African or black any more than European theologians can sanctify everything in their traditional culture. We cannot for that reason continue to ignore our history and be ourselves.

To suggest that the Bible is a source for black theology does not mean that we believe that Christ is no longer at the center of the Christian faith. The center is not identical necessarily with the circumference. The revelation of God is to each and to all. It is particular and universal. It is significant that the Bible allows for God's revelation to filter through creation, history and culture at the same time. Jesus Christ remains unique. The incarnation remains the highest peak of the Christian understanding of divine revelation. It seems to me that biblical interpretation must be prepared to give more attention to the history of religions while continuing to take seriously the biblical texts. The incarnation should still hold the central place in the understanding of the total revelation of God to all humans. The arena of God's salvific revelation is the locus of human existence at every place and time. Black theology must not break but, rather, expand the hermeneutic circle that begins and ends with the Bible re-interpreted. God has not been without witnesses among all humankind. Many Western theologians feel they have completed the circle by admitting the Asian religions in. Black theologians must reject this generosity; for unless the African religions and cultures are admitted, neither is black theology. Furthermore, we must insist that the spiritual and political dimenions of God's redemptive revelation are inseparable and interdependent.

The Maya and Aztec peoples of Mexico, traditional Africans and ancient Chinese, all hold that reality is a duality of interaction. This is different from a duality of dichotomy as expressed by Plato, Descartes and Kant whose seminal influence upon Western theology is beyond question. The yin-yang relation of the Chinese, the interaction of the male-female ultimate principles of the Maya and the sense of wholeness among Africans, are indications that humankind from earliest times has not been bound by the either/or of Aristotelian logic or the dialectic of Hegel. This holistic epistemology and ontology makes contact with biblical faith at such a crucial point that Western scholars may be forced to reconsider the superstructuring of thought which they have unwittingly imposed upon biblical exegesis and systematic theology. This has been exported, unfortunately, as a universal commodity in the theological centers and churches throughout the world.

Any conclusions we reach on method in black theology is provisional. The quest has just begun. We are presenting here an outline which must be filled in. To be dogmatic on such a vast subject would be to claim the omniscience which no human being has. We are encouraged, however, that the subject itself is becoming more clearly focused and is within our range of vision. We are now able to sketch the shape an adequate black hermeneutic should take. It is clearly different from Latin American models, though it shares much of the political focus of Latin American liberation theology. It is akin to theological developments in Africa, though it is by no means identical. It can learn from the contextualization of theology in Asia as well. Feminist theology has common interest with black theology as far as clearing up language is concerned, but since it is mainly sponsored by women who are neither poor, black or minority, there is an important difference. In short, we are breaking new but important ground, theologically speaking.

I will now share what I perceive to be some important characteristics of a viable black hermeneutic. First, it should have a universal vision. In speaking of "universal" here, we wish to avoid the Western "totalized" usage. Enrique Dussel has indicated that when we set ourselves up as a norm and then expect humankind to accept this as a supreme worth, we are guilty of "totalization."[55] Universal, as used here, would allow for contextualization of theology in each and every culture, whether European, African, Asian or Latin American. Universal includes all cultures, all ethnics and all religions.

Second, human rights will be central to a black hermeneutical perspective. It will include Jürgen Moltmann's contribution to individual and social rights, the rights of the living and the unborn based upon the *imago Dei*.[56] But it must go beyond reformed theology's range of vision. It must somehow embrace the spirit of cosmopolitanism of the Stoics who spoke of a divine spark in every human. Human rights must in no way be limited to those who are in a state of grace within the Christian covenant. It must be inherent in the light of God's creation in all humans, of all cultures and of all religions. A black hermeneutic cannot be hemmed in by dogmatic structures which draw a circle that does not include the entire human race. Hegel, in his *Philosophy of History*, writes eloquently concerning universal history. But world history for him does not include the religions and cultures of millions in Africa, the ancestral home of Afro-Americans. To add insult to injury he treats Egypt as if it were a part of the Orient.[57] The human family for us must be all of humankind. We must be concerned about human rights in this context.

Finally, we must include the holistic nature of thought and reality. A black hermeneutic must be able to mediate between extremes in thought and life. Howard Thurman recently expressed to me his interest in "mysticism and social change." His entire career has been based upon the relationship between spirituality and social activism, mainly within the black religious tradition. Others may stress the other side of the spectrum as Martin Luther King, Jr. did, but with a strong spiritual and evangelical thrust. This is the genius of black religion. The theologian of the black experience is charged with the responsibility of providing a suitable interpretation upon this experience. The secular and the sacred, the rational and the mystical, the individual and the social interact and are held in dynamic tension in one continuum of experience.

A black hermeneutical circle is essential to black theology. Much of the previous work has been preoccupied with content, but we must now forge a viable method for black theology. This task must be supportive of an even deeper immersion into the black religious heritage. The effort here is but the first fruits of a long quest.

NOTES

1. Juan Luis Segundo, The Liberation of Theology (Maryknoll, N.Y.: Orbis, 1976). See pp. 7-25

2. This paper by Jack B. Rogers is merely a preliminary unpublished draft. I am aware of its provisional character but I use it as a convenient discussion starter only.

3. Quoted by Segundo, op. cit., p. 7.

4. Ibid., p. 8.

5. Ibid., p. 9.

6. Ibid., p. 5.

7. African Christian Theology (Maryknoll, N.Y.: Orbis, 1977), pp. 34-36.

8. Ham and Japheth: The Mythic World of Whites in the Antebellum South (Metuchen, N.J.: Scarecrow Press, 1978). This study is published by the American Theological Library Association (ATLA Monograph Series, No. 12). See pp. 141-158.

9. Published by Orbis, Maryknoll, N.Y., 1974.

10. Published by the Fourth Episcopal District Press of the C.M.E. Church, Shreveport, Louisiana, 1977.

11. See C.B. Copher, "The Black Man in the Biblical World," Interdenominational Theological Center Journal (I,2, Spring 1974), pp. 7-16. C.F.R.A. Bennet, Jr., "Africa and the Biblical Period," The Harvard Theological Review (64, 4 Oct., 1971), pp. 483-500.

12. See C.H. Marbury, "An Excursus on the Biblical and Theological Rhetoric of Martin Luther King," in John Cartwright, ed., Essays in Honor of M.L. King, Jr. (Evanston,Ill.: Leiffer Bureau of Social and Religious Research, Garrett-Evangelical Theological Seminary, 1971), pp. 14-28. Cf. Thomas A. Hoyt, Jr., "The Biblical Tradition of the Poor and Martin Luther King, Jr., Interdenominational Theological Center Journal (IV, 2, Spring, 1977), pp. 12-32.

13. See Marbury, "Myth, Oral Tradition and Continuity: A Biblical-Theological Response to 'Roots'" The Church and the Black Experience Bulletin (Evanston, Ill.: Garrett-Evangelical Theological Seminary, Feb., 1977), pp. 19-22. Hoyt completed his Ph.D. thesis at Duke Divinity School on the "poor"in Luke and Acts.

14. *The Dark Center: A Process Theology of Blackness* (New York: Paulist Press, 1973), p. 3.

15. Ibid., p.11.

16. Ibid., pp. 15-29.

17. Ibid., p. 29.

18. Ibid., p. 31.

19. Ibid., p. 32.

20. Ibid., pp. 37, 164-167.

21. Ibid.

22. Richard E. Palmer, *Hermeneutics* (Evanston, Ill.: Northwestern University Press, 1969), pp. 20-21.

23. Ibid., pp. 24-42.

24. Pierre Thévanaz, *What is Phenomenology?* (Chicago: Quadrangle, 1962), pp. 42-45.

25. Palmer, *op. cit.*, pp. 42-43.

26. Ibid., pp. 44-45. Palmer's work is an excellent study of hermeneutics -- especially Schleiermacher, Heidegger, Gadamer and Ricoeur. It is recommended for further study.

27. See his "Structural Similarities and Dissimilarities in Black and African Theologies," *The Journal of Religious Thought* (XXII, 2, Fall-Winter, 1975), p. 18.

28. Ibid., pp. 20-21.

29. Ibid., p. 21.

30. Ibid., pp. 22-23.

31. Ibid., p. 23-24.

32. Ibid., p. 23.

33. Marbury, *op. cit.*, p. 19.

34. Ibid., p. 20.

35. Ibid., p. 21.

36. Ibid., p. 23.

37. Ibid., pp. 21-22.

38. Ibid., p. 23.

39. "An Excursus on the Biblical and Theological Rhetoric of Martin Luther King," op. cit., p. 16.

40. Ibid., p. 17.

41. Ibid., p. 18.

42. Ibid., pp. 19-21.

43. Ibid., pp. 21-22.

44. Cf. Hoyt, op. cit.

45. "Biblical Theology and Black Theology," Interdenominational Theological Center Journal, (III, 2, Spring 1976), p. 10.

46. James H. Cone, God of the Oppressed (New York: Seabury, 1975), pp. 97-99.

47. William R. Jones, Is God a White Racist? (Garden City, N.Y.: Doubleday, 1973), pp. 41-47.

48. See Aylward Shorter, African Christian Theology (Maryknoll, N.Y.: Orbis, 1977), p. 24.

49. See Basil Moore, ed., The Challenge of Black Theology in South Africa (Atlanta: John Knox, 1973).

50. See a response by Father A.R. Taylor in Impact (Vol. 8, No. 6, Aug.-Sept., 1978), p. 6.

51. Edward K. Braxton, "Toward a Black Catholic Theology," Freeing the Spirit (V, 2), pp. 2-6.

52. Braxton, "Black Theology: Potentially Classic?" Religious Study Review (Vol. 4, No. 2, Apr., 1978), pp. 85-90.

53. See "This Far by Faith: American Black Worship and Its African Roots," (Washington, D.C.: National Office for Black Catholics and the Liturgical Conference, 1977).

54. Eulalio P. Balthazar's contribution on the misuse of black and white symbolism in the history of theology is invaluable. His reliance upon process metaphysics as a way forward is unfortunate. Neo-classical philosophy is notoriously inadequate in treating cultural and ethical questions. My reference is to The Dark Center, op. cit.

55. Enrique Dussel, Ethics and the Theology of Liberation (Maryknoll, N.Y.: Orbis, 1978), pp. 17-21.

56. "A Christian Declaration of Human Rights," The Reformed World (Vol. 34, No. 2, June 1976), pp. 58-72.

57. G.W.F. Hegel, The Philosophy of History, trans. J. Sibree (New York: Wiley Book Co., 1944), pp. 198-199.

THE METHODOLOGICAL CRISIS IN BLACK THEOLOGY: MAJOR JONES, WILLIAM JONES AND JAMES CONE

This presentation may assume too much. I do not try to define or attempt to justify black theology since the movement is several years old and now there is substantial literature available on this segment of the worldwide liberation theology movement. In the United States, black theology antedates feminist theology and despite some efforts to replace it and tone it down it remains well established.

I. THE CRISIS IN METHOD

Black theology was born in crisis; its message and content were dictated by adverse circumstances. In the late sixties, black ministers were caught in the cross fire of the debate over violence vs. non-violence as a means of liberation. Black pride, consciousness and power had won the field. Integration associated with civil rights and the ethic of love were being questioned as the only way or even the right way for blacks to win their freedom.

Black communities, campuses and even families were torn apart. A division arose over ideologies and strategies that forced a cleavage between youth and age, light-skinned and dark-skinned, privileged and underprivileged. In this stormy situation, black pastors tried to help their people. Some were surprised that they were not respected. In many instances, their counsel was ignored. Angry black youth, inflamed by a dislike for racist oppression, left the churches in droves and rejected it as either escapist or racist, depending upon whether the church was black or white. Some perceptive black ministers banded together in an ecumenical body and announced through a nationwide press release that they endorsed "black power." Churchmen called upon black theologians to provide theological direction to this new approach to black liberation. At this time James H. Cone published his book *Black Theology and Black Power*. This work marked Cone as the pioneer in black theology and inaugurated the new theological perspective.

The urgency of the task at hand did not allow black theologians the luxury of time to develop a proper theological method. All black theologians at this early stage, myself included, accepted the challenge and began work. Given their sense of mission and the poignancy of their situation, they could not have elected to do otherwise. Their work was needed yesterday and tomorrow may be too late. All of us were aware of the several methodologies operative in the theological disciplines. It was not naivete which caused us to forego a preoccupation with method, but the urgency of the task itself. We were aware of course, that the time would come when a careful look at methodology would be required. In my judgment, this time has now arrived.

In this new movement, the first black religious interpreter who looked at methodology with serious concern was William Jones. He launched his program of reflection upon the black religious experience by providing a critique of several black scholars who had already written books on black theology. The razor-sharp logic of this youthful inquirer made it evident that black theologians were being called to greater accountability on the question of theological method. His first book *Is God A White Racist?* made it clear that, like every other black theologian, he, too, had problems. Some of these problems are emotional as well as deeply convictional and cannot therefore, as Jones seems to think, be resolved by mere logic. I believe his tendency to press for a careful methodology is healthy. By calling attention to this need and thus exposing the Achilles' heel of black theology, Jones has placed all black theologians in his debt. As a result of his piercing darts of criticism, we have all begun to enter the search for a proper methodology. This is a healthy means of advancing our common endeavor.

II. REPRESENTATIVE PROGRAMS AND THE QUEST FOR A METHOD

In this discussion, we will treat method as it has been developed thus far, principally by three black religious thinkers who are intensely involved in the present black theology discussion. My appraisal will include the works of Major Jones, William Jones and James Cone. It will be necessary for me to refer to my own program because it is often considered as a viable alternative to some aspects of James Cone's program.

1. Major Jones has published two books on black theology: *Black Awareness: A Theology of Hope* and *Christian Ethics for a Black Theology*. He is presently seeking to provide more insights on black theology. Jones, like other black theologians, attempted to attack the issues in his first book. Although he devoted a great deal of his exposition to history and to the nature and mission of black religion and church, his main focus is on the ethical question of means for black liberation. Major Jones, a friend and close associate of Dr. Martin Luther King, both at Boston University and in Atlanta, wavers between non-

violence and violence. While exalting love as the more excellent way, he is aware that unmerited suffering has not liberated the black masses. He is aware of the new mood among blacks and has to address those who, having given up on the goodwill of whites, have reached a point of utter frustration. He turned to Bonhoeffer's *Letters from Prison* for insights. Bonhoeffer's participation in the attempt to assassinate Hitler is seen by Jones as an example of what he calls an "ethic of distress."[1] Jones sees violence as an evil, but at times it may be the only alternative left when the system becomes so repressive that it renders the plight of the oppressed powerless and hopeless.

He believes that we should not embrace a situation-ethic at this point and attempt to justify our wrongdoing by sprinkling holy water on it. We should rather be honest, acknowledge the contradiction between what is right and what we are forced into by the circumstances. In this type of extreme situation we are informed that the only course may be to do what is necessary and ask God to forgive us.

We can appreciate Jones' dilemma. On the one hand, he perceives the importance of relating means to ends. He desires an ultimate "togetherness" between all human beings on a plane of mutual respect, but on the other hand, the real situation is so repressive as a result of systemic racism that it renders the plight of the black and the poor in our society almost hopeless. There seems to be no way to humanize life by employing the ethic of love. Jones has posed the issue sharply for us.

This basic argument is continued in his more recent work *Christian Ethics for a Black Theology*. Jones has pursued this ethical question relentlessly.[2] Whether we agree with his perspective or not, we cannot ignore the importance of the issue raised. What disturbs me is his inability to provide a helpful constructive statement so that blacks can move consistently from faith to ethics. Whether we find Dr. King's program tenable today or not, he deserves credit for providing a profound theological ethic to undergird his program of action. Jones does not seem to provide any connecting link between faith and ethics. While Kierkegaard spoke of the teleological suspension of the ethical for the sake of faith, Jones simply would suspend both, given adequate desperation and provocation. What is the value of being a Christian if under pressure one simply does what is natural anyway? Where is the enabling grace or power of God? Why cast this discussion in the mold of theological discourse? As Jones continues his reflection, we hope that before long he will cast significant light upon these matters.

2. William Jones has brought into sharp focus the theodicy question for black theologians and has done so with a keen eye on method. It is my impression that he should not have mixed theodicy and method. Jones does so, however, out of deep convictions which I can appreciate. He assumes that suffering is so entrenched in the black experience that a serious engagement with this problem must be the starting point of all black theology. Black theology after slavery is the same as Jewish theology after Auschwitz. Thus black theology and holocaust theology have much to learn from each other as his references to Rubenstein's writing indicate.

If Jones could have separated the issues and worked at method more from an epistemological point of view, it is my impression that his contribution to black theology would have been beyond price. He decided rather, to set up requirements for black theology which no black theist can approve without renouncing his faith, and on this basis assess the merits and demerits of their programs. By these standards all his associates are denounced. He then emerges as the only true interpreter of the black religious experience.

William Jones asserts that black suffering is multidimensional, that it is persistent and excessive, that it is undeserved and cannot be explained by any rational means.³ So far so good. With these assertions most black theologians would agree. But then he posits the assumption that God is to blame. He does not have faith in the integrity of the divine character. He does not see God's purpose in creation and providence as good and he does not commit himself to an affirmation of God's salvific purpose for man in Christ. He is free to assert that since there is no evidence in black history of God's liberating work, God is a white racist. His confidence is in the functional ultimacy of man. His optimism concerning man renders him either blind or indifferent to human transgression. He does not know that it is better to trust God than put confidence in man. That includes one's self as well as others. To affirm such trust in God takes faith and Jones appears short on faith.

It seems that William Jones should have discovered the limits of reason before attempting to deal with the most difficult theological puzzle of all -- evil and God. Philosophers and theologians have never been able to find the ultimate solution to this enigma within a mystery. Many a thoughtful person has wrecked his faith on this reef. Christians have been enlightened by their reflection upon the problem of evil, but it has been their faith in the love, justice and power of God which has enabled them to conquer and transcend the power of evil in their lives. Their faith-claim that God's love is stronger than death, as demonstrated through the cross and resurrection of Christ, has been for them "the victory which overcomes the world," and contrary to Jones' assertion, this faith may lead not merely to quietism but to activism to set wrongs right in this life."[4]

Thus William Jones, with his keen logical powers, has been most critical of the presuppositions of other black theologians. He does not seem however, to have delivered a serious blow against their programs because the others are aware that they stand within a theological circle. Out of this faith-claim, they treat the theodicy issue alongside many other theological concerns. As Jones assumes his constructive task and develops his own position more fully, his logical and critical powers probably will be more useful to himself and to others in this common enterprise. It is unlikely that the black theologian apologists will exchange their faith in the Living God for confidence in the functional ultimacy of man. When Jones has adequately developed his humano-theism it is not likely to resemble the faith that has sustained black people through the dark night of suffering.

3. We turn now to James Cone. In four major works produced in rapid succession, Cone has attempted to spell out his program of black theology. In *Black Theology and Black Power, A Black Theology of Liberation, Spirituals and Blues* and *God of the Oppressed,* Cone has hammered away at the tenets of his program. Thus, those of us who have followed his rapid ascendancy are fairly clear about what he has to say on the subject.

Cone's early works were neo-orthodox.[5] His doctoral research had centered upon Karl Barth's doctrine of man and he seems to be strongly influenced by Barth's work. My frequent references to his "Barthian" thorn in the flesh have been rejected. I will grant that Cone quotes learnedly from several other theologians, but he seems rather locked into this initial position. In fact, Cone's outlook seems to be rather akin to this theological perspective. Often a researcher selects his/her subject matter out of the affinity he has with the subject. This has been my experience often and Cone's subsequent development seems to confirm this tendency.

The early Cone drew heavily upon humanistic existentialists like Camus. Cone admits being part of the militant black movement in the late 60s. He gives a theological interpretation to the spirit of the black power movement. The rebellion and defiance of Camus in the face of unsurpassable odds challenged Cone. The attitude of facing death with dignity was attractive to him. He even suggested that death for freedom without the hope of future life was adequate for blacks. Cone later retracted this, especially after he had delved into black sources, as he did in *Spirituals and Blues*.

He was censured for his inadequate ethical perspective when he asserted that blacks should resort to "any means necessary" to win their freedom. The statement appears to be an ethic of no ethic. This was a reckless and irresponsible statement in the midst of a tense and explosive situation. Young angry black militants were seeking guidance. They asked for bread; he cast them a stone. A moral paralysis remains inherent in Cone's theological method.

Another difficulty is the ambiguity of Cone's definition of "blackness."[6] On one hand, Cone seems to conceive the term as having an ethnic or racial identiy. It refers primarily to skin color and is a frame of reference for a people enslaved and discriminated against in the United States. Cone's theology is seen as being anti-white, racist, separatist. His purpose, however, as I understand it, is to expose the bias in western thought and correct the omissions by calling attention to the contribution of the black religious experience. He has turned to black sources and has indicated a deepening immersion of his theology in this context. On the other hand, because he was so severely criticized for his identification of blackness with oppression, and his assertion that God takes sides with the black oppressed, Cone began to quote Tillich's ontological symbolism. He asserted that blackness was to be viewed as a universal ontological symbol of oppression. One must become black in order to enter the Kingdom, so to speak, but "becoming black" means assuming solidarity with the oppressed. Cone does not indicate that he is aware of the network of oppresions operative in the United States. He gives little or no attention to the implications of this "ontological symbolism of oppression" in the Third World. He only wants to say that blackness and oppression are inseparable in the United States and goes on to work his oppression-liberation model. Cone sees this as his strength -- this narrow focus on one concern. He sees my wider interests, for example, as a serious weakness. What shall I say, "one man's meat is another man's poison?" Isn't there a more or less adeqate manner of dealing with the oppression-liberation model in theological discourse in the context of a pluralistic society in this time of world history? I believe the answer is "yes" and I wish to argue this point later on. The shortcomings of Cone's provincialism are being exposed as black theology is forced into the broad climate of black ecumenism. When black theology informs action for liberation, there is a drive for operational unity. Furthermore, the tendency of black theology to reach into Pan-Africanism and to dialogue with Asian and Latin American theologians is placing a strain on Cone's rigid hermeneutical structures.

Christo-centrism is fine if it receives a proper interpretation. Of course, Christ must be the center of God's revelation to man in the faith-claim of Christians, but in my view, this does not exhaust the revelational possibilities of a loving, just and resourceful God. God is Maker of heaven and earth. He is the Lord of history as well as Redeemer and Sanctifier. The Author of nature is Giver of grace. God's revelation has a center in the Incarnation and, even there, Creation and Redemption are inseparable. God affirmed the goodness of creation by embodying the *Logos* in material form. Christ is the center and not the circumference of God's revelation to each and every people. God's revelation is particular and universal, but the movement of his revelation is from center to circumference. Cone is correct, I believe, in emphasizing the ethnicity of theology, but he is limited insofar as the universal outreach of his program seems to be short-circuited by this method.

Again the use of scripture in James Cone is suspect. One can forgive Albert Cleage, churchman and folk-theologian, perhaps for his misuse of the Bible. James Cone, however, must be accountable for the manner in which he uses it.[7] Other black theologians need to be led by his example, into a more abundant use of the Bible. From the beginning, the Bible is and has been a favorite religious textbook for black religionists and preachers. For this very reason, black theologians should handle the biblical message with due care. Cone's frequent reference to the Bible is a mixed blessing. We are pleased that the Bible takes on a central importance in his writings, but the manner of his interpretation is disturbing. Significantly, the biblical message is applied to the present situation of the oppressed for their liberation, but he often seems indifferent to sound historical criticism and careful exegesis. He is highly selective of his texts and their contexts and puts his blinders on if a given text does not say exactly what he intends. We are reminded that this very approach to the Bible has been used in the past to support slavery and discrimination, not to mention sexism. Even a black theology should be oriented toward the unity of the Bible and the whole gospel. We find the priestly as well as the prophetic, the social as well as the personal, internal criticism of our own people as well as external criticism of those who oppress. In a word, we find the bitter with the sweet and the gospel remains a two-edged sword. There are stories in the Bible, but it is not all story. The literary examination of the Bible, with which Cone is quite familiar, reveals that the Bible is more like a library with many editors and authors than a homogeneous work by one story-teller. For the sake of the liberation of the oppressed in-depth and in the long run, we must be faithful interpreters of the biblical texts. To this end, we must unlock the biblical message in all its disturbing clarity and bring it to bear upon what needs to be done to redeem ourselves and humanize the social order.

My final observation regarding Cone's program has to do with the epistemological question. We recall that he reveals a deep indebtedness to theological method in the neo-orthodox mood, a movement which he almost escaped because of his youth. The giants in this movement were all in semi-retirement and some were deceased by the late 60s when Cone emerged from his doctoral studies. He encountered them second-hand through teachers who continued to pass on their legacy, as well as through his research. Neo-orthodox theology provided for Cone an anchor in the Christian faith and in the church. Without this foundation, deep and secure, in the "faith once and for all delivered to the saints," it is likely that we would have lost James Cone forever from the ranks of theologians. An anti-church approach to black power would possibly have claimed him but for this base of operation.

This too is a mixed blessing. It is important that Cone sought to provide a theological interpretation of black power as a member of the age class of angry young militants who assumed the mantle of leadership in the black movement during those troubled times, but his development so far has indicated that he is locked into the tight hermeneutical structures of that beginning, and for this reason, he is in serious trouble. While white scholars have accepted Cone as the spokesman for black theology (when they considered the movement worthy of any attention), black theologians have persistently made the point that James Cone speaks mainly for himself. Fred Herzog, Rosemary Reuther and Peter Hodgson, to name a few white authors, have taken Cone quite seriously. Sometimes white scholars seem to select Cone as the chief representative of the black theology movement for negative reasons. Here I do not speak mainly of those white scholars just mentioned, but in some cases, Cone has been set up as the "straw man" of black theology. There are, as all well know, serious questions in the method, content and implementation of his program, and therefore if it ends up in logical inconsistency and moral paralysis, one need not read further into the black theology literature. It can be dismissed summarily for lack of substance. How does one explain the fact that black theology is not central to theological education programs in the nation, to my knowledge, except in the two major black seminaries -- Howard School of Religion and The Interdenominational Theological Center in Atlanta? It is certainly not because James Cone has not been heard and read in most of the theological schools in this country and in numerous colleges and universities as well. Is it because his theology, though read, has not been taken seriously? If so, this is not Cone's fault; other black theologians have not been accepted any more readily and neither have the theologians of liberation in general. Our main focus, at this point, however, is to expose deficiencies in Cone's theory of knowledge.

A leap of faith dimension seems to be inherent in Cone's thought. Reason does not have a high place in his theology. He has a good grasp of philosophy, but this knowledge he uses mainly to discredit the use of reason in the interpretation of matters of belief. A theologian, as theologian, must work with conviction, I believe, out of a belief-system. Faith should have first place, therefore, but there should also be a quest for understanding concerning what one believes. This means that theological assertions should be carefully and critically examined by means of all our logical and critical powers. What I observe is that Cone often resorts to the argument from ignorance. It is one thing to accept the finitude of the human intellect in aspects of belief which transcend the reach of the mind. It is quite another matter to buy into a sub-rational stance. In the latter instance we accept beliefs blindly without attempting to think about them. This is inexcusable, the shadow of Kierkegaard, notwithstanding. For Cone, admitting that something cannot be subject to thought, provides an escape for a dogmatic assertion that something he affirms should be taken at face value, without question. Of course, he deposits revelation as the basis of his assurance, but divine revelation also requires interpretation, and we are challenged to take our heads as well as our hearts into this enterprise. Edgar Brightman, I believe, quotes Barth somewhere as saying, "God speaks, man listens," but in fact Barth speaks and the Barthians listen. This is exactly what comes through in much that Cone writes. Cone often writes as if God is speaking to him and only to him as a theologian of the black experience. All other theologians, including his brother Cecil, hear a different drummer.

No theologian, it seems to me, is entitled to privileged information from God. Each theologian belongs to a community of believers. His role is to interpret the faith for that community, but he is painfully aware that many believers in that community may know more about God than he will ever know. The theologian, therefore, who is faithful to his task, must learn from the religious experiences of the believing community and enlighten that community regarding its own faith claim. This means that a theologian must be prepared to encounter what Eliade calls an *hierophany* -- he must allow the experiences of the believing community to reveal themselves to him and he must be prepared to describe and interpret what is there. Cone, on the contrary, in his research into black sources, seems to impose ready-made structures of thought upon new materials and new experiences. He does not learn

Hermeneutics and Method 43

from these. His insights seem static. He always seems to find what he is seeking. For this reason, one does not find the freshness and evidence of growth one expects in a new book from his pen. *God of the Oppressed* is his latest and most mature work, yet one could anticipate, with minor exceptions, the content of this work.[8] His autobiographical sketch is new. One is hopeful regarding his use of the sociology of knowledge for ethics, but this does not meet the test. His Christology is stated more clearly, but it does not open up the possibility of dialogue with Africans who are seeking values in their traditional religions or with black sects and cults at home. Yet liberation from oppression is a common theme. What we have is a monologue. What we need is a black ecumenical theology and an operational unity. In his latest work, he still criticizes white theologians for their blindness; yet he seems to write mainly to impress white scholars. His tirade against black theologians seems to have the ring of condescension. The only thing new is that for the first time Cone is aware that he must deal with some of the telling criticisms meted out by other black scholars. Perhaps this is the best evidence we have that other black theologians are being read and heard.

The either/or approach to thought seems to dominate Cone's program. This is characteristic of the Western logical method. A thing must be one thing or another and very often this includes playing opposites over against each other. Oppression is played over against liberation, life over against death and liberation over against reconciliation. There is another model of thinking, the both-and model which mediates between extremes in thought and action. The biblical as well as the African perspectives seem to be wholistic rather than dichotomous. Thus far Cone's constructive thought as well as his critiques seem to employ the either/or model. This indicates to me that, in spite of all his references to the black experience, his pattern of thought is shaped almost completely by philosophy and theology in the North Atlantic community. Given the tightness of his thought-structures and his dogmatic mood, there is little hope for a breakthrough at this point.

III. A BRIEF CONSTRUCTIVE STATEMENT

A black theological program should be expected to take the motif of *liberation* quite seriously. Our experiences of oppression make this a very demanding concern. The issue is clear. On this point, there is almost universal agreement. Major Jones has raised the issue of using "salvation" rather than "liberation" as his crucial theme. He has merely introduced the issue thus far. I await further explication of his meaning before commenting. Generally speaking, this drive for liberation seems to be the central distinguishing mark of the movement. Other liberation theologies are based upon other types of oppression i.e., sexism or classism. Black theology has clearly singled out *racism* as its target. Indeed, it cannot do otherwise for *racism* is the root oppression in the black experience.

Since we are created by God, the author and maker of heaven and earth, racism should be seen as a theological problem. We are as God has made us out of a creative purpose. Our racial characteristics are a given from the hand of the Creator. To place more value upon one individual or group than upon another is to choose the judgment of the creature over that of the Creator who made human beings in his own image, placing them at the apex of his creation, and affirming the goodness of all that he had made. Racism is, therefore, self-idolatry, self-glorification, the worship of a particular color of skin. Black theologians agree that racism is more than a sociological problem.

The awareness of social sin is another characteristic of black theology. Sin and salvation have horizontal as well as vertical dimensions; this is true not just on a one to one basis. A careful analysis of racism leads to the inevitable conclusion that we have to do with a systemic evil affecting all segments of our society. Its consequences affect its victims-- a whole people for a life-time. Every aspect of life is impeded by the strictures placed upon blacks by whites. The penalization of blackness goes into the past and reaches forth into the unforeseeable future. The beneficiaries of this society are also rendered unhealthy by the fact of racism. Anyone who is unmoved by the unmerited suffering of a whole people or who assumes the right to privilege because of his/her status in a society that rewards whiteness, is morally and religiously stunted. This is a society in which it is hard for blacks to forgive and for whites to repent. Black theology sees clearly the need to interpret sin and salvation in a more comprehensive manner than is usual in most theological programs. Black theology is *ethical* as well as *evangelical*. It cannot be either without being both at the same time.

Another common characteristic of black theology is its advocacy of wholeness. We see clearly the need for viewing persons in community. The value of a religious perspective which is concerned with the whole person and all of life is affirmed. The body/soul, secular/sacred, priestly/prophetic cleavages so characteristic of much theology is disowned. We see the African and biblical outlook as lending full endorsement to this more comprehensive view of persons-in-community. Thus we have embraced an approach which accepts ethnicity. American society is a "tossed salad" and not a "melting pot." We live among unmeltable ethnics. Our alienation is the greater, however, because of slavery and discrimination based upon race. We move, therefore, from the particular to the universal. Just as the melting pot theory of society is a myth, so is the concept of the universal, as used by theologians, a myth. No interpretation of the Bible or revelation limited to scholars in the North Atlantic countries is truly universal. It is true that all humans must operate out of some center, but the center is not the circumference. Black theology has the possibility of pointing the way to a true universality for Christian theological ethics. Out of our suffering as a people, we have developed a sensitivity to suffering everywhere. Being in the west but not of it, we have an affinity with both the west and the Third World situations. This has profound implications for a breakthrough in a theology of liberation for all peoples.[9]

Dr. Basil Matthews, a native of Trinidad and professor at Howard University, has just passed on to me for review the fruits of his careful research on the thought processes of peoples of African descent in Africa, the Caribbean and the United States.[10] According to Matthews, blacks personalize their learning. Knowledge must be recognized as a personal human experience. The black person internalizes his thought. For him, knowledge is not an abstraction which stands on its own outside of the experienced reality. Knowledge passes through human experience and is processed by the person with his whole being. Black thought is a lived event. Matthews quotes approvingly from the African philosopher, Leopold Senghor, who asserts that the African builds himself into the wholeness of reality by or through affective identification by means of imagery. This is thinking with soul. Hence the unusual manifestation of symbols and metaphors in black thought. According to Senghor we have here to do with the totalized or symbolic all-in-oneness of the African concept which emerges from the immediacy of the black affective intellectual perception. Matthews refers to this as cosmic thinking. He traces his thesis through black literature, especially speeches and sermons. His point is that we encounter a black cognitive process, a way of thinking and perceiving reality which is pan-African. This is to be contrasted with the one-thing-at-a-timeness, the fragmentation of the field of perception and the disruption of the rhythm of movement characteristic of much Western analytic thought.

My independent studies have led me to conclusions similar to Matthews'. I discovered the tendency toward intuition and wholeness of thought and noted the preponderance of perception over conception in black thought. This, I believe, is a constructive trend in reflecting upon African modes of thought. It is not sufficient that we criticize the Western giants like Hegel. Roy Morrison, a black philosophical theologian, seems obsessed with exposing the deficiencies of Hegel. Once he has done his critical task in designating Hegel as a racist, it is my hope that he will turn his considerable philosophical powers to our common task of forging a life-view and a world-view supporting the meaning and liberation quest of black people.

In conclusion, it is to be expected that black theologians like others, will differ among themselves. Some will differ on substantive points. But it is a youthful movement and many of the more important contributions to the development of black theology have yet to be made. Our differences are not to be seen as devisive. We have a common goal and are joined in a common struggle. Whatever conflict there may be is in the head and not in the heart. Together, we are seeking to develop a theology which will give substance to faith and provide evidence of hope for the black and the poor in our midst and indeed for all humankind. We believe that the world also needs love. How could a Christian believe otherwise? But for us, love must always be expressed in the context of liberation from bondage. By this liberation, we do not mean only spiritual freedom between man and God, but freedom from the bondage of the whole person in the social context. For us the gospel as Good News liberates persons and communities from systemic, cultural and institutional structures of oppression. Only thus may the kingdoms of this world become the Kingdom of our God and his Christ.

NOTES

1. Major Jones, Black Awareness: A Theology of Hope (Nashville: Abingdon, 1971), pp. 98-106.

2. Major Jones, Christian Ethics for a Black Theology (Nashville: Abingdon, 1974), pp. 122-150.

3. William R. Jones, Is God a White Racist? (Garden City, N.Y.: Doubleday, 1973), pp. 17-23.

4. Ibid., Ch. XI.

5. James Cone, Black Theology and Black Power (New York: Seabury, 1969). This work essentially brings together Barthian dogmatics and the ideology of Black Power. There is also a strong emphasis upon Existentialism, especially that of Camus.

6. James Cone, A Black Theology of Liberation (New York: J.B. Lippincott, 1970), pp. 54-66.

7. Ibid., pp. 92-101.

8. James H. Cone, God of the Oppressed (New York: Seabury Press, 1975). Cone's autobiographical sketch in this book is helpful. He adds the sociology of knowledge dimension to his method. We meet a more mature Cone, but I do not see this work as a radical transformation of theological output.

9. A thorough discussion on my views stated here may be found in the following works: J. Deotis Roberts, Liberation and Reconciliation: A Black Theology (Philadelphia: Westminster, 1971), pp. 13-25 and J. Deotis Roberts, A Black Political Theology (Philadelphia: Westminster, 1974), pp. 74-90.

10. The comments here are the results of several conversations I had with Dr. Basil Matthews while we were faculty colleagues at Howard University. He had produced, at that time, small installments in writing, but not produced a major work to my knowledge.

*BLACK LIBERATION THEISM

Provisional definitions of "liberation" and "theism" are essential to our discussion. "Liberation" is now loosely associated with a new consciousness during the postcolonial period in the Third World. Black liberation is often viewed in the broader context of pan-Africanism as a bold program of human liberation. "Liberation" is tied to a rapid, even a revolutionary social transformation. The word is usually used to mean setting free the oppressed from various types of bondage.

"Theism" is related to an understanding of the god-idea. Philosophical as well as theological treatments of theism are common, but treatment of theism should have a concern for a god as an "idea", if not as a personal reality. Theism may emerge from reflection upon a metaphysical or ethical ultimate as in the context of revelation it may develop into faith. It may exist in the form of deism, polytheism, pantheism, monotheism or in other combinations. In all cases *theos* or *deus* is implied as the root word. That is to say, some understanding of a personal god or abstract being in singular or plural form is implied. Whether we are concerned with atheism or deism, the key concept is "god." Without a god-idea, theism is not present. God is the presupposition of philosophical theism and the faith-claim of theological theism. My own understanding of God may be placed somewhere between monotheism and panentheism. I choose to stand in a theological circle based upon an affirmation of faith in the God of the Bible who is revealed supremely in the Incarnation. This is a convictional and not an evaluative statement vis-á-vis other expressions of theism or nontheism.

Among representative black theologians, one finds the Christocentric theism of James Cone, the humanotheism of William Jones, and the mediating theism of J. Deotis Roberts. In my theology, the word "mediating" is used to describe my position as mid-way between Cone and Jones yet, while bridging basic differences, still independent and distinctive. In Jones, one finds a religion of reason exalting the functional ultimacy of humanity for its own liberation. In Cone, one encounters a leap of faith that places great weight upon God's commands and promises but has little to say about human ability and responsibility in effecting the liberation of the oppressed.

I wish to indicate here how reason and revelation, faith and works are related. These merge, not as we reject God but rather as we discover "the human face of God" when we encounter his liberating work in our midst and join him. Isn't it possible to see God as concerned about human liberation without denying his transcendence and omnipotence? Is it necessary to minimize God in order to accept the dignity of the human? The deification of humanity is as serious a problem as the iconization of God. Humanity without God is unable to save itself or redeem the social order. Human beings before God and laboring with God are ennobled and empowered to do good and be co-laborers in the humanization of humankind. Human beings in relation to God and through grace are allowed to be co-creators and co-laborers with God.

I A CRITIQUE OF JONES' HUMANOCENTRIC THEISM

What William Jones calls humanotheism seems limited to a select few among blacks in the middle class. Many of these blacks cannot handle the razor-sharp logic in Jones' position. They have a rather affective grasp of a worldview or a religious affirmation. Jones does not make contact with the mass religious or secular movements in the black community. He is too rational and he presents a religion without revelation. Most mass movements are highly emotional and are often theocentric though not necessarily Christian. William Jones's critique of existent programs does not radically change the present omissions in black theology. What we need on the one hand is an open door to non-Christian movements involved in Black liberation. On the other hand, we need a way of entering into meaningful conversation with African traditional religionists as a part of the quest for our Afro-American religious roots.

What Jones has set out to do is to address a highly select group of black people who are secular in outlook, optimistic about human self-sufficiency, and capable of serious abstract thought. He provides a program of philosophical reflection on the black religious experience. His is a philosophy of religion in black perspective. Only when the God-question becomes a matter of faith in revelation as well as an axiom of religion do we have a theological concern for theism.

References to non-western religions without a god-idea -- Theravada, Buddhism, classical Confucianism, or the religious concepts of the Greeks -- do not seriously alter the case. One can, of course, find all sorts of germinal concepts among the Greeks depending upon the people and periods being examined. The roots of religion, theism, humanism, and ethics were all explored by them.

The study of black religion must be pluralistic, allowing for programs in philosophy of religion as well as theology proper. William Jones is a philosopher of religion who is in conversation with black theologians on common concerns. He is alone both in his perspective as a scholar and in regard to the religious community he represents. This makes his contribution most valuable. That he be called a black theologian or that his program be designated as black theology is not essential. At the moment he wavers between a secular humanism and what he calls humanotheism. Theology does have a special meaning whatever the character of the experience being reflected upon. Theism can be treated philosophically without reference to the faith community or its faith-claims. Theology refers to reflection upon the faith of a believing community. The term "theology" implies not only the idea of God, but also faith in God. This is true whether we speak of Judaism, Islam or Christianity. Black Jewish theology needs to be distinguished from black Christian theology. Black Protestant theology differs from black Roman Catholic theology. My understanding of what William Jones provides is in the nature of black religious thought rather than a black theology.

A black theology may be biblical or philosophical as well as systematic. Biblical and philosophical black theologies still require that the idea of God center in faith in the revelation of God. More specifically, black theologians need to decide first of all whether they are "church" theologians. If they are, it is necessary for them to take seriously the Bible, the tradition, and the total revelation of God as Christians understand these concepts. A black Christian theology will have its own distinctive character. On the other hand, there will be an openness to others who do not accept the fundamentals of the Christian faith-claim. There have always been Christian humanists, but for the most part they have accepted the doctrine of God, although they may have problems with the Trinity, the divinity of Christ, the traditional doctrines of humanity, sin, and so on. They have stood for "the human face of God" and they have been strong on the human goodness and responsibility. They have embraced activism as a very important ethical stance. The traditional "natural theology" position has contributed much to both a universal understanding of religion and moral endeavor. This humanistic strand of Christian thought has permeated Protestantism and Roman Catholicism without giving up faith in the revelation of God.

Theology includes epistemology but it is clearly more than that. It goes beyond a neat abstract edifice, however neatly packaged. If it is only a rational structure, it is the dry bones of faith. It involves a reasonable understanding of what happens when a human being puts ultimate trust in the living God. While there are other theologies related to other religious systems, it is clear to me after some careful study of these other theologies, that there is something distinctive about the Christian understanding of God. My task as one who affirms the Christian Creed, is to treat this position from the "inside". The God of the Christian faith cannot be found as the conclusion of a syllogism. While the "reasons of the head" may satisfy philosophy of religion, theology includes the "reasons of the heart" as well.

There is a need to engage that considerable audience of blacks who are non-Christian (secular and religious) outside the black church. This includes a host of our finest black youth. Many of my close ministerial associates cut loose from me when I wrote my first volume on black theology. Later some of these same pastors invited me in for workshop sessions. Since their youth have been leaving in droves, it has finally dawned upon them that a church without youth has a past but no future.

Many persons and groups are committed to the liberation of blacks even though they claim to reject the Christian Creed. We need to understand the sects, cults and whatever other religious movements which are at work in our midst. Since black theology must develop within the context of black religious experience, sociologists and historians of religion can help us understand the nature of black religion. Black religious experience is the "stuff" through which the Christian faith is sifted to provide a black theology. All theology is the reflection upon the faith response to a religious ultimate. Black Christians in their reflection upon their faith, respond to the Christian God experience, His presence and power radiating through their own *lebenswelt* -- living world. Faith is expressed in the experience of black suffering, the sorrow, joy and hope we have carved out of a position of powerlessness in a society saturated with systematic racism.

All blacks share a common racial experience: Christians, Muslims, Jews, sects, cults and even secular-minded blacks. When James Cone asserts that to be black is to be blue, he reaches into the experience of us all. Black experience needs proper analysis and interpretation. This is the province of the history of religions. Those who study "religion" in its universal dimensions can contribute much to our understanding of black religious experience.

The real breakthrough will center in the bridge-making task of linking African traditional religions and black religion in the New World. This connection is of vital importance for black theologians both in their constructive task and in their encounter with African church leaders and theologians. Black theologians need to develop their program so that it will be open to dialogue in two directions beyond their faith-claim.

On the one hand, they must be mindful of blacks who are non-Christians but religious and others avowedly secular but who are allies in the liberation struggle. On the other hand, they must be aware of the African roots of their heritage and the spiritual riches that can flow into their understanding of faith from this source. The encounter with African religions and the heritage undergirding them can contribute much to our spirituality, our worship and our sense of the unity and wholeness of our personal and corporate life.

II. A CRITIQUE OF CONE'S CHRISTOCENTRIC THEISM

The contribution of scholars like Leonard Barrett of Temple University and Charles Long of Chicago University are beyond estimation. Theologians find Gayraud Wilmore's work invaluable. The influence of Long upon James Cone is now beginning to be clearly manifest. Unfortunately Cone is writing on the subject-matter known best by Long who is a reluctant writer. This is not as helpful as it would be if Long were writing on such things as "spirituals" and "folklore." James Cone imposes ready-made theological structures on this material that do not fit. He does not have the skill and the investigative knowledge needed to do the anthropological, phenomenological, literary and historical interpretation necessary. It would be best to allow the myths, symbols, and meanings to emerge from the phenomena itself -- black religious experience. If this were allowed to happen it would be possible to begin the process of indigenizing black theology.

At the moment Cone is not ready to learn what he needs from black sources. He quotes incessantly from the sprituals, blues and folklore in our Afro-American past and ends up exactly where his major works in theology leave us. His works are too similar and are being produced too fast to allow time for any signficant growth in what he produces. Until William Jones' work was published recently, Cone had not been carefully criticized in print by any black scholar and white theologians had only aimed a few cautious broadsides at him. Vigorous constructive criticism is essential for the development of any theological program.

Cone's Christocentric understanding of revelation does not allow him adequate room for growth even after the research on the black sources has been done. Without a re-examination of the foundations of his program, I cannot see the possibility for the openness to black religious experience necessary to relate to non-Christians in the black community or to Africans. Once Cone limits his understanding of the revelation of God to God's revelation in Jesus Christ he cuts off conversation with all those who do not accept this affirmation as normative. Add to this the dogmatic manner in which he asserts the finality of God's revelation in Jesus Christ and his insistence upon the affinity of blackness to this revelation, and one becomes aware of the inadequacy of Cone's position and his inability to move in the direction we need to go.

III. LIBERATION THEISM: THE MIDDLE WAY

We must expand our understanding of God's revelation in nature and history. God is the author of nature, the maker of heaven and earth, the Creator-Spirit and the Lord of history. His benevolent providence unfolds as history's purpose finds it meandering way from creation to consummation. God unveils his purpose in all things, in all places, through all time and among every people.

This position is not problematic for us, once we are aware that the God of creation is the God of re-creation. The Creator is the Redeemer. The Incarnation, the Word made flesh, is the "materialization" and the "inhistorization" of God's saving purpose and activity in time and among humans. Creation and history are the media through which God makes himself known. To hold this more expansive view of revelation is not to reduce God's revelation in Christ, but it is really a robust affirmation that he is Lord of all. The Author of nature is the Giver of grace and the Lord of history. This is to emphasize the "Godness of God."

At the same time, there is opened up to us the context in which black theologians may enter into a meaningful dialogue with non-Christian religionists as well as with the secular. Black theologians in asserting the liberating work of God will need to hold out the possibility that this work can happen outside as well as inside the black church. Black Christians would do well to heed the summons of the theologians of revolution when they insist that we should seek to find where God is at work making life more human and join Him. More of God's liberating work may be happening where the black Congressional Caucus is active or where a black mayor is pleading for laws to control handguns or to deliver goods and services to the black poor than when we participate in our feast days and solemn assemblies. Let us not forget that the Lord of the church was crucified not on an altar between two candlesticks, but outside the city gates between two thieves.

The Atlanta statement on black theology was forged out of a meeting of minds of black religious scholars and other church leaders. For some reason, we have drifted apart. Black theology is becoming more abstract and moving further away from the churches and their leadership. I am disturbed by this trend. This came home to me in a meeting with African scholars at Union Theological Seminary in New York. During the meeting, as well as in correspondence between us and the All-Africa Conference of Churches, no distinction like this is made. Again as I met with the National Committee of Black Churchmen, I saw few scholars, and at the meeting of the Society for the Study of Black Religion I saw few church leaders. Furthermore, the leadership of the scholars seems to be gravitating toward those black professors who have plush professorships in Ivy League universities or ranking theological seminaries which are predominantly white in outlook. Could it be that while we talk black we really prize the fact that the white world has cast the mantle of respectability upon us? Could this be similar to the problem of a black congregation that insists upon a white pastor? Whatever the reason may be behind this situation, there must be deep psychological wounds that need to be healed. The unfortunate fact is that we are getting away from the mass experience of our people who need to be liberated from all forms of oppression and we are not being informed by those persons who are in touch with the black masses. If this trend continues, black theology will not be church theology; it will be ivory tower theology and we will have joined the bandwagon of most American and European theologians who are addicted to an arid theological scholasticism.

I am pleading for a theology of the black experience that grows out of the soil of our heritage and life. For us, faith and ethics must be wed. There can be no separation of the secular and the sacred. Jesus means freedom. He is the Lord of all life. His healing touch makes us whole in mind, soul and body. The church is the agent of social change as well as the ark of salvation. The right to material goods and services stems from our humanity. Our people are to be equally devout as prayer leaders and precinct captains. Our churches must no longer be comfort stations where we administer spiritual aspirins or hospitals where we administer salves to wounds that require surgery. The black church, a sleeping giant, must become a household of power supporting those social, economic and political programs that make life more human for our people. To this end we need a theology emerging out of our experience of the Christian faith that informs our worship, our life and our witness in the world.

IV. THE CONSTRUCTIVE TASK

Black theology is to be indigenized theology. Therefore, it needs to make a careful study of the particular character of the black religious experience. It is rather morbid to characterize all black experience in the context of conscious suffering. This is to overlook the joy and hope that are written largely in the black experience. We have the gift of laughter and we have been able to sing the Lord's song in a strange land. Gladness and celebration are so much a part of black religion that one cannot describe the phenomenon without mentioning these ingredients. More accurately the black religious experience is a "sorrow-joy" experience. But the experience, when it is intense, is weighted heavily in the direction of release and hope rather than in the direction of doubt and scepticism. Only thus have black people been able to maintain sanity and trust in life.

Thus black theologians must be anxious to let the experiences that blacks have had with life under difficult social circumstances, provide their myths and the symbols for theological discourse. The black experience is a melody of aspiration, liberation, protest, survival, meaning. We have known great suffering, but we have known the meaning of victory over suffering through faith as well. This means that God as Lord of history and the Christ of Good Friday and Easter can be understood right out of the black encounter with life.

Black theology is to be *political* theology. All of life and the whole person must be in focus at all times as black theology develops. We take our direction from African traditional religions. Religion is a seven-day-a-week living experience for Africans. The health and wholeness, family and social life, economics and politics are as sacred as tribal ritual. Life is religious and religion is life. Out of economic necessity, slavery-supporting Christianity made a distinction between freedom of the spirit and physical bondage. Unfortunately, Platonic dualism and theological scholasticism provided theologians with a frozen dogma. Paul's conservatism and legal doctrines aided in establishing the permanent split between spiritual and physical liberation from which American Christianity has not recovered. To blindly follow this false trail is not to the advantage of black theologians. The recovery of the wholeness of the person that we find in the Bible, together with the African roots of our religious experience, provides a good foundation for a new departure toward a theology of liberation for all oppressed people everywhere. A political theology will overcome quietism and the privatization of religion and open up the possibility of a secular/sacred merger as well as a personal/public ethics.

Black theology is to be *church* theology. The black churches have preserved the African temperament of black religion. It is logical that black religious and cultural nationalism will find a strong ally in the black church. Furthermore, the black church is the one major "political" institution under black control. As a political, economic, social and cultural institution it is unrivaled, and it has deep historic roots in in the aspirations of black people for liberation from all types of bondage. Black theology can be authentic only as it sinks its roots deep in the history, life, and witness of the black church. The raw materials for a black Christian theology are embedded in the black church. Therefore, black theology must incorporate the experiences flowing from churches and their members. The folk religious tradition that has been chronicled in black sermons, in the spirituals and the gospels, as well as in the oral tradition, is the stuff of black religious experience. The contemporary experience of the black churches as they participate in the humanization of black life must be considered. Endless conversations must take place among black laypersons, ministers, and black theologians if black theology is not to die still-born as a futile and abstyract dialogue among a handful of so-called "black theologians." If our task as black scholars who happen to be theologians is to be fruitful and authentic we must stay in touch with our people.

Black theology is to be *community* theology. We desire that all our people be set free. This means all black people. We cannot write off those who are followers of non-Christian movements. We must seek a fuller understanding of all the "isms" in the black community and constantly assess why some other movements are more successful in liberating black people. We must determine whether there are deficiencies in our theology and in the manner it is being applied in practical situations. We must also look carefully at the programs of other liberation movements at work in the community and seek an "operational unity" with these groups even if we cannot arrive at an ideological unity.

Black theology is to be *ecumenical* theology. We separated from the white churches primarily for *social* rather than *theological* reasons. Until recently, black churches have not been interested in serious theological construction. What we do now must not open deep wounds of doctrinal differences. We can do without charges of heresy. A remarkable unity in the black consciousness of Christians has elevated our struggle for liberation above any form of sectarian pettiness. Even the critical and constructive stage of black theology upon which we are entering should center in substantive matters of thought rather than dogmatic polemics. We must be open to black theologies, allowing for different spiritual and intellectual autobiographies of the several theologians providing their programs. We must not, however, spare each other that rigorous constructive criticism without which there can be no maturity. A remarkable meeting of minds has taken place among black Roman Catholics, Baptists, Methodists and other Christian denominations regarding our common foe (racism) and our common heritage. The black religious experience is the context out of which we are developing a fresh interpretation of the Christian Faith. Black ecumenism is a reality among black church leaders and theologians as we together chart the course of black liberation.

Black theology is to be universal. In speaking of the indigenizing dimension of black theology, we implied its ethnic origin. Black theology should bring liberation in touch with reconciliation. Only thus may liberation be elevated to its highest theological and ethical level. When reconciliation is properly understood in theological terms, liberation takes on its distinctive Christian character as well. We are able to consider reconciliation in terms of its this-worldly and social consciousness aspects as well as in terms of the personal and other-worldly interpretation of it given by the white oppressor. We also are able to view the possibility that the oppressed may need to be set free from their self-imposed fears and chains. The means that we choose for our own liberation will be seen in the context of reconciliation. If an experience of total reconciliation of the estranged groups is the final goal, then all matters must be placed in Christian theological perspective. Means, values and results are to be explored theologically and ethically. The liberating experience of reconciliation will be one in which black theology will speak redemptively to all sorts and conditions of men, women and children the world over.

We have provided in this essay provisional definitions of our liberation and theism, and have attempted to clarify positions regarding other faith-claims and the points of departure of some of the most outspoken black theologians. Adequate treatment of these differences or similarities has been offered, however, but at least the dialogue has been initiated. The details of the program await further investigation.

NOTES

* This chapter first appeared in <u>The Journal of Religious Thought</u> 33, No. 1 (Spring-Summer 1976): <u>25-35</u>.

BLACK THEOLOGY IN FAITH AND ETHICS

Black theology is a constructive restatement of the Christian faith in the light of black religious experience. This is the positive case for our tasks as black Christian scholars. Negatively, white oppressors of blacks during slavery and subsequent discrimination to the present have provided "a mark of oppression" in the black person's life. This has produced among blacks a psychology of survival to which religion has contributed. The scholarly task emerges out of the sheer omission of the black religious experience in all major works in Christian theology by white scholars. In this sense all previous American theology has been white.

We may illustrate the need for black theology by a brief look at black history. The war in U.S. history that provided an end to slavery is recorded as "a war between the States" or as "a civil war." The name given to that war really depends upon whether the white historian lives to the north or south of the Mason-Dixon line. But to the black scholar it might rightly be called "a war of emancipation." Most U.S. history, until this period of black awareness, has been a record of "white history." Although not labelled such, this is exactly what it has been. Black writers who are attempting to correct these omissions have the advantage of being honest. It is interesting that some white liberals, together with some blacks who have been whitewashed, rushed in at once to write what they designated integrated history. To the credit of writers of black history, they rejected this concept. A massive job of research and writing is needed before the record can be set straight. This task has only begun.

Similarly, there is a need to correct the omissions of "white theology" by a "black theology." Black theology is not inherently racist any more than the black church is. The black church first came into existence out of a need to overcome the injustices, inhumanity, and the indignity of being in a white church. The black caucus within white churches and the black churches themselves exist, presently, out of sheer necessity to overcome white racism within the churches and to provide for black cultural expression and empowerment programs to fight injustices against blacks. While the white silent majority advocates "law-and-order-without-justice" and "God-and-country", the black church remains a strong prophetic Christian voice.

Amid political repression, economic deprivations and wholesale attacks on the humanity of blacks, the black church is preoccupied with fundamental issues like survival and liberation in a white racist society. Black theology is "church theology." Its task is closely linked with "black ecumenism" and the mission of the black church.

A. REREADING THE BIBLE

The Bible is a book well-loved in the black community and within the black church. Black saints and sinners alike quote from its pages. The Bible is the religious textbook for blacks. Even black Muslims quote from the Bible more than they do from the Koran. This indicates that black Muslims are really Christian heretics rather than Islamic sectaries. The Bible has made an unusual impression upon blacks in this country. The Bible is the theological textbook for all Christians; but it has been misread to blacks. It was first misread to them by white preachers and then by black preachers. White preachers read opiate passages to blacks to make them satisfied slaves and docile servants. Many black preachers read similar passages to make them good Toms and to provide sedatives for the pain and suffering caused by racism. Add to this the escapist pie-in-the-sky interpretation of the Bible and one becomes aware of the reason for an outright rejection of Christianity by young militant blacks who cannot accept this version of the Bible.

But the Bible needs to be reread by black theologians for positive reasons as well.[1] A real feel for the Bible exists in the hearts and lives of blacks. The Bible goes to the center of the black religious experience. This is especially true of the Exodus, the prophets and Jesus. Carter G. Woodson, a student of African as well as Afro-American culture, has made the point that blacks have an "Oriental mind." This explains why illiterate black slaves understood the Bible better than the learned white preachers or missionaries who taught it to them. Another point needs to be made. The Bible has a lot to say about liberation (deliverance from bondage), about justice, love and mercy, and about the oppressed. The privileged need definitions, rationalizations, logical convictions and clarity of language to understand liberation, justice and mercy. The oppressed person has an immediate "intuitive understanding" of these words. A black reared in this country does not need a constitutional lawyer or a professor of logic to explain justice or injustice. From early childhood the impact of these words has been plain. Thus, when the Bible speaks of love, justice and mercy, its message goes right to the soul of blacks.

Blacks who reread the Bible today, conscious of their past and their present, will be greatly rewarded. Its message to blacks is personal and social. The Bible speaks existentially to individual blacks, but it also addresses all black people. For example, the bondage of Israel becomes their bondage and the deliverance of Israel their deliverance. When we reread the Bible, (notwithstanding Paul's conservatism -- e.g. "slaves obey your masters"), we discover that the Bible holds to a holistic view of humankind. Biblical anthropology conceives of the human being as unified -- body, mind and spirit. It follows that there is no way for an enslaved person to be free. The faulty theology, written into law, that asserted that a slave could remain chained in body and free in spirit is to be condemned as a demonic distortion of the biblical message. Much Christian paternalism dressed in evangelical zeal and parading as home missions among blacks, reds and browns in this country is informed by the same bogus theology. Blacks, Spanish-Americans, and American Indians are still the heathen near at hand for the missionary who did not get off to Africa.

B. RECONCEIVING THE FAITH

Bishop Joseph A. Johnson speaks of "detheologizing" the faith. His approach is analogous to Bultmann's demythologizing the New Testament.[2] I prefer the "reconception" principle. Bishop Johnson, a black New Testament scholar and noted preacher, has done a worthy job of reinterpreting the Christian faith in the light of the black religious experience. His meaning is too negative. I see this "detheologizing" as precisely the weakness of James Cone's approach. Black theology must not be a simple reaction to white oppression. It is rightly interested in eradicating the misinterpretations of theology that have provided an ideology for the oppression of blacks, but it must do more than this. It must be a constructive restatement or "reconception" of the Christian faith in the light of the black religious experience. Just as Pettinger is busy reinterpreting Christian faith in the light of process philosophy, so black theologians have the task of reinterpreting it in the light of their racial experience.

For blacks, religion is not an ultimate trip of a dropout generation. It is an experience of meaning providing what Tillich calls "the courage to be." It equips blacks who know the real meaning of "threatened being" with resources for social and psychological survival. The often shallow and faddish theological styles of white theologians are inadequate to deal with the religious experience of blacks. There is a lack of vital theological thinking going on in this country that is valid for any American -- black or white. Black theology may yet be a pioneer in pointing the direction for all important theological reflection. It is existential. It is a theology of survival, of meaning, of protest against injustice and inhumanity. It is a theology dealing with the issues of life and death.

In this "reconception" process black theologians will become modern apologists in the best sense of that word.[3] They will seek to be true to the givenness of the eternal message of God's redemptive revelation in and through Christ. Blacks in the context of the black experience will provide the situation in which they will pursue their task. The vital issues of the Christian faith will be reexamined and reinterpreted in terms of bondage and deliverance. Black theologians must deal with the hard questions and the problems of an oppressed people who now seek liberation in a society that remains racist.

Is it possible for blacks to affirm their personhood in this time of repression? Law and order we must have, but not without justice. Just and equal treatment based upon the God-given dignity of all is the basis of all morality. Thus our reconception of the faith will seek to answer the question of how we may be fully *human* and Christian at the same time. The mission of black theology is plain. In this time of black consciousness, power and liberation, it is the only alternative to a mass exodus of blacks from the Christian faith. If a radical distortion of the faith were needed to make the point that black theology is making, then it would not be worth the effort. The fact is, however, that our new humanity in Christ is what the Gospel is all about. We become *dignified* and *free* persons through our saving relationship with Christ, and this has a great deal to do with how we ought to treat one another. *Liberation* leads to *reconciliation*.

A black theology has to take into consideration the cardinal beliefs of the Christian faith: God, humanity, Christ, church and kingdom.[4]

The question of God is crucial for those who seek to be themselves as blacks and at the same time be true to the claims of the Christian faith. Blacks assume that God exists. Africans and Afro-Americans live in "a pool of divinity." The supernatural world is just as real to blacks as the natural. Religion is as native to blacks as breathing. This does not mean that blacks are always well-informed concerning the deity or spiritual realities so native to their experience. The God of Israel and of Jesus, the God of the great prophets of social justice, made an immediate appeal to Africans in bondage in the New World. This God replaced the "High God" and the lesser spirits, for he was "far" and "near" at the same time. The further the gods of the jungle disappeared from their present lives, the more precious the God of the Bible became to them as a divine friend, enabling them to endure the loneliness, ruthlessness and pain experienced by them in this Babylonian Captivity. This is the "faith of our fathers living still."

The black person's God is a God of love, mercy, justice and power. He is Creator, but at the same time is a benevolent and provident God. The real God-question for blacks is not "does God *exist*?" It is rather "does God *care*?" In the language of a Spiritual we sing:

> Over my head, I see trouble in the air,
> There must be a God somewhere.

And again:

> God of our weary years,
> God of our silent tears.
> Thou who has brought us this far on the way,
> Thou who has by Thy *might*
> Led us into the Light
> Keep us forever in Thy hand we pray.

Black theology has to deal likewise with human nature and sinfulness. But its major concern is human *dignity*. Blacks are "nameless," anonymous, "nobody knows their name." They are the one who lives underground and often finds themselves to be "nobodies," a mere face in the crowd. The Christian faith addresses these truly forgotten Americans, the blacks, and tells them to lift up their heads; for in the sight of God they matter. They are indeed somebodies. They are no longer slaves, but sons, heirs. We are: "a son of God, . . . an heir through Christ" (Gal. 4:7, K.J.V.).

In this manner black theologians can make fruitful use of black consciousness and black pride. They can give theological direction to the blacks who live inauthentic lives -- because they have accepted the whites' assessment of their "itness," their "nobodiness." The christian understanding of God's gift of life and of grace leads blacks to self-acceptance and the courage to be. They know that their life contains value, dignity and worth; for the gift of life and of grace can only be bestowed by the Lord of life and the Bishop of our souls -- Jesus Christ Our Lord.

But black theology must be realistic. Sin is a universal human experience. All saints are not black and all sinners are not white. All are one in separation from God and others through sin. We all have chosen the lesser good when a greater good is both known by us and possible by us. Repentance is required of us all. The sin of racism, like all sin, can be both personal and social. People may consider themselves free from prejudice in one-to-one relations with blacks and yet support institutions and enjoy privileges made possible by their participation in an unjust society, and this often without a word or deed of protest.

Forgiveness is based upon a consciousness of sin -- a broken relationship with God and with one another. Sin includes pride, selfishness, and a perversion of will. The sin of racism involves the worship of the finite -- white skin. The crucial problem of racism is that it has created a climate between blacks and whites in which whites *cannot repent* and in which blacks *cannot forgive*. Yet there can be no liberation for blacks or whites unless whites repent of the sins of racism -- both personal and social. There can be no reconciliation between blacks and whites unless blacks forgive.

When we look at what God does for us in Christ, we become aware of the fact that we are heirs of a grace that we do not deserve and have not earned. God does not treat us as we deserve. We deserve death and yet He offers us life. As we look at the Christian creed, then, we observe two things: that without repentance there is no forgiveness, and that forgiveness is a gift of grace. Unrepentant sin is said to be unpardonable sin. Racism is such an unpardonable sin for racists who are unaware of the sin implicit in the worship of white skin as well as a corresponding hatred for their brothers and sisters in black skin. They are really saying "evil be thou good." Their moral perception is so blurred that they have lost the powers of moral discrimination. Many whites are unpardonable sinners in the area of race because they are not aware that they have any sins that require repentance. They are guilty of the sin of the elder brother. They are self-righteous. Some blacks, on the other hand, now hate whites for what they have done to them so intensely that they have become thoroughgoing separatists saying, "All whites are racist." They feel justified in looting, burning, etc., for they feel that they are no longer duty-bound to honor "white ethics." Whites themselves, in relation to the race issue, have made a mockery of their own moral codes. These blacks cannot accept "good-will" because they associate all whites with the unmerited suffering they have endured at the hands of some whites. The "law of retaliation" is their creed. They seek to treat whites as if they were nonexistent or reduce them to an "it" and therefore deny their humanity. Once you deny human beings humanity, you no longer need to recognize them as persons. They become nonpersons and may be treated as such. These blacks are creating for themselves a new racism so that injustice merely changes hands. They are also guilty of an unpardonable sin. In their case, they cannot forgive. But according to the Christian Creed we must forgive our brothers and sisters before we may expect forgiveness from God. Black Christians are called upon to be open to those who seek genuine reconciliation. They must be aware that the ultimate judge of human actions is God alone.

A new understanding is needed of the meaning of Christ. Just as a growing boy has difficulty identifying with his mother, however loving, because he is a potential man, even so a black man, conscious and proud of his black heritage has difficulty accepting fully the white Americanized Christ as Saviour. A people seeking to overcome an identity crises needs a Saviour who identifies with their plight. They need an existential Christ whom they may address as "my Lord and my God."

For blacks the "white hippie" Christ is not a proper symbol of the mediator between God and humanity. He does not belong to the slums. He belongs to the suburbs. How then may he be compasionate unto salvation for blacks and the poor? He does not live in their world nor does he share their experience. But the Jesus of the Gospels is truly for blacks "a God with us." Thus black theologians must re-discover the "humanity of God." This is precisely the meaning of the Incarnation. This Jesus, whom shepherds, tax collectors and common people accepted as their master, appeals to the blacks who are powerless, poor and oppressed. This Jesus was born among the lowly and the meek. He was born in a barn and wrapped in a blanket used for sick cattle. He was crucified in the market place between two thieves and cast upon a dump outside Jerusalem. In his birth, life, ministry, death and resurrection, he cast his lot with the sinful, the needy, the oppressed. The quest of the black Christ has rightly rediscovered this Christ by rereading the Bible and reconceiving the faith. The spirit of God is the spirit that rested upon this same Jesus. The Spirit of the Annunciation, of his baptism and of his adoption is the Spirit who guides, comforts and strengthens black pilgrims in their progress toward the heavenly city.

Finally, we shall touch upon the quest for black peoplehood. We are a people severed from our cohesive tribal and familial roots in Africa, brought in chains to this country where we were further splintered up, scattered and abused. Our family life has never recovered from the shock of slavery. The slender shreds of family life that survived the bondage and human torture of the cruel slave system were subject to another severe test during the northward migration of blacks from plantation to ghetto. The northward movement was characterized by "lonely women and roving men." Most relations between men and women were tenuous. The results as we know, were women as heads of families, parents-without-partners, children without fathers. It is a short step from this to the chaotic delinquency and the crime we witness among blacks in the inner cities. In addition to these, we have a vindictive and repressive prison system bent on retribution rather than rehabilitation: a welfare system designed to drive the devoted father out of his home, as the victim of an economic system that denies him the means of supporting his family; and the general problems of housing and education that pass these social debilities and ills from one generation to another. This is not an *excuse*, but a *description* of a *real* situation that needs to be corrected primarily by the just use of *white power* . What is needed to alter this picture is not merely the concern and action of churches, but of the institutions of society as a whole, including the government. A type of domestic Marshall Plan is required.

In the midst of all this, the black church and its faith have stood as a buffer between blacks and their cruel social environment. When family life was little known among blacks the church gave them a family. In the fellowship of the church the black male affirmed his manhood. Whereas during six days he was "a boy," on Sundays, at least, he was somebody. Black women found emotional release and healing in black worship and fellowship so that they could endure their living hell without fainting beneath their burdens. Thus the church as a people of God, as a household, and as a family, has real significance for blacks who now seek to rediscover their humanity in order to be free.

In conclusion, we, as black theologians, must not be ivory-tower or armchair scholars; we must provide an ideology to make possible rapid strides toward social justice and equality for our people. Liberation and reconciliation, given the proper theological interpretation, must be held up as twin goals. Black theology is a theological ethic, a political theology.

American race relations have been based upon a superordination of whites over blacks. The basis of peace between the races has always been *accommodation* of blacks to the underdog position. Whenever blacks affirm their personhood or peoplehood, seeking freedom and equality, the white response or "blacklash" has been conflict and even violence.

Liberation in black theology will be based upon *equity*. Equity is different from *equality*.[5] Equality is based upon integration that assumes that *white is best*. It is a one-way street that demands that blacks make themselves acceptable by white standards and embrace white values. This demand assumes that black is undesirable and inherently inferior. Blacks are expected to disrobe themselves of their culture and history, and declare a poverty of culture. They are to consider themselves bankrupt and exemplify cultural nudity in order to be integrated into the white church and the majority society.

This is no longer possible for blacks who are conscious and proud of their culture. They refuse to consider white as inherently good, beautiful and superior. They assert that black is beautiful, that blacks have a worthy past and a noble heritage. We are no longer a people with amnesia. We remember our Afro-American past and henceforth assert that this past and this culture must be recognized and contribute to the enrichment of our pluralistic society.

This is the meaning of the "black caucus" and "black ecumenism." The Consultation on Church Union is not a primary concern for blacks. A super church would merely add to the frustration and anger of blacks who even now feel swallowed up and powerless in the white church. Only black Methodists and those blacks who are a "caucus" within white member bodies of COCU are involved. The majority of blacks never left major black denominations to enter the white church, which never had the will to purge itself of racism. The present "black mood" has created a climate of mistrust between blacks and whites to such an extent that blacks in COCU are saying that they must get together themselves or get out. They do not want to be the victims of a "divide and rule situation" within the new superchurch, when the only hope of their people is in a responsible use of collective power for liberation. It will be well for a strong caucus movement to remain in COCU and keep the pressures on for reparations, restitution, and empowerment programs. Furthermore the young, the black and the poor are the conscience of America. The white church must not be allowed to rid itself of guilt by a single handout like the pittance the bishops offered the Black Catholic Caucus.

It will be well if the blacks stay one as "the church within the church." When good white liberals say, "If the blacks want to keep to themselves, it is all right with us, we can do without them," this reveals how superficially they understand their own guilt and participation in racist insitutions that create and sustain intolerable and inhuman conditions for blacks. If they cannot work effectively in the black community, indifference is no solution. Let them go to work humanizing white power on behalf of blacks and all oppressed people. Black Christians have a prophetic mission to remain with the white church as a "plague" to prevent good, God-and-country, law-and-order-without-justice white Christians from being at ease in a racist Zion. Whites need the black presence to keep them aware of the seriousness of racial sin and of the fact that without repentance and forgiveness of this sin there can be "whiteanity" but no true Christianity. In this sense black Christians may be in some cases a new Israel, a chosen people, who may yet challenge the church in this country to be the church.

Obviously the real power base of the black Christian witness is the black church in the black community. The black church is a slumbering giant in the cause of black liberation. It has not yet flexed its moral and spiritual muscles in this cause. Black theology is addressed to all blacks -- to those in white churches, to those in black churches, and to those in no churches. To the extent that black theology is ecumenical it attacks racism in all Christian bodies and calls all blacks together in the fight for freedom and humanity.

Reconciliation is the goal of black theology. But reconciliation is built on liberation.[6] The brokenness within the body of Christ, resulting from racist oppression of blacks, cannot be overcome by sentimentality and empty promises. Black theology believes in a God who is lovingly just. The love, justice and power of God are the basis of all morality, social as well as individual. Thus blacks must be set free. They must be treated as persons. Their dignity is secure in creation and redemption, in nature and grace. They are children of God by spiritual adoption. Their new humanity is freedom. Their inner freedom cannot exist apart from outer freedom. Equity and justice for blacks are God-given, not human-bestowed. They are their crown-rights. Any reconciliation that is truly Christian between blacks and whites must be between equals. In Christ the dividing wall is removed and love unites the estranged. Christ is head of the church. He is liberator and reconciler. As his disciples, black and white, we are called to a ministry of freedom and reconciliation.

NOTES

1. J. Deotis Roberts, Roots of the Black Future: Family and Church (Philadelphia: Westminister, 1980), pp. 98-107.

2. Bishop Joseph A. Johnson, Proclamation Theology (Shreveport, La.: Fourth Episcopal District Press of the C.M.E. Church, 1977), Ch. II.

3. Roberts, op. cit., pp. 15-22.

4. See my Liberation and Reconciliation: A Black Theology (Philadelphia: Westminister, 1971), Ch. V, VI and VII.

5. Roberts, A Black Political Theology (Philadelphia: Westminister, 1974), Ch. X.

6. Roberts, Liberation and Reconciliation, Ch. II.

PART II

LIBERATION AND CONTEXTUALIZATION

OPPRESSION AND LIBERATION IN WORLD HISTORY

A few years ago Reinhold Niebuhr, the great political prophet and theologian, warned this nation about its "prides." He spoke of the pride of wealth, the pride of race and the pride of power. He noted that while European monarchs have become honorary figureheads, disrobed of their real power now invested in parliaments and prime ministers, U.S. presidents are becoming tyrants. His warning was as a voice crying in the wilderness, unheard and unheeded. He also kept a critical eye on the sermons preached in the White House and alienated himself from the company of God-and-country middle Americans who blindly celebrated the coalescence of piety and politics on the Potomac. Recent events have vindicated Reinhold Niebuhr's role as a prophet without honor.

I. THE REVOLUTIONARY QUEST IN INTERNATIONAL FOCUS

Paul Lehmann, a long-time associate of Reinhold Niebuhr, has written a powerful book entitled *The Transfiguration of Politics*. Lehmann is concerned with the presence and power of Jesus of Nazareth in and over human affairs. This is a bold, even an explosive book. Lehmann looks at Hannah Arendt's work, *On Revolution* and applauds her for observing that revolution is born of the passion for humanization. He does not accept her conclusion, however, that the American Revolution was the only successful one in view of the fact that it did not devour its children. Lehmann is concerned about the relationship between revolution and humanization and he longs for a revolution that will keep its promises to humanize life. According to Lehmann, revolutions have a saving possibility. Faith has to do with retelling the story of Jesus of Nazareth from the perspective of those who have been repressed by the Establishment. The story of Jesus must now be retold under the "kiarotic" and apocalyptic pressure of the history of revolutions so that history may be saved by the power of the story. Lehmann would have us discover the power of Jesus' presence to shape the passion for humanization that generates revolution. Christians are the true revolutionaries because their ultimate commitment is to keep revolution, truth and life effectively together. In this way freedom for revolutionary action can be bound up in faith with freedom from the coercion of revolutionary action. Ultimately the vocation of a valid revolution is to bring about love.¹

Lehman asserts:

> The Christ story is the story of the presence and power of Jesus of Nazareth in and over the ambiguity of power in human affairs. It tells in word and deed of the liberating limits and the renewing possibilities within which revolutionary promises and passions make room for the freedom to be and to stay human in the world.²

Whether one agrees with Lehmann or not, we must admire his courage and conviction, to say nothing of the mature scholarship of the book.

In a recent work Sidney Lens analyzed the practice of capitalism and socialism in global perspective.³ According to Lens, Karl Marx had planned that his ideology would be most applicable in those countries where material development had reached an appropriate level. But most recently social upheaval has been centered in the less developed countries. At the present time, many countries are experiencing what Lens called "a double revolution". Karl Marx outlined a socio-economic cycle of birth, growth and decay. The middle class, or bourgeoisie, aided by the peasantry, would seize power from the feudal class. A class struggle would ensue between the bourgeoisie and the peasants. This would be followed by a revolution of the majority, the proletariat, against the minority, the capitalist class. A new social order would thus emerge designated as "the dictatorship of the proletariat."

According to Lens, the revolutions of this century often move in another direction. Peoples rise up against the alliance of foreign imperialists and native reactionaries to liberate themselves. They leap from feudalism to socialism. Thus the revolutions in underdeveloped countries resemble the pre-Marxist revolutions. The difference is that international capitalism has intervened and that the amount of money needed to provide a modern economy is many times greater than it was 150 years ago. Lens provides a careful evaluation of Marxism under Lenin, Trotsky and Stalin, and analyzes the social upheavals in Asia, Africa and Latin America. He is especially impressed by "the human face" of socialism in Yugoslavia under Tito. He sees it as humane, pragmatic and creative in its expression. It includes "self-management" and "social ownership." The surpluses go to the worker and society as a whole rather than to the individual entrepreneur or shareholder. Along with this sharing of wealth is a decentralization of decision-making.

According to Lens, capitalism cannot keep its promise to solve basic economic problems for two reasons: (1) there are limits to growth; the supply of food and natural resources is not inexhaustible, and (2) The flow of goods and capital will not be indefinitely uninterrupted. Capitalism may be somewhat tamed and controlled by domestic law and politics, but it is inherently uncontrollable on the international scene. The self-interest of one country is not compatible with the self-interest of another. A nation may even indulge in military aggression in its own economic interest. A case in point was Kissinger's rash statement that the U.S. might, under extreme circumstances, declare war in order to get oil from the Middle East. Furthermore, multi-national corporations easily become super-governments in themselves and operate beyond divine and human laws.

The maximization of profit is the guiding motive of capitalism. This selfish motive, even if it is wed to the Protestant ethic, can lead toward an ecological crisis as well as a political-economic impasse. What we need, according to Lens, is a collectivist élan rather than rugged individualism, for we must maintain a balance between natural resources, technology and population. A humane and just social order will not develop from the profit motive. What we have is a situation in which 5 or 6 per cent of the world's population uses one half of its resources. One fourth of humanity lives in affluence while three-fourths live in appalling poverty. Lens is prophetic in observing that history is crowding the human race toward a more humane social structure and time is running out.

Len's mature study serves here as a basis for exploring the revolutionary human quest for liberation in international focus. He provides a great deal of worldly wisdom from the sphere of political economy that theologian-ethicists sorely need. We must have some acquaintance with the "mathematics of power" if we are to make any dent at all in the arena of social and economic policy-making that affects the nature and destiny of people and communities.

Nevertheless we must say that Lens does not give adequate attention to the ideological foundations of communism, with its myths of the inherent goodness of collective humanity destined for utopia, or its negation of the God-idea and an anthropology rooted in the *imago Dei*. Neither a romantic view of humanity that does not deal realistically with the radical nature of sin nor a stress on the human person as a collective being that disregards personal dignity can serve as an adequate corrective for the rugged individualism of capitalism with its emphasis upon the maximization of profit.

On the other hand, the Protestant ethic, as used and abused by many capitalists, cannot be the ultimate solution for the social and economic woes of "the wretched of the earth" or the "have nots". There is a need for equity in the economic order if life is to be made human for the masses. This can exist only where there is a compassionate concern for the wellbeing of both individuals and communities through the sharing of wealth and power. In Christian theological ethics there is a realism about sin and redemption that is essential to all futuristic planning. Without such realism, romaticism prevails, whether the context be capitalism or socialism.

II. THEOLOGIES OF LIBERATION FROM OPPRESSION IN WORLD HISTORY

Arend Van Leeuwen quotes approvingly from Bishop Leslie Newbigin as follows:

> What is happening now . . . is that the peoples who have no history are being drawn into the history of which the centre is Jesus Christ and that is the only history. In other words, that which has been static, or at least cyclical, in which the only movement was round and round, life and death, rise and fall -- that is being drawn into a movement which is linear and dynamic, which is moving irreversibly and can never be back where it was before. The ferment of change which arises from the impact of the Gospel, or at least of the kind of life which is given an irreversible direction to that which was once static or merely cyclical. When I say the impact of the Gospel or of that kind of life which has its origin within Christendom, I include technology, western political ideas, Communism -- all those things which have come into the eastern world from the West and have their roots in the Christian tradition.[4]

Van Leeuwen himself has contrasted what he calls the "ontocratic" East and the "theocratic" West. By the former he means a cosmic totality, while the latter implies heaven, Spirit and the kingdom of the Lord. He is forced to admit that technology has divided the theocracy of the West into sacred and secular components. But he still lauds Western civilization and asserts forthrightly that the end of Western domination does not mean the end of the expansioin of Western civilization. This conquest, he asserts, is greater than before. In the past nations of the Third World were forced to embrace Western values, but now they are eagerly taking the initiative to acquire them for themselves.

Liberation and Contextualization 75

It goes without saying that the writer has a Western bias. He is not satisfied with stating facts, for he is working from a thesis that demonstrates the cultural captivity of Christianity in the West. He has the mentality of a Western missionary who transplants Christianity to Asia or Africa. He does not appear to appreciate the possibility that Africans may discover Christ for themselves in their own culture and history and that this may be in God's plan. Like most theologians of mission, his perspective links Christianization and development. The new direction, however, is *indigenization* and *liberation*.

III. INDIGENIZATION AND LIBERATION

"Liberation" is the term that sums up the new mood among peoples of the Third World. *"Development"* is the term most useful for the more powerful nations which have economic interests in the so-called underdeveloped countries. *"Liberation from oppression"* is a formula for the multitudes in overpopulated and poverty-stricken societies in Asia, Africa, Latin America, the islands of the oceans and oppressed minorities (or majorities) everywhere. The human race is yearning for freedom and a humane existence.

Religion is a power at the center of this ferment for human liberation among all nations and peoples. The work titled *The Religions of the Oppressed*[5] provides an account of a widespread nativistic reaction to oppression in the post-colonial era. The tension that built up during the colonial period increased with the rise of nationalism and its cultural concomitants until it broke and was released like a mighty flood. Today there is a close affinity between *liberation* and *indigenization*. Reconceived religions are providing motivation for nation-building. Vital religious movements and theological systems cannot divorce themselves from the quest for personal identity and political self-determination around the globe.

Liberation from oppression is a serious concern among the masses everywhere, but the social context is different in various parts of the world. Blacks are a majority in South Africa, while they are a minority in the United States. Oppression is called segregation in this country; it is known as apartheid in South Africa. But racism is a form of inhumanity. It is unjust and un-Christian in any land and among any people because it dehumanizes both the oppressor and the oppressed. As long as it is sustained neither can lay hold of their full humanity nor can they acquire an authentic existence.

Harold R. Isaacs notes a connection between the experience of untouchables in India today and that of blacks in the United States.[6] Having studied oppressed groups in the United States, Israel, India, Malaysia, the Philippines and Japan, he points to what he calls "a universal reach" for new sources of self-respect in human affairs. New racial, cultural and national identities are being formed everywhere. The postscript to Isaac's book is most disturbing. He reports that the research for the book is ten years old. Whereas the so-called ex-untouchables have grown in number during those ten years from sixty-five million to eighty million, their status remains the same. They are ex-untouchables by law, but they still remain untouchables in fact. Not surprisingly, some two million have already embraced Buddhism, a casteless religion, which in some areas, has entered into social criticism and action. The liberation imperative is at work here and those in power should now heed the warning signs.

In the summer of 1971, while on a travel-study tour of several African societies, I vistied Addis Abba. Like most black Americans, I had looked to Ethiopia with pride. Hailie Selassie was a sage and wise man who had brought gifts to Howard University. His kingdom was the oldest dynasty of Africa that remained, into this century, undefeated by the West and never subjected to or humiliated by colonial rule. The Italians made an attempt to dominate the Ethiopians during World War II, but failed to gain a permanent foothold there. Furthermore, Ethiopia was seen as an ancient Christian kingdom. Even Islam which had been so successful amid Coptic Christianity in Egypt, was not able to uproot this ancient Christian Orthodoxy in Ethiopia. Coptic Christianity, now the Ethiopian church, was the established form of religion. The king and court loved, respected and supported the priesthood and the church.

All appeared peaceful, and downtown Addis Abba looked modern and properous. My experience for the first few days was limited to guided tours provided by the Ministry of Tourism. But my practice on such trips has always been to get out in the field and meet the people, to observe and listen to the masses. I was jolted by my visit into the peasant territories. And then as I conversed with law students and theology students my sensitivities were further heightened regarding the suffering of the masses.

Those theology students who spoke of social, economic and political change did not expect to be ordained priests. They saw the church as indifferent and insensitive to the poverty and suffering of the masses. For all practical purposes the church had become a department of the state to give sanction to the established political order. The king and those in power, they said, had amassed great wealth. The masses had been abandoned to their lot of misery. Being motivated by a political understanding of the gospel, the seminarians expected to work and serve among the disinherited.

A few days later I went for a stroll in the park. A group of hungry boys approached me. They wore rags, they were obviously undernourished, and they complained that they had pains in their stomach from lack of food. It is difficult to resist such an opportunity to express Christian compassion, but one soon learns that under such circumstances, it is wiser to turn off compassion. Even a rich person could not begin to feed the hungry and clothe the naked under such wretched circumstances.

Not long thereafter I took the bold step of going behind the large walls erected around the bazaars and shacks in the heart of the city. This was off-limits for those visitors who have a mere commercial or cultural interest in travel. Behind those attractive walls I saw teeming thousands of humans living under animal conditions, in pigsties of squalor, in sharp contrast to the pomp and circumstance of palace and church, king and priests. As I pondered this tragedy in human contrast, I was accosted by children who clung to me like leeches, begging and pleading for handouts. As I painfully scolded them or sent them away, I noted one lad who persisted. He continued to follow and I saw in his eyes the pain and the hope of a revolutionary. Most children gave in, they accepted their fate, but here was one who was born to rebel. I said to myself, he will be a liberator if things remain as they are. When he becomes a man he will change conditions, by violence if necessary.

The crisis has erupted; the rest we read daily in our newspapers. How sad it is that those in power in that ancient kingdom and the mighty everywhere do not read the signs of the times and do not share the resources and the power to make life more human for the masses of people around the globe. Too often the evangelists and the missionaries become priests in the king's court.

Just as Amos was rejected at Bethel, even so prophets in our time will not be invited to preach in the White House. The Mormons have enshrined their patriotism and piety in a multi-million dollar monument near the nation's capitol. In spite of the architectural and aesthetic splendor it represents, to the black oppressed minority, it is only a monument to institutional racism. Here is an American Success Story, the very finest expression of the merger of the American dream and theology. But *it is not* a Christian church -- whatever its pretensions. No church can be Christian that does not recognize the equal worth of all persons because they share the same created nature and have all alike been redeemed by the same grace.

These examples provide a contrast: on the one hand, we see a state that uses a church to sanction oppression and, on the other, a church that theologizes a race of people into inferiority and yet views itself as ultrapatriotic, expressing the finest in the history and culture of a nation. Against these systems of oppression we offer a theology of liberation. We believe that the human quest and history itself are on the side of human liberation. The time has come when the gospel must go political. Moltmann is correct: We must now be concerned with the "crimes of history" and let the oppressed go free.

IV DEPRIVATION AND MILLENNARISM

A. deWaal Malefijit relates "millenarism" and "deprivation."[7] Millenary movements often involve active struggles for greater political participation or independence. These movements usually demand intense commitment and unconditional faith and loyalty from their followers and are often action-oriented. By concerted, communal efforts, people seek to hasten the coming of the millennium. Thus millennary movements are powerful potential agents of social and political change.

Deprivation regularly attends the rise of religio-political movements. Deprivation exists when there is a discrepancy between legitimate expectations and actuality. The reference may be to differences between the past and the present situations, between present and future, or between one person's lot and another's. The deprivation may relate to material goods, to status, to behavior, to worth, and so on. Usually personal dissatisfactions alone are not sufficient to set such movements in motion. People will follow prophets only when they strike responsive chords and promise the alleviation of commonly experienced social deprivations. When the framework of authority is disrupted, the disoriented classes will revolt, or if revolt is not possible, they will follow one who formulates a new and better order.[8]

Some programs of theology must tackle liberation and indigenization at the same time. Examples could be found in a wide spectrum of areas around the world. P.D. Devanandan and M.M. Thomas of the Religion and Society Institute at Bangalore, India, are representative of this outlook. Devanandan was aware of the Indian situation -- of nation-building and the

Hindu renaissance. He accepted the challenge to the Christian community to participate in this process of nation-building. In his thought he combined his reflections on what he called "common humanity" and "new creation." Devanandan pleaded for a constant probing into religious consciousness and the structure or constitution of human nature that make both response to and rebellion against God possible. He was also preoccupied with the meaning of revelation. Revelation, as viewed by Thomas and Devanandan, was concerned not merely with the relationship between man and God; it also implied a

> transformation of human nature and human relations so that it is proper to include the new structures of Christian community as part of the deed of God in Christ.[9]

Devanandan developed his view of "common humanity" within a Christological frame of reference and spoke of both Christians and non-Christians as being subject to Christ's concern for all. This enabled him to link "common humanity" with "new creation." Christ inaugurated a "new creation" with cosmic dimenions which manifests itself in changing political relationships in our time and which implies the manifestation of "common humanity."

"New creation" was used in reference to contemporary secular-theological emphases by M.M. Thomas, who applauded the value of a secularization that liberated people to become properly involved in social developments. Devanandan pleaded for a Christian participation in nation-building implied by an acceptance of Nehru's idea of a secular state. Thomas and Devanandan shared a view of "open secularism" that expressed itself in a common, or inter-religious, grappling with problems and responsibilities of modern human existence. They saw the real task as that of helping Hindus to redefine the meaning of religion.

Devanandan made use of Hocking's reconception principle as a basis for inter-religious dialogue. Assuming the all-inclusive character of various religions, which he eloquently described as an interplay of creed, cultus and culture, he pleaded that adherents of various religions, in a period of change, should reconceive the characteristics of their own religion with reference both to the demands of the changing situation and to what the other religions may contain of spiritual treasures. He provides a classic example of such reconception of Hinduism in his study *The Concept of Maya*.

What he sought through this Christian-Hindu dialogue was increased Hindu concern for the liberation of people from the prevailing social conditions that limit possibilities for fulfilling human destiny. His work, however, transcended the social and political dimensions of the process of reconception and anticipated a theology of real interfaith dialogue. He did not give up his all-inclusive Christological affirmations. He gave little attention to the religio-phenomenological implications of the Christian-Hindu conversation. This he left to scholars like Hendrik Kraemer and J.B. Carman. His real concern was the reconception of Hinduism, with special reference being given to the politico-ideological implications of the Christian relationship to reconceived Hinduism.[10]

V. DETENTE IN OUR RELIGIOUS CONVERSATION

The detente in our religious conversation must be in the context of an all-inclusive humankind. The transcontinental dialogue must be more than Euro-American or East-West; it must be Pan-African and Pan-American as well. All humans are religious and therefore inter-religious dialogue must drop its exclusivism and pro-Western bias and embrace all humans. *But charity begins at home.* So, for example. in *Black Religion* Joseph Washington alerts us to a fourth religion in America beyond Protestantism, Judaism and Catholicism: black folk religion. We will not pursue this further at this time because we will be treating the matter more fully in Chapter 5.

We are just coming to grips with ethnic pluralism and religion. Authorities on world religions, even in this country, have virtually ignored the religious experience of native Americans. Anthropologists have turned mainly to Africa, South America, Australia and Oceania for examples of religious systems similar to those very much alive among American Indians.

In *God is Red*, Vine Deloria, Jr., a native American trained at a Lutheran theological seminary, has produced an informative and disturbing book. It is a work that breathes the air of liberation and indigenization in this time of world history.

According to Deloria, native Americans have a casual attitude toward history in contrast to Christian thought and belief for which time is central. The contrast between Christianity with temporal interpretation of history and the American Indian tribal religions with their spatial emphasis is clearly illustrated when we understand the nature of sacred hills, sacred rivers, and other geographical features sacred to Indian tribes.[11] He observes that changing the conception of religious reality from temporal to spatial terms involves severely downgrading the teaching and preaching aspect of religious activity. Rearrangement of individual behaviorial patterns is incidental

Liberation and Contextualization 81

to communal involvement in ceremonies and continual renewing of community relationships with the holy places of revelation.[12]

We conclude with this observation drawn from Deloria's book:

> World history as presently conceived in the Christian nations is the story of Western man's conquest of the remainder of the world and his subsequent rise to technological sophistication.... A major task remains for Western man. He must quickly come to grips with the breadth of man's experiences and understand these experiences from a world viewpoint, not simply a Western one.[13]

NOTES

1. Paul Lehmann, <u>The Transformation of Politics</u> (New York: Harper & Row, 1975), pp. 10, xii, 69-70.

2. Ibid., p. 20.

3. <u>The Promises and Pitfalls of Revolution</u> (Philadelphia: United Church Press, 1974).

4. Van Leeuwen in C.C. West and D.M. Paton, eds. <u>The Missionary Church in East and West</u> (London: SCM, 1959), p. 82.

5. V. Lanternari, <u>The Religions of the Oppressed</u> (New York: Knoft, 1963).

6. <u>India's Ex-Untouchables</u> (New York: Harper, 1974), p.7.

7. <u>Religion and Culture</u> (New York: Macmillan, 1968), pp. 339-41.

8. Ibid., pp. 342-43.

9. See Carl F. Hallencruz, <u>New Approaches to Men of Other Faiths</u> (Geneva: WCC, 1970), pp. 56-62.

10. Ibid.

11. Vine Deloria, <u>God is Red</u> (New York: Grosset & Dunlap. 1973), pp. 111, 117, 138.

12. Ibid., p. 81.

13. Ibid., pp. 122-23.

THE ROOTS OF BLACK THEOLOGY:
AN HISTORIC PERSPECTIVE

My purpose is to explore the historic roots of black theology. This is no mean assignment -- it is an awesome task. Given the limitations of space and time given to this task, my conclusions can be only exploratory and provisional. But it is a work that must be done and it is a privilege to begin so noble an endeavour.

I shall now indicate how we expect to approach our subject. First, I will suggest that the origins of black theology are hidden in the oral tradition of black religious experience. Second, oral tradition surfaces in folkloric references in sermons and other folk expressions. Third, I will trace the ideological basis for black theology. Fourth, I will look at black theology itself as a formal program with special reference to its method and content. We will conclude with a critical assessment of the past and present status of the movement. Having charted out an ambitious course, the task now begins.

I. THE ORAL TRADITION

What we now call black theology is about a decade old. When we make this assertion, it is necessary to indicate what we mean by black theology. First, I want to state what I do *not* mean by black theology, for this will set our definition in its proper context. We do not have in mind basic religious beliefs which are abundant in the oral or written tradition of blacks, though elements of black theology are found there. Neither do I have in mind a popular or journalistic notion of "black theology" which turns out to be an expression of black folk religious beliefs. What I do have in mind is a formal and systematic interpretation of a creed of doctrine worked out by persons who are practising theologians with the knowledge and skills of this discipline. Furthermore, black theology is thus for the expression of a faith for black Christians who belong to congregations of Christians. It is an expression of the Christian faith in the black experience for all black Christians -- including those in white denominations. Black theology is one which has special reference to those blacks who are deeply embedded in the black congregations in black communities. Essentially it is black church theology. The black church is the center and context of black theology, though it is compelled to enter into conversation or dialogue beyond this foundational setting.

With this preliminary look, let us explore the origins of black theology in the oral tradition. This tradition goes back to Africa as W.E.B. DuBois reminds us in his classic discourse on "black spirituality."[1] Africa has much of its cultural history encouched in an oral tradition. African religions are not religions of the Book as are semitic religions and many Middle Eastern and Asian religions. African religious beliefs are not easily understood by means of Western logic and metaphysics. Scholars, black and white, whose sole intellectual equipment consist of the historical-critical method of biblical exegesis or whose thought-structures are shaped by Aristotelian logic or Platonic metaphysics are ill-equipped to unlock the message of the African background to Afro-American thought and belief.

I do not attempt to reopen the Pandora's box of puzzles arising out of the Frazier-Herskovits controversy. In several writings, I make it clear that we begin with the assumption that there are "Africanisms" in black religious experience.[2] There are traces of a "world-view" or "life-view" of an African temperament within the collective unconsciousness of blacks. This temperament radiates throughout all black cultural expressions whether in religion, literature, art, music or drama. It is the quality of "soul."

Sir James Frazier did not give adequate attention to the fact that blacks were never fully accepted into mainstream American culture. Our very survival, therefore, depended upon the cultivation of a subculture satiated with religious experience. In a real sense religion preserved and nurtured black soul culture. The religious element in black religious experience is not merely as a "compensatory" factor as Mays seems to argue,[3] but as a powerful incentive to protest social injustices, as recent writers like Harding[4] and Wilmore[5] indicate. In sum, the "soul" quality of black religion within black culture is the basis for continuity of the African-Afro-America connection. The sources of both consolation and radicalism in black religious experience are rooted in this context.

Since there exists such tribal diversity among Africans and their religious systems, phenomenology of religion, social psychology and anthropology as well as ethnohistory are indispensable tools of investigation. C.H. Long,[6] a black historian of religion, and Joseph R. Washington,[7] a sociologist of religion, have done some creative excavations in these areas, but I am not happy with their conclusions. Long is too skeptical or cautious regarding the "African Connection," while Washington is downright confusing on the issue. Both men reject the validity of the apologetic use of this material by black theologians. Presumably both scholars have bought into standards of theological discourse set by scholars in the North Atlantic community. Long and Washington have a closed mind on the subject and have not come to grips with the bold thinking of theologians in the Third World as well as their black colleagues. Cannot theologians have a breakthrough as well as phenomenologists and sociologists of religion? I fear that these fine scholars, along with some others, have unwittingly fallen into the trap of white scholars who summarily dismiss all black scholars according to standards which they have set up. It is time for all scholars -- black and white -- to be mindful that all scholarship is culture-bound and may be used as an instrument of oppression.

II. THE ROOTS OF BLACK THEOLOGY

The indigenous base for black theology is found in our oral enthno-history. It is found in the exhortation of black preachers and the simple folktales of unschooled black people. It is found in popular literature and in classic prose, poetry and drama. In a word, the roots of black theology is deeply embedded in the soil of black culture.

There is a great deal of contextual theology in the following:

> You are de same god, Ah
> Dat heard de sinner man cry.
> Same God dat sent de zigzag lightning tuh
> Join de mutterin thunder.
> Same God dat holds de elments
> In uh unbroken chain of controllment.
> Same God dat hung on Cavalry and died,
> Dat we might have a right tuh de tree of life --
> We thank thee that our sleeping couch
> Was not our cooling board,
> Our cover was not our winding sheet. . .
> Please tuh give us uh restin' place
> Where we can praise Thy name forever,
>
> Amen.[8]

God is eternal, the same yesterday, today and forever. He hears the sinner's cry of repentance and forgives sin. He is the creator of the elements in the entire cosmic realm. But humans have a special place in His creative and redemptive plan. God suffers for us. The author of the above hymn to Calvary is proof of God's intention that all might be saved. The hymn concludes with a paean of praise for awakening from sleep to greet the light of another day. Yet the hymn expresses the hope that springs eternal with the assurance of everlasting life. It is unusual to find so much material for theological reflection tied up in such a small neat bundle.

Dr. Martin Luther King, Jr. once recalled that he walked beside an elderly woman in the Selmar March. He asked her if she was tired of walking. Her reply was: "My feets am tired, but my soul am rested." In the midst of great suffering we have been blessed with a sense of humor, "the gift of laughter." We have been able to rejoice in the mist of tears. This sorrow-joy experience is noted in this excerpt from the spiritual "There's A Little Wheel A-Turnin."

> Oh, I don't feel no ways tired in my heart,
> No, I don't feel no ways tired in my heart,
>   In my heart, in my heart,
> Oh, I don't feel no ways tired in my heart.[9]

John J. Jasper (1812-93) was a slave during his youth. A fellow slave taught him to read. He started reading out of the New York Spelling Book until he was able to read the Bible. Within months he was converted and soon after that he was called to preach. He was no doubt a biblical fundamentalist innocent of any natural scientific knowledge, but his sermon, "De Sun Do Move" is a theological credo in itself. He has no reservation in affirming the creative and redemptive purposes of God. God is creator, Redeemer and Judge.

> My Lord is great! He rules in de heavens, in de earth and down under de ground. . . . [10]

It is instructive to note how much traditional folklore is satiated with religious meanings. In an Afro-American folktale, Uncle Pleas always prayed "Oh, Lawd, kill all de white fo'ks, and save all de black. He prayed under a large oak tree every night. The master discovered what he was doing. One night the master got to the tree first and took several rocks up with him. When Uncle Pleas prayed this night and repeated his usual refrain three times, the master let two or three rocks fall on his head. Uncle Pleas was frightened for he thought that God was throwing the rocks. He called out, "Look out dere, Gawd! Stop dat th'owin' dem rocks. Don't yuh know white from black?"[11] The theological implication of this bit of folklore can lead some very seminal discussions in black theology such as in *God of the Oppressed* or *Is God a White Racist?* by William Jones.

The explorations of the black theologian into folk materials is rewarding, but it must be done in such manner that the theologian may get in touch with people who are in touch with

God. A most valiant attempt to get at this folk base for "Black Beliefs" radiates in the works of Henry Mitchell, but what he has done is not black theology proper. He has, however, been working incessantly at the sources.

My own work in this area has been mainly encouched in my study of folklore.[12] James Cone tapped a rich lode of raw deposits for black theology in his study of spirituals and blues.[13] The problem with theologians looking at this type of material, however, is that they often see what they look for. The study I made is not so much theology but literary criticism and phenomenology of religion. Cone's study, on the other hand, is mainly a theological interpretation of the material. My only point is that the theologian must consciously lean away from this material with his convictions until the sources speak to him. In the language of Eliade, the folklore must confront him as an *hierophany*; it must show itself. Once the theologian is able to describe what he has discovered in the phenomenon of the mass black religious experience, he can properly begin the hermeneutical task of interpreting and communicating what he has found.

III. THE IDEOLOGICAL BASIS FOR BLACK THEOLOGY

It is important to now look briefly at the ideological basis for a black theology. Blacks deny that there are "ideas" in black experience. It is time for us to come to grips with the fact that we have an epistemological component in our experience. Our task is to discover and describe this core at the center of black thought and treat the thought at the heart of black religious experience.

Black theology is often rejected both for not being rooted in black folk religious experience and for being a formalistic program of systematic theology. Ideas have consequences. Thought is a basis of action no less than it is for reflection. Anyone studying the social upheavals in the Third World during the post-colonial period can make this claim with hard evidence. We make a serious mistake when we restrict black religious experience to the affections alone.

A wholistic approach to the existing individual requires that the head, heart and will be moved by a source of belief. The question cannot be limited to the emotional quality of soul. In black experience there is a cognitive as well as volitional content of the soul quality. Knowledge can be intuitive as well as rational. The existentialists insist that "truth is subjectivity" -- it is participation of the knower in what is known. Most African/black thinkers appear to assume an existentialist posture. This is even true of those scholars like

Nathan Scott who keeps his distance from all other black scholars no less than Howard Thurman, the black mystic-poet-religious philosopher *par excellence*.

An equally important characteristic of black thought is its sensitivity to community. *Ujamma*, "familyhood" or network of kinship ties, informs the best in African/Afro-American thought and practice. We have only begun to unpack the significance of the image of the black extended family for a doctrine of the church in black theology. This is crucial not merely for the depth and intimacy of fellowship, but also for the political and social mission of a fellowship made of an oppressed people seeking liberation here and now. Spirituality, fellowship, ethics and social action are all bound up with a theological exploration of communalism in the African connection of Black Churches.

The prophetic vision has been more clearly lifted up in black theology. It builds more securely upon the radicalism in black religious history. The spiritual component in black religious experience has been virtually neglected in the quest for a more "political" message. I have not been unmindful of this element and for this I have been critized severely by William Jones.[14] I shall not follow this quest for meaning, consolation and spirituality here. It does exist and it has been the means to sanity and wholeness for a people victimized by injustice and inhumanity in America.

Here we will be brief in presenting some evidence for the assertion of radicalism in black religious history. This is not to ignore the "compensatory" or reactionary characteristics of our history. By means of documents and interpretation the works by S. Stuckey[15] and R.F. Betts[16] trace "the ideology of blackness." Stuckey presents and interprets such seminal documents as "The Ethiopian Manifesto" by Robert Alexander Young; "The Appeal" by David Walker; "Address to the Slaves" by Henry Highland Garnet and "The Political Destiny of the Colored Race" by Martin R. Delany. Betts has brought to this discussion materials from Edward W. Blyden, Marcus Garvey and Malcolm X, to mention only a few. What we meet here and elsewhere is a series of installments upon a whole tradition of black radicalism in nationalistic "manifestos" providing a pattern of reflection upon ideologies of black liberation. What is remarkable is the manner in which religious convictions inform this entire tradition. Religion behind this tradition is derived from Christian and non-Christian sources. Black ecumenism growing out of the thirst for freedom has never been provincial. It transcends sectarianism as it focuses upon liberation. It provides a basis for an "operational unity" against a common foe -- racism, and for a unified goal -- liberation.

Liberation and Contextualization

Black religionists, especially ministers, deeply supported abolitionism, the convention movement, economic development and moral uplift in the 19th century. Religion has been a factor in the history of the NAACP as well as the Harlem Literary Renaissance. "Black power" was manifest in the labor involvement of A. Philip Randolf and the ministry of Adam Clayton Powell, Jr. All of the currents of thought and activism filtered into the Civil Rights/Integration period which reached its nadir in the decade from 1954-65. The history of the black power/conscious movement built on these ideological and activistic foundations. The current approach to black liberation may be reformist and not revolutionary, but it plugs into this same history of thought and faith among blacks. The black theologian, as interpreter, must bring the deeper understanding of the gospel to this sustained push for freedom incorporated in our history. We affirm that faith in God has brought us "thus far on the way" and this faith will lead us on.

Before moving rapidly into the evaluation of existing programs of black theology, we need to look at the recent historical antecedents which gave rise to this program. We see three distinct and yet continuous ideological stages reading from 1954 to the present. First, from 1954-65, we meet the civil rights/integration stage. Second, from 1966-72, we encounter the black consciousness/black power phase. And, finally, from 1973 to the present we entered the "political" involvement period. My chronology may be questioned, but my preoccupation is with the kiarotic content of this history.

The civil rights/integration stage begins with the Supreme Court desegregation decision of 1954. It was an ethical as well as a legal decision. It assumed the equality of all people before God and before the law. Dr. Martin Luther King, Jr. became the theologian/preacher/leader of the entire movement. His *Letter from a Birmingham Jail* and *I Have a Dream* messages gave classic expression to the ethico-religious foundations of the civil rights/integration stage. This terrain is so familiar that we need only point to the tie which Dr. King forged between the legal and religious basis for civil rights and the goal of both secular and religious integration. Unfortunately, Dr. King remains an unsung theologian even among his peers. Black theologians need to correct this ommission in their historical perspective in order to lay a solid historical foundation for their own work. Only those who take black religious history seriously are able to understand Dr. King's message and mission profoundly and to provide the necessary internal criticism upon its theory and praxis.

The black consciousness/power movement reched its peak around 1968-69. Black churchmen first took note of it in 1966.

Dr. King had to deal with some of its implications during his last years. He did not fully understand it, but shaped some of his policies by a conscious reaction to it. He opposed its aspect of "black racism" and its potential for violence as a means. For some, the riots of the late 60's justified his caution. Others claim that the absence of his leadership together with the repression of the Nixon White House as creating "a spiral of violence."[17] The vicious cycle of violence runs its inevitable course from injustice to rebellion to repression. White middle America saw this period of history as moving from black power in its violent expression to a legitimate white backlash in the form of "law and order" in the able care of the Nixon White House, the Burger Court, the F.B.I. and the C.I.A.

Black religion and black theology saw black consciousness/power through different eyes. We saw the affirmation of blackness as leading to a re-definition of our own being as persons and as a people. Through this re-definition of our existence we found a way to self-respect and self-determination. We no longer accepted the image of ourselves in the white mind. Theologians and churchmen among us saw this black consciousness/power movement in its cultural and historical context as a part of the entire religious heritage of blacks. Furthermore, as they re-read the Bible and re-conceived the faith, they were able to see more clearly what God through Christ is doing in the world to make life more human. Even if Cecil Cone sees this movement as relegating black theologians to a bygone phase of the black liberation movements, I would argue that black consciousness/power is to be taken side by side with the affirmation of the sovereignty of God. We must not exalt the almightiness of God to such an extent that we end up in moral paralysis.[18] To think well of God is not to think less of the human if we understand the meaning of *imago Dei* and what it means to be co-creators and co-laborers with God. The title to Cecil Cone's book is misleading. He does not write about the identity crisis in black theology, but about the identity crisis of black theologians. In varying degrees all blacks face some identity crisis because of the "doubleness" in black existence, so well articulated by W.E.B. DuBois. There is no reason why theologians should escape this. A theological assessment of this identity crisis, in personhood and peoplehood would have been invaluable. Part of my purpose here is to stimulate this type of investigation.

Finally, the last and the continuing stage of the black movement which theologians of the black experience need to consider is what Preston Williams correctly refers to as "reformist" rather than "revolutionary." More and more of the black leadership from the civil rights period and the black power stage is to be reformist and participatory. There is a turn toward political involvement. The goal is neither integration nor separatism, but the affirmation of black ethnicity within a pluralistic culture. Blacks are embracing the best from the civil rights and black power periods but more and more using the power acquired within the "system" to make it more humane. Those who acquire status and influence may no longer receive accolades from the black masses for their ascendency. They are now being held accountable for their use of power and priviledge to set their brothers and sisters free.

In the document *Gaudium et Spes*, ("The Church and the Modern World"), Vatican II called the theologians of the Catholic Church to the task of reading the signs of the times. Black theologians will be irresponsible and unworthy if they do not see this as central to their task and program.

IV. BLACK THEOLOGY

There are two things to be discussed at this point, blackness and theology. "Blackness" has to do with an awareness of belonging to the Afro-American heritage. It is far more than consciousness of a color of skin. It involves a new definition of self, a different self-understanding and a sense of worth. It symbolizes that our dignity as human beings is no longer at the mercy of the image of black in the white mind. Nonetheless, "black" is also a "dirty" word in our culture. It is defined by Webster as ugly, evil, fiendish and everything undesirable. Blacks have re-defined this term and "transvaluated" it. A word which is shameful, a badge of inferiority, of ostracism, is now shrouded in a halo of glory. This is not unlike the arch symbol of our faith -- the cross. The "curse" of the cross has been translated by Christians into the ultimate salvific symbol of our faith. Foolishness has been transformed into the very power and wisdom of God. Blackness has been re-defined in like manner into a meaningful symbol of black theologians. But blackness associated with oppression is negative. It is that from which we desire to be delivered. Blackness is a whole set of positive and negative experiences deeply embedded in Afro-American history and culture.

We are able now to accept our humanity as it is in God's creative and redemptive purposes. We are sons of God. We are children of God. This is God's good pleasure. The way we understand our personhood and our peoplehood sets us upon a quest for a beloved community. We can now put our liberating in theological perspective.

Black theology addresses itself to a liberating understanding of reconciliation. We understand the pain and wrath of God as well as His love and mercy. We see the revelation of the character of God as justice and power as well as love. God's providence is understood in relation to the crimes of history as well as in reference to personal transgressions. Jesus becomes a radical and he is understood as the oppressed one or as a suffering slave because of his involvement in the liberation of the oppressed. Reconciliation is not merely vertical, it is horizontal as well. It involves understanding what God is doing in the world to set humans free and join him in the liberation push. It means opposing power structures that dehumanize life. It involves a political, social justice understanding of the faith that resists the institutional and cultural manifestations of oppression based on race. Reconciliation does not exist apart from sharing power. It requires a new white consciousness that includes cross-bearing the willingness to accept all men as equals in a new relationship. It means whites giving up self-glory, the worship of white skin, and participating in a new humanity in which there are no slaves or masters but human beings.

Black theology is theological ethics. Its mission is to humanize life as well as liberate the oppressed. It must maintain a balance between liberation and reconciliation. The outlook of black theology is expressed in terms of hope. Blacks are a people who have not only survived but have woven a living hope out of the crucible of suffering. While others are giving up because of corruption in high places, we have moved beyond the despair of the Long Hot Summers of the late 60s. We are seeking and acquiring political, economic and social power. While some theologians are still implying that we are not interested in "winning," black leaders and those who elect them, are. We must not get out of touch with the people and especially when they may understand the faith better than we do. Almost to a man, the black elected officials are advocating the humanizing of life for everyone. Most of them are conscious of being black and take a strong stand for the liberation of blacks but do not seek revenge on others. They seek a leveling of society, a sharing of power, goods and services, but in the context of a togetherness on a higher level between equals.

Theologians are called to direct black power and white power to ends that are mutually beneficial to all people. Could it be that the legacy of Dr. King or even that of Jesus is more present in the secular order than among the anointed? If black theology is to be more than an abstract enterprise for the edification of black theologians themselves it must begin to read the signs of the times to see what God is doing in the liberation struggle. These black secular leaders appear to be strange prophets who are "doers of the word and not hearers only." They are acting as if they understand how love, justice and power mingle in the nature of God and in the Christian ethic; for they are working out a liberating approach to reconciliation in the social order. While some black theologians are talking about dying for freedom, these men and women are delivering bread and butter and providing employment and welfare cheques in the language that the black poor trust and obey.

NOTES

1. The Souls of Black Folk (Greenwich, Fawcett Pemier Books, 1968) pp. 104-151.

2. "Black Theological Ethics: A Bibliographical Essay" in Journal of Religious Ethics (March 1, 1975) p. 73-83.

3. B.E. Mays, The Negro's God (Boston: Chapman and Grimes, 1938).

4. Vincent Harding "Religion and Resistance among Ante-Bellum Negroes" in A. Meier and E. Rudwick (eds.) The Negro in the Making. Vol. I, New York: Atheneum, 1969. pp. 179-197.

5. G.S. Wilmore, Black Religion and Black Radicalism (New York: Doubleday, 1972).

6. "Perspectives for a Study of Afro-American Religion in the United States" History of Religions (February 1, August, pp. 54-65) and "Structural Similarities."

7. Black Sects and Cults (New York: Doubleday, 1972) Ch. I.

8. "Same God," L. Hughes and Arna Bontemps, eds. Book of Negro Folklore (New York: Dodds, Mead and Co., 1958) p. 257.

9. Ibid. p. 305.

10. Ibid. p. 228.

11. Ibid. p. 76.

12. "Folklore and Religion", The Journal of Religious Thought (26/2, Summer, 1970) 5-15.

13. Spirituals and Blues (New York: Seabury 1972).

14. Is God a White Racist? (New York: Doubleday, 1973) Ch. X.

15. The Ideological Origins of Black Nationalism (Boston: Beacon, 1972).

16. The Ideology of Blackness (Lexington, MA: D.C. Health, 1971).

17. Helder Camara, Spiral of Violence (Denville, NJ: Dimension, 1971), Ch. I.

18. Identity Crisis in Black Theology (Nashville: A.M.E. Press, 1976).

THE FUTURE IS NOW:
CONSERVATISM, LIBERALISM AND LIBERATION

> It was the worst of times;
> It was the best of times.
>
> Charles Dickens

Harry Emerson Fosdick once preached from the text: "One day is as a thousand years," then added, "There is no democracy in days." A single event, such as the publication of Karl Marx' *Communist Manifesto*, the crucifixion, or the freeing of black slaves, may have more significance for generations unborn than whole centuries in a stagnant period of history. We are living in such a time.

The population explosion with its hunger pains, the energy crisis, pollution, violent revolutions, genetic engineering, racism and many other problems await our urgent attention.

I. NEW THEOLOGICAL INITIATIVES

Much talk is heard these days about "contextualizing" theology. Shoki Coe, an Asian theologian, has suggested this very strongly. He has rejected "indigenization" as a proper term, much as Latin American theologians have found "development" a misnomer for their liberation program. Coe reasons that indigenization is the glorification of a static past, whereas what Asians want and need is a dynamic future. He does not deny the value of reflection upon the cultural traditions of a people; he encourages this. What he desires to overcome is a form of static traditionalism which locks a people into the past and excludes them from participation in a creative and changing future.[1]

An African theological student in an American seminary seemed to be saying something very similar when he complained that his white professors were using anthropology to unlock the past while he longed instead for social and political perspectives designed to humanize life for his people now and into the future.

Alistair Kee, referring to this same situation, observes:

> The older forms of theology have stemmed largely from the initiatives of European anthropologists who have encouraged Africans to look to their cultural heritage in the past. The new form of African theology springs from a new consciousness among Africans of their political situation and far from being about the past, is oriented towards the future.[2]

Latin American theologians are using "political" as a sweeping word, so broad in meaning that it covers all material concerns. The social and economic factors of human life are subsumed under the term of political. Perhaps it is possible to view social and economic forces under the umbrella of the political, but for the sake of a critical analysis, it does not seem advisable to do so. Isolating these factors for discussion makes it possible to combine them with more force.

Andrew Young, former Ambassador to the United Nations, recalled in an address how he had personally experienced the economic plight of blacks, an insight which is evident in his political outlook. As a close aide of Dr. Martin Luther King, Jr, he rejoiced in the successes of the civil rights movement. His euphoria evaporated, however, leaving him with sober realism, when he decided to dine with his family in an exclusive restaurant in downtown Atlanta. Upon receiving the bill, Young observed that blacks were not economically prepared to take advantage of many of the new opportunities resulting from the freedom movement. As a consequence, Young, developed a great sensitivity toward the economic condition of the black masses. He was able to associate the wholesale poverty among blacks with their political apathy and powerlessness. He realized that the improvement of the economic situation among blacks and other poverty-stricken Americans is directly proportional to their development of political power, a development all too often prevented by abuse of political influence. It was only logical that he should make an immediate association of economic with political rights. He later described his "ministry" in Congress as that of "feeding the poor." It is but a step from these concerns at home to his larger interest in human rights and hunger on a global scale. We might properly speak of political economy in considering this direct interaction of economics and politics.

Problems in the area of social welfare complete the trilogy. The social, political and economic factors of a nation are interdependent. In our society, class and race play a significant part in determining social patterns. Education and housing are directly related to economic means. We can properly speak of socio-economic layers in our society. Just as political attitudes determine the content of bills passed in Congress, state-houses, and city halls, so sensitivity or lack of sensitivity to social ills plays a large part in determining the political outlook and the economic state of the masses. A mutuality exists, then, among the political, social and economic factors which shape our life styles.

II. A CONCISE CRITIQUE OF AMERICAN CHRISTIANITY

Why are conservative churches growing? Harvey Seifert, among others, has been very perceptive of this trend. This movement needs to be evaluated today against the background of what must be done if churches are to fulfill their true mission. As Seifert observes:

> Present differences may be short-lived, with the long-term prospect quite a different one. There are reasons to believe that conservative churches are only delaying their crisis. . . In times of uncertainty and threat, a frequent reaction is to move back toward past situations in which one used to find security. When individuals feel bewildered and powerless, they may turn to sectarian churches for sanctuary, a safe retreat from the storm. Unfortunately this tends to give religious approval to features of the traditional American way of life which must now be challenged if we are to avoid disaster. Some conservative church congregations may be growing for the wrong reasons, while some liberal congregations may be declining for the right reasons.³

According to Seifert, liberal churches may learn from conservative churches some things that deserve careful evaluation.⁴ In conservative churches, religion seems important. It is a source of strength, presents a clear, confident message, brings assurance and is filled with emotion. It provides a warm and intimate fellowship, inviting loyalty and extreme dedication.

Liberals, on the other hand, may be luke-warm to religion while stressing other crucial causes. While conservatives are aggressive soul-winners, liberals often wait for visitors to find them. Liberal theology is frequently complex and abstract over-awing the average churchgoer. Liberals raise disturbing issues out of the gospel while often neglecting to comfort and reassure their seeker. Liberals often use polished preaching, refined liturgy and anthems while shunning informal and simple forms of worship. Laughter, tears and amens are for those who have no other language and yet these are not the hall-marks of the liberal church. Relationships between persons in liberal congregations are more casual than communal. Friendship does not grow beyond the country club or coffee table. The poor, less educated, racially exploited are often ill at ease in this climate. Then, too, liberals often ask members to witness to a wide area of interests, while conservatives seek dedication to a specific issue.

While Seifert is helpfully critical of liberals, he is equally perceptive in his evaluation of conservatives. Among the latter, there is frequently an autocratic and charismatic leader. Usually an absolute demand for conformity is present which always precipitates the schismatic spirit. Ethical demands are one-sided and frequently personal, while the serious social ills of our time are a matter of indifference. Lack of support for social involvement lends credence to the quietism. A withdrawal from secular life to a spiritual sanctuary leads members to regard the latter as a safe retreat from the world. Seifert writes:

> Conservative churches have been good at stimulating support for the church, or at evangelism and missions. . . . They can learn from the liberal church that the work of the church is also being done when one joins other agencies to organize social protest movements or to change the policies of corporations.[5]

In my judgment, Seifert's assessment is valuable so far as it goes. What he has provided is a rather accurate description of the WASP situation in the United States. My own researches into the religious expression of black folk reveal many exceptions to this liberal-conservative look at American Christianity. Seifert has provided helpful insights, however, toward a serious theological critique of the American church situation. This is a significant contribution to the self-understanding of American churchgoers. We are suffering from the lack of an adequate foundational theology for the social and ethical involvement of christians. Thus the effectiveness of churches in mission to whole persons and total communities is seriously in doubt.

III. THEOLOGY GETTING DOWN TO CASES

John C. Bennett observed recently that U.S. economic difficulties are compounding the usual problems that socially conscious churches have in arousing compassion for the poor. As he points out,

> The middle classes that largely determine the mind of our churches do not appear to be poor or

oppressed to others and yet very often they feel themselves very much harassed and even victimized . . . . They have a high standard of living but they are usually in debt for it. They have to pay more than they can really afford for their housing, and the costs of higher education and medical care become very great burdens.[6]

Bennett goes on to assert, however, that the two major barriers to perception of the plight of the poor are "compartmentalized Christianity" and "conservative individualism." As he notes:

It is the easiest thing in the world to be a sincere but compartmental Christian who never raises any new questions beyond those to which he or she may have received answers in early formative years . . . . When others at a later time raise new implications of Christian theology and ethics, they become a threat.[7]

Bennett is right in asserting that we must not allow our middle class debts and burdens to becloud our vision of the meaning of real poverty. Furthermore, we must not allow our passion for individual freedom to be separated from a quest for social justice. We must not permit the affirmation of equality of opportunity to obscure the need to overcome inequality of condition. Bennett sees black, feminist and liberation theologies as keeping these issues alive.[8]

Some so-called Chrisitans in our country have made the judgment that human suffering in some lands should not be alleviated. Tragically some theologian-ethicists have joined this company. Whole populations in Fourth World countries are said to be expendable. Fourth World countries are designated by economists as such because of their despicable poverty -- a poverty so widespread that even massive aid programs could not save them.

The principle of triage is being offered as a formula. The term comes from the French *triere* meaning to pick or select. This formula is used for medical screening of patients to determine priority for treatment. It has been applied in sorting casualties of military and civil disasters into three groups: (1) those who will be expected to survive regardless of treatment; (2) those who will be expected to die regardless of what is done for them; and (3) those who will die unless given immediate aid.

Now this principle is being offered as a manner of dealing with world hunger. Historically, it is associated with the theory of Thomas R. Malthus (1766-1834), a minister, author, professor of history and political economy. Malthus asserted that there is little hope for social happiness since population growth exceeds the food supply. He suggested that famine would solve the problem since many people would be eliminated through starvation. Charles Darwin (1809-1882) was among the few who took this theory with great seriousness.

Over Since the Great Depression, however, several people in science, religion and public service has reviewed the Malthusian thesis with careful concern. At the present time, the human family faces malnutrition, hunger and outright famine. Overpopulation among nations seems to be the main culprit, but poor distribution of resources and the depletion of sources of energy are increasing dangers. Therefore, the principle of triage is being explored.

When we apply triage to social decisions, it raises serious ethical and theological questions related to scarcity and the just allocation of goods and food. The greatest danger is that we may decree like Goethe's Faustus, "Evil be thou good!"

Clearly, this formula of selecting who should starve should not be used in devising a solution to world hunger. This answer is too callous and is being offered by the wrong people. The application of this principle would insulate us from the horrors of famine and lead us to abandon the search for constructive alternatives like seeding the oceans and farming the deserts, as well as more effective use of family planning. The most alarming feature is that this suggestion is being offered by fellow Americans who are mainly male, white and comfortable. Accordingly, those of us who are out of the mainstream have good reasons to ask how long it will be before we, too, following this same insensitivity and logic, become expendable *en masse*.

To understand this case more clearly, we should look briefly at a proposal by Garrett Hardin who offers "a case against helping the poor." Hardin, a social biologist, presents this solution to the energy crisis. He works against the selfish and rapacious use of resources which will victimize every one if there is any unrestricted consumption of resources held in common. This he calls "the tragedy of the commons."

He is correct in warning us of the limits of growth and that we face a shortage of both energy and food. We can accept these facts and still recoil at his proffered solution. He would apply "a life boat ethic" to world hunger. For instance, if too many people crowd into a small boat, it will sink and all will die unless some voluntarily give up their lives, or are thrown overboard to drown. We should observe that it might be considered an act of heroic martyrdom for a father to give up his life for his infant son, but it would be an act of selfish savagery for a stronger man to throw a weaker companion to the sharks. What is most shocking, perhaps, is not the proposal itself, for in an imperfect world less than perfect decisions are often made. What is most alarming is that the advocates of life-boat ethics are prescribing this solution for the weak and powerless, not for themselves.

Father Joseph Fletcher, for example, feels that people in Bangladesh, the Sabel and Haiti should be allowed to starve unless they curb their "callous progenitive habits." He goes on to assert that aid to these peoples is counterproductive, because sharing increases the suffering and death among them. It is our commitment to life, according to Fletcher, which will not allow us to feed the hungry in those places. He states that "to help these people in such countries is morally wrong."[9] This is the same writer, who as a theologian-ethicist, gave us *Situation Ethics* in which he insisted that we are to be guided in our ethical decision by the "most loving thing to do." I am not able to see how allowing a whole population to be wiped out through starvation is a loving deed.

Fortunately, presented in the same symposium are other opinions. Stuart W. Hinds writes:

> Persons and nations cannot live merely for the sake of their survival alone. The time has come at last when pressured by the forces of nature and history, we must learn to live for one another.[10]

Walter Harrelson makes a similar point:

> Biblical religion . . . invites human beings to seek to preserve all life; to find a solution to world hunger; to recognize that repentance opens the way to life; to bear in mind that some cannot live at the expense of others; that we live together or perish together, and that living or dying we are the Lord's.[11]

Black ethicists need to enter this discussion before it is too late. We must not allow those who are incapable of developing solidarity with the oppressed to dominate such a far reaching concern as world hunger. Our destiny as blacks in the First World is bound up with our kin in the Third and Fourth Worlds so inextricably that what happens to them will inevitably happen to us. I am reminded of what James Baldwin wrote to Angela Davis when she was in prison. In essence, he asserted that all blacks were in some sense destined for the same fate, that of "political prisoners." He indicated that, "if they come for you in the morning, they will come for me at midnight." If the people of Haiti are permitted to starve, genocide may soon be the fate of blacks in Harlem. Writers who are prepared to sacrifice whole populations as the moral thing to do cannot be trusted to write all of our theological and ethical guidelines.

IV. THE QUESTION OF MEANS: VIOLENCE VS. NON-VIOLENCE

Another crucial issue facing a theology of deliverance from systemic oppression is the question of means. This is sharply focussed when Christians of a non-violent persuasion face those who contend that sometimes violence is justified. This is difficult to sort out. Both camps are concerned about the validity of the christian ethic. Those who opt for non-violence are certain that love in its highest expression will not allow for violence, which usually includes the taking of human life. Those who advocate violence, for the most part, do not see it as a panacea; they see it as an action of last resort. Violence, they believe, should be used only when all alternatives have been tried, but they reckon without the possibility that man's inhumanity to man can be so devastating that violence *will* or indeed, *must* happen to make possible meaningful human existence. Exploitation based on race or class can become so severe and widespread that the choice of violence is determined more by the circumstances than by the choice of the oppressed. For the exploited, in their powerlessness, all options for constructive social change have been closed. As in the past black slaves could find freedom only in death so for them the choice seems to be liberty or death.

We have here attempted to place the issue rather sharply. We are not prepared to offer a solution. A careful analysis of these problems is needed on both sides. Clearly, however, what seems called for is a more comprehensive understanding of violence. Violence means more than one-to-one physical assault. It can be *covert* as well as *overt*, psychological-economic as well as physical, and systemic as well as personal. Inevitably, it marks the beginning of a vicious cycle. As Helder Camara explains it, violence tends to spiral. The spiral begins with injustice which leads to revolt; revolt leads to repression; repression establishes an even more severe form of injustice. In this way, the history of unjust societies becomes a type of self-fulfilling prophecy.[12]

Non-violence seems to have some slight chance to be effective where a certain "repressive tolerance"[13] allows minor changes to take place, but even these cosmetic measures may be disallowed when the status quo is threatened and substantive changes in unjust structures are demanded. A case in point is the recent revelation of how the "system" in this country opposed the Martin Luther King non-violent leadership.

What seems to be called for is an assessment of the means of liberation by those who are oppressed. Most people writing treatises on non-violence are too comfortable. They are mainly concerned with telling those who are the victims that they must be willing to suffer still greater abuse, even though their suffering has already made them "hollow men." Why don't they address the oppressors concerning the humane use of power? The fact is that these erudite scholars, be they theologians or ethicists, do not tune in on the problem; they do not have the proper solution. Their words and ideas are empty for those who have endured "ethnic suffering" generation after generation and see no possibility of relief.

James Cone sees violence as built-in to the system:

> Violence should be put in its proper perspective. It is embedded in American law and custom. It hides beneath such slogans as "law and order," "freedom and democracy" and "the American way of life". . . . I am speaking of white collar violence, the violence of Christian murderers and patriots -- citizens who define right in terms of whiteness and wrong as blackness. These are the people who hire assassins to do their dirty work while they piously congratulate themselves on being "good" and "non-violent." [14]

Cone sees the distinction between violence and non-violence as misleading. He argues that oppressors do not qualify to discuss it. He would like to speak rather of justifiable or unjustifiable use of force, and of whether the means are proportionate to the ends. Only the victims of injustice, according to Cone, can provide the answer.

A balanced and critical assessment by the World Council of Churches' indicates that oppressors are more diligent in criticizing the violence of the victims of oppression than they are critical of the systemic forms of violence.

> Violence must be recognized in all forms of suffering endured by the victims of racism and in the dehumanizing consequences of discrimination and segregation. To deny a person the right to work in order to sustain his or her life or to shorten a person's life through malnutrition or the denial of proper health and medical care are as violently destructive of human life and personality as are the more overt acts of violence directed against groups.[15]

The Commission on Faith and Order states that it shares the agony of Christian pacifists who are caught between "their commitment to non-violent action as the strategy for overcoming racial injustice and the element of violence in concrete movements of human liberation."[16] In fact, they endorse non-violent action as the proper Christian approach to overcome racist oppression. Yet they conclude:

> We are also called to stand firmly on the side of the oppressed, even though violence may at times be present, for our goal is to achieve a more just society in which such desperate acts of violence on the part of the oppressed will no longer be necessary.[17]

While the latter statement seems to waver in regard to means, it does come down clearly on the side of justice and humane treatment for all people. Any adequate treatment of this subject would need to look at human rights and the relation between Jesus and freedom. In my judgment, serious research and dialogue is needed both on the part of those requiring deliverance and on the part of those holding power regarding what it really means to be Christian in all human relations, both personal and social.

NOTES

1. In G.H. Anderson and T.F. Stransky, eds. Mission Trends 3 (New York: Paulist, 1976), pp. 19-24.

2. A Reader in Political Theology, ed. Alistair Kee (Philadelphia: Westminister, 1974), p. 117.

3. New Power for the Church (Philadelphia: Westminister, 1976), p. 57.

4. Ibid., pp. 58-62.

5. Ibid., p. 67.

6. Los Angeles Times (Nov. 20, 1975, Pt. I, 31).

7. Ibid.

8. Ibid.

9. Soundings (LIX:1, 1976) p. 66.

10. Ibid.; p. 50.

11. Ibid., p. 99.

12. Dom Helder Camara's Spiral of Violence (Denville, N.J.: Dimension Books, 1971) as discussed by Robert McAffee Brown, Religion and Violence (Philadelphia: Westminister, 1972) pp. 8-12.

13. Ibid., p. 11.

14. James H. Cone "Black Theology on Revolution, Violence and Reconciliation," Union Seminary Quarterly Review XXI:1, Fall, 1975): 10-12.

15. "Racism in Theology and Theology Against Racism". Report of a Consultation by the Commission on Faith and Order and the Programme to Combat Racism (Geneva: World Council of Churches, 1975), p. 13.

16. Ibid., p. 13.

17. Ibid.

*CONTEXTUAL THEOLOGY:
LIBERATION AND INDIGENIZATION

This is the time of world history in which the entire human situation must be explored. Our exploration must move, however, from the particular to the universal. The universal is abstract; the particular is concrete. Such an approach implies a serious encounter with ethnic theological programs everywhere. The context of belief, life and action must now be given priority.

I. THE CONTEXTUALIZATION OF THEOLOGY

Today Christian theology is required to take the world of all people seriously. All must be reached in their *lebenswelt* if faith is to be a live option. Theology as developed in Europe and America is limited when it approaches the majority of human beings. Any "universal" arising out of the experience of such a small sample is a myth. Christian theologians unaware of the ways and thinking and believing of peoples elsewhere in the world make only a false claim to universalism.

There is no completely universal perspective, since all human thought and belief is limited by structural bounds. There can, however, be an openness to the universal. When it is objected that we are dealing with a universal revelation, we must raise the issue concerning the finite human understanding through which God's self-disclosure is communicated. The eventual locus of divine revelation is our personal, social, cultural and ethnic existence.

Christian theologians may generally be numbered among the colonizers of the peoples of the Third World. Though many have been "God's colonizers" not by intention but by default, the results have been the same. My recent research on Albert Schweitzer provides me with some concrete evidence. The treatment of his theology in the Atlanta centennial celebration during April 1975 led me to this conclusion. Schweitzer, as a theologian went beyond most of his peers in his involvement in Africa. Paradoxically, it is the manifestation of this European mind in an African context that dramatizes the pro-Western orientation of his so-called philosophy of civilization.

Aristotelian logic and Platonic dualism do not exhaust the thought structures of the human race. It is the height of self-pride for those who are limited to an exposure to these categories of thought and their derivatives to speak *ex cathedra* for all Christian believers. It is more honest to admit our particularities.

My eyes have been opened by a discovery of the thought and belief of Asian and African peoples. The study of religion in general is the key to a deeper understanding of a particular religion. It is of some interest that Paul Tillich should say to Mircea Eliade late in life that if he had an opportunity to begin all over, he would study the history of religions first. This encounter is personal for me. I assert categorically that the study of world religions is a great resource for a more meaningful theological understanding today. It is essential to do independent study, travel and field work in order to appreciate more completely the unity and diversity of the various religions and the systems of doctrine flowing from them.

Christian theologians and missionaries have often been the "colonizers" of the minds and spirits of non-Western people. They often dismissed non-Western religions as heathen. They thought they paid the highest compliment by accepting a non-Western religion as a mere preparation for the gospel. They were not aware that the very gospel that they sought to transplant was blighted by the "Constantinian Captivity" of the church. In their pharisaism, they did not observe anything of worth in other religions or the cultures that sustained them.

My appreciation has been deeply enriched regarding the universal reach of the human spirit by my encounter with giant intellects and cosmic spirits in Asia and Africa. I have argued that theologians can have their lives and thoughts enriched by this experience precisely because they view the faith of other people from inside their own system of belief and thought.[1]

The search for a cosmic Christ has broadened my horizon. The Christo-centrism of my approach has not diminished, but I now see Christ as Giver of grace, Author of nature, and Lord of history as well. The Incarnation remains the center of God's redemptive revelation. The circumference of revelation, however, has been expanded. Through Jesus as the Christ we discover the meaning of God's all-pervasive cosmic revelation. This revelation is manifest in creation and providence in all times and among all peoples.

My studies in Christian Platonism, centering on the Cambridge Patonists, during my doctoral program at Edinburgh and Cambridge Universities, have made me sensitive to this vision. The discoveries of William Temple *(Nature, Man and God)* together with my conversations with Canon C.E. Raven, a theologian and scientist, opened my mind to this new perspective.

Islam as I met it in South Asia and the Middle East pointed to a legal and political outreach of religion that did not reject the mystical. One encounters Islamic theologians, past and present, who, in their own lives, blend the spiritual and political dimensions of faith. This led me to look again at the priestly and prophetic unity in biblical faith.

All encounters with religious experience are invigorating for theological reflection. The *élan vital* of preliterate religions, the *Tao* of Laotzu, the *Jen* of Confucius, the Compassion of Buddha, the Brahman of the Hindus, are examples of the richness of these explorations. More recent reflections upon the African roots of black religions have also been a great source of insight and inspiration. African religions combine the semblance of the family system of Confucianism with the deep spirituality of Hinduism and Buddhism. In my view, the African perspective provides a basis for a holistic interpretation of religious experience.

What we are developing is a theology of liberation. If theology is to be more than dry bones for faith, if it is to address humans of flesh and blood, if it is to deal with the ultimate issues of life and death, it must be more than a logical statement of doctrine, though it should include that. Theology cannot be truly universal if it refuses to deal with the particularities of the human situation. It must now, however, rest with the particular; it must move from the particular to the universal. In moving to the universal, it must not abandon the concrete particular, for that is where we meet the human situation. There is no *abstract* universal that makes any difference in the relief of human misery. There is no universal revelation that separates salvation history from world history. Systematic theology must become theological ethics. It must speak not merely from the ivory tower, but from the market place. Theology, to be worthy of the name, must now address impersonal realities as well as non-believers.

II. THE INSEPARABILITY OF THEOLOGY AND ETHICS IN THE BLACK RELIGIOUS EXPERIENCE

Theology and ethics are inseparable in the black religious experience. The context of the faith of black people is a situation of racist oppression. Religion, and especially the understanding of the biblical faith, has been the source of meaning and protest for blacks. Our religious heritage has nurtured and sustained us through our dark night of suffering. Without this profound religious experience and the churches that have institutionalized it, blacks might not have survived the bitterness of American oppression.

Consciousness is not adequate by itself to liberate a people. It must be empowered. Thus, there has been in black religion a concern for operational unity in order to provide a united front against racism. Black theologians cannot enter into the quest for the personhood and peoplehood of their people without having their ethical concern sharpened. I have argued the case for the ethical dimension of black theology.[2] In fact, any theology worth the name must now make contact with the human situation in the context of world history. When one takes the biblical faith and the Incarnation seriously into account today, the result is a theology of liberation. Whether we find ourselves (as theologians) in the camp of the oppressor or the oppressed, what we have to interpret is a gospel of liberation.

My own pilgrimage has been an extended one. It began with a search for a reasonable faith. Emotional piety and intellectual honesty provided a serious conflict. Much of my life has been given to wrestling with truth. The encounter with natural sicence, literary and biblical criticism, and philosophy accelerated the crisis. The support that sustained life's purpose in the passage through doubt to a more mature faith has been the Bible, reinforced by a steadfast sense of being called to a ministry in the church. This philosophical orientation led me into philosphy of religion and later into philosophical theology. Much of my early research and writing was preoccupied with epistemological questions of faith. This is evident in my books *Faith and Reason*[3] and *From Puritanism to Platonism in Seventeenth Century England.*[4]

My responsibility has been that of a theologian of the church. As a systematic theologian in a theological school within a predominately black university, I have sought to interpret the faith for future leaders in the church. Most of my students have been black or non-Western. Their ministry, therefore, has been to all sorts and conditions of humans. Almost from the start I was challenged to match intellectual honesty with the social and political imperatives of the gospel. It became clear to me that while faith should have the priority, reason should be included. Augustine, Anselm and Pascal led me to a faith seeking understanding. Or put another way, these theologians helped me to find my way.

From the Detroit Conference on Theology in the Americas (August 1975) we learned that the North American reality is different from that in Latin America.[5] We also discovered that while the *mood* of black and Latin American theologies are similar, the context is quite varied. While oppression is most pronounced in the form of classism in Latin America, racism is its principal manifestation in the United States. Black women experience a double oppression. Racism is destructive of the entire black family and community. We may observe, then, that in this country we are faced not merely with an overlap or network of oppression. There is beyond this, in the experience of blacks, a hierarchy of oppression. Racism is the most systemic, historical and far-reaching form. Blacks are constantly faced, as a people, with the threat of extinction. On the one hand, genocide could result from repression of a revolt arising from sheer frustration. On the other hand, the negative effects of oppression of blacks for such a long period may have triggered the self-destructive tendencies now evident in widespread drug abuse and black-on-black crime.

Existentialism seems to be attractive to black religious thinkers. The experience of racism has caused blacks to develop an introspective mood. We are a long-suffering people. Our psychic health has been sustained by a faith that has defied all human limits of endurance. Amid despair and powerlessness, we have carved out meaning and sanity. We have been able to hold life together through faith even though we have not had the ultimate control over our destiny or the issues of life and death. Existentialism, "a creed for crises," has been useful to blacks as they have faced the extreme situation in this country. I have sought to establish these aspects of the psychology of black religious thought.[6] The existential posture of Augustine's "self-understanding," Pascal's "reasons of the heart," Bergson's "duration," and William James' "stream of consciousness" have left deep a deep impression upon my mind and spirit.

The discovery of Kierkegaard was a moving experience. His analysis of human existence seemed unusually profound, but his revolt against reason repelled me. The affirmation of the individual seemed wholesome up to a point, but he did not give sufficient attention to interpersonal relations. His critique of religion and society stirred up my prophetic instincts, but there was an absence of a profound theological ethic as he insisted upon a teleological suspension of the ethical for the sake of faith. From this melancholy Dane, however, radiated a penetrating insight into the human "sickness unto death," which was put into a profound psycho-theological context for me in Tillich's *Courage to Be*.

This existential posture of my thinking has been mixed with a strong mystic bent. Howard Thurman's writings have been a great inspiration. I find the manner in which he combines a deep spirituality with a passion for social justice extremely attractive. The question of how one maintains sanity in a society bent on inhuman oppression based on race is a personal matter that must be faced before one can find health and wholeness as a person within a community of persons.

III. HOLISTIC THINKING IN BLACK THEOLOGY

This type of theological discourse requires unitive thinking. It transcends the split in thought and life of much Western thinking. The discovery of the total person, the corporate personality, and the unity of humankind leads directly to an understanding of salvation as liberation.

The existential theologians taught us a great lesson, that theology can begin with the human situation as the locus of God's revelation. But for the most part, they overlooked the collective dimensions of human nature. They unwittingly played into the hands of those who espouse a privatized expression of faith. The theologians of hope, on the other hand, emphasized the collective aspects of human life. These theologians analyzed human solidarity in oppression and expressed faith in political terms. The individual human being was exchanged for the social human being. Anthropology was replaced by eschatology, but the either/or mold of Western thought was evident in them, and the holistic outlook in the Third World (including the Bible) was not predominant.

An adequate anthropology will take the insights of Freud and Marx with all seriousness, but will go beyond them. The *imago dei* is at the heart of the Christian understanding of the human being. It is the relation of the human person to God which is the "wholing" dimension of human nature. It is essential to move from the human to the divine and view the human in the context of this encounter. If the weakness of traditional theologies has been God-talk may it not be that the shortcoming of much theology today is that Feuerback's observation is being fulfilled: Theology is becoming only anthropology? While it is the person who is being approached by God's revelation of his saving grace, we should be assured that it is the whole person who is being considered. The human person is a child of God at the same time that he is a fellow to all humans.

Liberation and Reconciliation: A Black Theology[7] was my first comprehensive effort to provide a theology of the black experience. This book was dismissed by some as a social treatise. It has been of some interest to me that other theological programs have developed out of a dialogue between the social sciences and Christian belief and have not lost their recognized theological character. This is true of existential theology in relation to the depth psychology. It holds for Latin American liberation theology and the theologies of hope in relation to Marxism. And yet a theology that emerges out of the identity-crisis and the social pathology created by racism is ruled out of court by the theological guardians at the gate. There is a sense of urgency surrounding the theological task of black theologians. They will not be silenced by the criticisms of the theological élite; for we are convinced that we have found a different and vital way of doing theology.

A Black Political Theology[8] builds upon the earlier work. In this more recent book there is an attempt to develop a theological ethic. The context of black theology is racism in the midst of ethnic pluralism. We are oppressed in a society that is highly developed economically, technically and militarily. While Third World countries experience oppression externally from the United States, we as blacks experience oppression internally as victims of racism. A whole set of problems crush our people. We must not, however, mistake the effects for the cause. If there is no root and branch dismantling of racism, then unemployment, illiteracy, all sorts of crimes, economic deprivation and political indifference will continue to destroy our people.

We have not until this day participated fully either in the democratic process or in the prosperity of this nation. America has been more like Babylon than the "Promised Land of Freedom and Brotherhood." In this centennial era, it should be remembered that there are millions of citizens who have been excluded from the American Dream. These have not known this nation as "a righteous kingdom," but more as an anti-Christ. What will America do to correct this situation today and in the future? What will America do about its "prides" of race, wealth and power? These concerns should lay the foundation for a home-grown theology of liberation.

It has been the genius of black religious experience to speak to personal and social needs. Without this bifocal religious affirmation of meaning and protest, we could not have survived the harshness of our oppression in the American environment. W.E.B. DuBois illustrated this as he wrote *The Souls of Black Folk,* in which he speaks mainly to personal faith. In his *Litany from Atlanta* he raises the theodicy question as he cries to a God of social justice. This is the faith of our black fathers living still. The "Second Reconstruction," through which we are now passing, underscores the need for the faith "that has brought us thus far on the way." It is a faith that is not content with things as they are. God is a God of Promise and we struggle for the freedom of this God who makes all things new.

We need a theology to address the whole person. Human life must be understood from the depths. Economic analysis treats only one important dimension of the human situation. Human suffering is most profound when it is deeply personal. We must, however, consider the existential and the political aspects of human existence together -- both are important. They are interchangeable and yet, as we have seen, human nature is more than either in the Christian perspective.

Christology is the capstone of a theology of liberation. The God who wills and acts for the liberation of the oppressed does so as we encounter him through the words and deeds of Jesus as the Christ. It is in and through Christ that we know God, the meaning of history, and of life and death, and the direction of events in human communities. Christ is the center; he is the Liberator. It is through the incarnation that we discover how we are to become co-laborers in the liberation struggle. Salvation is the result of participation in the liberation struggle. Christ frees us that we may free others. Christ is the center, but not the circumference of God's universal revelation. God's revelation is in all nature, all history, and among all peoples. Our task is to observe where God is at work and join him in the liberation of the oppressed. We all must discover God in Christ at work where we are and move from that center, being guided by the Spirit, toward making life more human. It is thus that we are set free as humans both from the slavery of sin and the sin of slavery. It is thus that we participate in a liberation-situation in order to uproot the systems of bondage: that there may be no slaves or masters, but a cohumanity in Christ Jesus our Lord, in the church as an extension of the Incarnation that embraces all people.

* First published in The Christian Century (Jan. 28, 1976), pp. 64-68.

NOTES

1. "The Theology of Religion," *International Theological Centre Journal* 1, no. 1 (1974): 54-68.

2. "Black Theological Ethics: A Bibliographical Essay," *Journal of Religious Ethics* 3, no. 9 (1975): 69-109.

3. *Faith and Reason* (Boston: Christopher, 1962).

4. *From Puritanism to Platonism in Seventeenth Century England* (The Hague: Martinus Nijhoff, 1968).

5. See Sergio Torres and John Eagleson, eds., *Theology in the Americas* (Maryknoll: Orbis Books, 1976).

6. "Religio-Ethical Reflections Upon the Experiential Components of a Philosophy of Black Liberation," *International Theological Center Journal* 1, no. 1 (1973): 80-94.

7. *Liberation and Reconciliation: A Black Theology* (Philadelphia: Westminister, 1972).

8. *A Black Political Theology* (Philadelphia: Westminster, 1974).

*CHRISTIAN LIBERATION ETHICS:
THE BLACK EXPERIENCE

In a casual conversation with Jürgen Moltmann, in his office at the Protestant Faculty at Tübingen, I was led to certain valuable insights: (1) that in discussing human rights, we must include social rights as well as individual rights; (2) that black theology must look at its own roots in the radical wing of the Reformation, i.e. Anabaptists; and (3) we will have to do our own reflection and not rely on the conclusions of Euro-American scholars.

The black experience of the Christian faith has been different. Our response to the Christian faith has related to our experience of unmerited suffering as a whole people at the hands of fellow human beings, many of whom confess faith in the Christian God. Our response has deepened our spirituality and sharpened our socio-ethical consciousness. Therefore, we are aware that blacks have a contribution to make to Christian social ethics which is profound.

My main vocation is that of a theologian, but thus far blacks in the field of ethics are reluctant writers. The task will not wait. Black theology is in essence theological ethics with a strong awareness of the Bible as a primary source. In fact, it is the reading of the Bible in the light of the black experience which is the foundation for the entire enterprise.

Liberation ethics as well as liberation theology is rooted in an experience of oppression in which a group of people suffer; their suffering may be based upon class, sex, or race. A liberation ethic emerging out of the black experience must be an ardent and uncompromising foe of racism. It cannot ignore class or sex as forms of oppression, but it must keep a single-eyed vision upon racist oppression. Moving from this center of perception, it can and should be sensitive to, concerned about, and active in the alleviation of other forms of oppression. But its primary agenda must always be racism. Even when there are coalitions with other groups, the black agenda must be a root and branch attack against racism.

I. SOURCES AND METHODOLOGY

William C. Settles, Jr., writes about the religious survivals of slave revolts:

> The historical experience of African peoples with religion has been incantatory. Religious ideas have been the instrument of ritual and ritual the rhythm of being. Religious ideas have lived: they have been purposeful rather than mechanical, imminent rather than transcendent. On the Old Continent as well as in the new world of enslavement, religion has been invoked, called upon by the faithful and embodied by them.[1]

Settle compares the impact of religion upon the Haitian slave revolution on August 14, 1791, with Nat Turner's rebellion in 1831 in Southampton, Virginia. The plantation settings were different, but both regimes exploited Africans; and within these locations some leaders, through their understanding of their plight wedded with the religious consciousness, had developed their ideas of liberation and dared to act upon these to find freedom for their black followers.[2] A group of black religious scholars have written in a forceful manner regarding this protest characteristic of black religion since 1966. Vincent Harding, Gayraud Wilmore, and Eric Lincoln are among these.

Charles H. Long has written about the essence of the religious experience of the Afro-American. He describes Africa as a religious image, the involuntary presence of blacks, and the experience and symbol of God. Long goes so far as to suggest that a new interpretation of American religion would result from a careful study of the black religious experience.[3]

Long is joined by Cecil Cone, who is mainly concerned about the celebrative characteristic of the black religious heritage. Cecil Cone does give some attention to the doctrine of God as an almighty sovereign power in the black experience of the Christian faith. In his critique of the "black power" element in James Cone, Joseph Washington, and J. Deotis Roberts, he exchanges the prophetic for the priestly, a price too high to pay, for black religious experience contains both in abundance. Fortunately, the writings of Howard Thurman stand as a corrective to this one-sided view. As a master of spiritual disciplines, Thurman has a deep social awareness in this thought and life. This, I believe, flows from a profound reading of the black religious heritage.

The Bible was soon embraced by black slaves. The Africans brought with them a highly developed and sophisticated awareness of creation as divinely ordered. Robert Bennet says:

> With his deep sense of God as creator, the slave
> heard in the Bible. . . not a new word but ideas
> with which he was more or less familiar. The new
> faith was not etched on a *tabula rosa*, nor was it
> merely seized upon as a means to survival."

Bennett sees in Scripture the message that God acts in the course of human events to bring about divine purposes for humankind. Our reading of Scripture, according to Bennett, is to the effect that it is God's intention that humans are to be free and live in a just society. Black awareness in black history is an assent to God's justice within creation and an affirmation of God's lordship within history. America's problem, therefore, is not the black presence, but the white refusal to accept that presence. Black theology, according to Bennett, has the task of developing a contemporary expression of salvation history. White racism and black suppression are to be brought together. Bennett concludes:

> The same hermeneutical process which confronts us
> with the message from Scripture also suggests those
> categories by which we can deal creatively with the
> word being spoken by the black experience. It is
> assumed that God's final self-revelation given in
> Jesus Christ and under the old and new covenant
> has consequences for the whole course of human his-
> tory, and that word and event continue as a potent
> influence in conveying that revelation. As we deal
> with blackness and black history as potent word and
> event, we come to see Scripture as relevant. . . .It
> leads us to discern and accept God as speaking to
> us in the givenness of our situation.[5]

Whatever we do with method, we must somehow bring the experience of ethnic suffering by blacks and the Christian ethic together. We must also keep the liberation motif at the center of our focus. The individual approach to ethics is inadequate. We cannot neglect personal piety and ethics. But we must develop a community ethic. Here Paul Lehmann's vision will be useful. Our context must be the African-Afro-American religious connection wedded to the biblical faith. The social analysis of Marx and Weber must help to provide structures and categories for our thought. The serious work of Martin Luther King, Jr., must be mined and brought up to date in the post-black power era when we confront a new form of racism which is more subtle and stubborn and widespread than any variety of racism we have faced thus far. "New occasions teach new duties," and the black exponents of a Christian social ethic must be perceptive readers of the "signs of the times."

II. THE THEOLOGICAL BASIS OF HUMAN RIGHTS

Jürgen Moltmann may well set the stage for this part of our discussion. In an essay on the theological foundations of human rights Moltmann says:

> Human rights are ultimately grounded not in human nature; nor are they conditioned by individual or collective human achievements in history. They reflect the covenant of God's faithfulness to his people and the glory of his love for the church and the world. No earthly authority can legitimately deny or suspend the right and dignity of being human. It is in the light of this covenant as fulfilled in the cross and resurrection of Jesus Christ and in the power of the Holy Spirit outpoured upon all flesh that Christians express solidarity with all those who bear a human countenance, and more particularly, a willingness to stand up for those whose fundamental rights and freedoms are robbed.[6]

Moltmann's discussion hinges on these important considerations: (1) the equal dignity and interdependence of men and women; (2) the equal validity and interdependence of personal rights and social rights; and (3) the equal dignity and interdependence of the present and future generations. His theological argument is based upon his explication of the biblical and theological understanding of the *imago Dei*. His orientation is Reformed, and the argument is cast in the mold of an exclusive Christocentrism. His structures and confession of faith are, in my judgment, too limited to guarantee human rights for humanity has a whole, the majority of whom stand outside this confession. We need a cosmopolitan and humanistic understanding of revelation and ethics, similar to that provided by the Stoics in classical Christian thought, to meet our needs today. Indeed, the legal, political, and moral context for natural law and human rights is precisely this in a historic sense. The structures for ethical discussion by all who stand within the Barthian tradition to which Moltmann and James Cone both belong are too limited to meet the demands for a theological and ethical exposition of human rights for our time. Any black ethicist should clearly see that his ethical outreach should be beamed at the mass of black folk at home and people in the Third world with whom he is wed by cultural ties, racism, and poverty.

As we look at the history of ethics we find two American ethicists whose perceptions are helpful -- Walter Rauschenbusch and Reinhold Niebuhr. Rauschenbusch had a keen awareness of social evils and applied the gospel in this direction.

Unfortunately, he was too optimistic about human nature and too enchanted with American democracy to deal realistically with either. Furthermore, he did not isolate racism as a serious problem to be addressed. Glenn R. Bucher, writing on the omission of racism on the agenda of the advocates of the social gospel, tries to explain rather than excuse them. He argues that most of them, if not all, did their work in the urban north.⁷ The fact that they did not readily link poverty with racism indicates that they were white rather than black.

But Rauschenbusch's importance for the black ethicists may well consist of two factors: (1) his awareness of the collective nature of evil and his willingness to initiate social reforms with the desire to bring the kingdom of God to earth; and (2) his advocacy of cross-bearing for the cause of social justice. He writes: "Social regeneration involves not only growth but conflict. The way to the Kingdom of God always has been and always will be a *via dolorosa*. The cross is not accidental, but is a law of social progress." ⁸

Reinhold Niebuhr, on the other hand, is too pessimistic concerning human nature. He leaves us with many ambiguities in our moral perception. In protesting against liberalism he swings, I believe, too far in the other direction. He ends up with a "possible impossibility" and an unfortunate cleavage between the manifestation of love and the pushing and shoving of justice. But along with that pessimism concerning man there is a realism which the black ethicist needs to take quite seriously. One of the most helpful aspects of his thought is the distinction he makes between individual and social ethics. While I would hesitate to contrast the two, I am grateful for his separating these problems for definition and analysis. He argues for a sharp distinction between the moral and social behavior of individuals and of social groups -- national, racial, and economic. This distinction, according to Neibuhr, justifies and necessitates political policies which would be necessary and even embarrasing if applied to matters of an individual ethic. Niebuhr writes:

> The inferiority of the morality of groups to that of individuals is due in part to the difficulty of establishing a rational social force which is powerful enough to cope with the natural impulses by which society achieves its cohesion; but in part is merely the revelation of a collective egoism, compounded of the egoistic impulses of individuals which achieve a more vivid expression and a more cumulative effect when they are united in the common impulse than when they express themselves separately and discreetly.⁹

Niebuhr's analysis of collective evils enabled earlier black scholars to have a deeper insight into racism as a cultural, institutional and systematic evil. William Stuart Nelson, Benjamin E. Mays, and others of that generation added Niebuhr's contribution to the insights they had gained from the social gospel in their opposition to racism. Their ethical thought was enriched by their knowledge of black religious experience, their encounter with black people, and their response to racist oppression.

Niebuhr, more than Rauschenbusch, attacked racism in a forthright manner and instructed black leaders concerning the best approach to overcome it. Niebuhr tries to deal realistically with racism as a stubborn collective evil. He understands that blacks must oppose this evil and steer a course between resignation and violent rebellion. He rightly suggests that power must be pitted against power in the black struggle for equality. Niebuhr goes on to say that

> it is hopeless for the Negro to expect complete emancipation from the menial social and economic position into which the white man has forced him, merely by trusting in the moral sense of the white race.[10]

He admits that there are individual whites who identify with the cause of racial justice.

> The white race in America will not admit the Negro to equal rights if it is not forced to do so.[11]

The full force of Niebuhr's observations on race were never really taken into account until the black community and churches encountered black power. Even such an astute thinker as Martin Luther King, Jr., who read Niebuhr both carefully and critically, did not take these insights with great seriousness until he met the advocates of black power in debate and again as we search for strategic instruments for black liberation as we confront new phases of racism.

III. THE LEGACY OF DR. KING

It is my contention that any viable position in liberation ethics in this country must take seriously the legacy of Martin Luther King, Jr. Thus far the pacesetters in the field have almost ignored his rich contribution, both his thought and his action. James Gustafson has a long chapter on theological ethics in America in one of his books.[12] I have searched in vain to find King's name in those sixty or more pages. The author

Liberation and Contextualization

would swear that he is not a racist, but the document speaks for itself. He is not alone. There are black writers who give King's ethics little if any attention. They are too busy quoting from white ethicists. Since our main task is to come up with some perspective in black liberation ethics, King's work is the more dispensable.

He is the bridge between the older generation of black religious thinkers and the present situation. George Kelsey, Benjamin E. Mays, Mordecai Wyatt Johnson, and Howard Thurman are among those who laid the ethical foundations for King's work. King, in his account of his intellectual development, does not pay adequate respect to black thinkers who prepared the way for him. At the time when he wrote, most black scholars would have claimed respectability by quoting white sources; why should he be the exception? And yet with our new consciousness of the importance of our "roots" we would be remiss if we did not examine his works in the context of the black heritage. Without the black church tradition there would not have been a Martin Luther King, Jr., as we know him. Without a religious experience that steeled black sufferers against hardships and inflamed their consciences against injustices, King would not have emerged as it were from the womb of the black church. Crozer and Boston only refined what he brought with him. Furthermore, his effectiveness as a leader among blacks, even among whites, may be explained only in this way.

King's pilgrimage to nonviolence is well known. It would take too long to restate it here. What King sought was a method to overcome a systemic evil -- racism. All of his white teachers had failed to indicate how the ethic of Jesus could deal with overcoming a massive social evil like racism. They had done their exegesis of scripture and their theological reflection in such an individualistic manner as to render the Christian ethic ineffectual in dealing with a social evil like racism. In the West, Marx and Reinhold Niebuhr have been helpful, but King rejected both on theological grounds -- his understanding of God and man.

King describes nonviolent action as follows: It opposes evil actively. It is a method which is active spiritually. Nonviolence does not seek to humiliate an opponent but cultivates understanding. It attacks the forces of evil rather than the persons who are evildoers because they themselves are victimized by evil. Nonviolence accepts suffering without retaliation. King held that undeserved suffering is redemptive and can educate and transform human nature. Nonviolence avoids internal as well as external violence. One must refuse to hate.[13]

For King, love is the message; white nonviolence is the method. He gets love from his understanding of Jesus and the method from Ghandhi. He integrates these in his own thought, life and program. Unfortunately, King accepts the Lutheran version of *agape* of the Lundensians rather than doing his own exegesis. The result is interpreting love as a giving love devoid of the input from *eros* and *philia*. Another weakness is the failure to reconcile justice and power in the theological grounding of his ethics. Unless we work at these deficiencies in King's ethical program, we will not have an adequate ethical perspective for the present and the future. Thus an affirmative attitude toward King's contribution does not require an uncritical acceptance of his position as a norm for all times to come. The genius of the norm which black Christians have used in the fight against racism has been the adaptability to new occasions and new duties.

Here the insights of John Bennett on "middle axioms" prove useful. Our norm is the black experience of the Christian faith. Our goal is human liberation from racism among other social and personal forms of oppression. For us personal ethics must be subsumed under community ethics. The main focus of black liberation ethics must be social without neglecting a profound concern for personal ethics. We, therefore, have a norm and we have a goal. The middle-axiom thesis provides a means whereby the norm is brought in contact with a situation (racist oppression) to lead toward a goal which is racial justice/equality.

As we reflect upon King's program and seek to update his unusual contribution to ethical thought and action, we must find a way to modify the norm and the goal as we confront a new type of racism initiated by "benign neglect" and culminating in the Bakke case. The new racism is subtle, respectable, highly intellectual and nationwide. The white conscience no longer exists, or if it does, it does so in a callous, self-righteous and antagonistic form. The white liberals are tired, and many are now avowed racists. A Latin American theologian could have been describing churches in the United States when he said that in the face of the poverty-stricken masses the churches are too feeble to even deny their Lord. A colleague said to me recently, white churches are seemingly condemned to hypocrisy on racism.

The picture is dismal, especially when figures are translated into kith and kin and people you care about. But blacks have been in the freedom struggle a long time. In developing a strategy to move forward black church men and women, black ethicists and theologians have a major role. Our inspiration comes from our faith in the Lord of the church and from a communion with black saints and martyrs of the past. They did not fail their generation; we must not fail ours.

NOTES

1. "African Religious Survivals as Factors in American Slave Revolts," The Journal of Negro History, LVI (1971), 97.

2. Ibid., pp. 103-4.

3. "Perspectives for a study of Afro-American Religion in the United States," History of Religions (August, 1971), p. 66.

4. "Black Experience and the Bible," Theology Today, XXVII (1971), 426.

5. Ibid., p. 433.

6. "The Theological Basis of Human Rights," The Reformed World, XXXIV (1976), 51-52.

7. "Social Gospel Christianity and Racism," Union Seminary Quarterly Review, XXVII (1973), 153.

8. In Benson Y. Landis, A Rauschenbusch Reader (New York: Harper, 1957), p.97.

9. Moral Man and Immoral Society (New York: Scribner's, 1960), p. xii.

10. Ibid., p. 252.

11. Ibid., p. 253.

12. Christian Ethics and the Community (Philadelphia: Pilgrim Press, 1971).

13. King, The Pilgrimage to Non-Violence, Stride Toward Freedom (New York: Harper, 1958), p. 102.

* First published in Religion in Life (Summer 1979).

PART III

BLACK POLITICAL AND SOCIAL THEOLOGY

*THE IMPACT OF THE BLACK CHURCH

The black church was born in the African forests and has been an extended family during our experience of our sojourn in the New World. The black religious experience, both oral and written, is the essence of our heritage. In a recent conversation, one of our greatest black churchmen, Rev. Dr. Thomas Kilgore of the Second Baptist Church of Los Angeles and president of the Progressive Baptist Convention made the observation:

> Our black religious heritage is too rich to be consigned to history. It must be preserved for our posterity.

He pledged his moral support for those who are busy recording our religious heritage. I was greatly encouraged by these remarks.

Black theologians have talked a lot about our blackness, but have been writing mainly for a white readership. We must consciously change our style and we must seek now to reach our non-theologically trained constituency beyond the halls of ivy. All blacks share a common black religious heritage. It is this common experience that we are called to make plain. I have elected to divide my subject-matter into three parts: (1) the history of the black church experience; (2) the theological understanding of the church in the black experience; and, (3) the mission of the black church.

I. THE HISTORY OF THE BLACK CHURCH EXPERIENCE

Africans always have been a deeply religious people. Religion in Africa is a social force for cohesion. It provides an interpretation of ultimate reality and it supplies meaning for every phase of the life cycle. African religion forms a complete belief-system with its own theology, ritual, faith and life style.

Osadolor Imasogie, a Nigerian religious scholar, provides us with a brief but helpful discussion on African traditional religion. He also indicates how this contextual religious experience is transformed by the encounter with the Christian faith.

Against the protest of many Western writers, Imasogie argues for a common African religious experience. He takes the position that, though there are differences, they are overshadowed by beliefs held in common -- e.g., the eternal Supreme Creator. The differences, he suggests, are determined by socio-political and geographical situations.¹

Imasogie rejects Geoffry Parrinder's characterization of African religion as he also rejects the conclusions of Father Schmidt. Schmidt discovered the idea of a Supreme Being among the Pigmy people of Central Africa. This was a gain over Emil Ludwig's view that since the concept of deity is philosophical, Africans were incapable of discovering it. While Schmidt argued for the presence of this belief, he misread the content of the belief. Indeed, it seems that all Western scholars fall short at this point. The Supreme Being was understood to be a deistic god -- a god who was a creator but not a provider. God was believed to be one who created the world and removed his presence and power from this world. It was, therefore, left to the lesser spirits to control affairs among humans in this world.²

It has been left to African scholars to clear up this confusion. Indeed, there seems to be almost universal agreement among African theologians that European scholars misread the African understanding of God. Our writer quotes from John Mbiti as well as from his fellow countryman, E. Bolaji Idowu in asserting that God is one and that the lesser spirits and the ancestors are understood as messengers and instruments of this one God. Furthermore, this God is not only the Creator, but the one near at hand as Provider. This God is also in some sense the Redeemer in the African religious consciousness.³

C. Eric Lincoln renounces the white man's racial and cultural arrogance as he dismissed the black man's religion during slavery. Lincoln says:

> The African he dismissed arbitrarily as heathen did . . . believe in a supreme God. . . . What the white man dismissed as African ancestor worship was a highly sophisticated expression of love and respect for the family, and a recognition of the continuity of its relationships. . . . What is more, the African moral codes were consistent with the notion of One God of all people.⁴

James H. Cone is correct in saying that the black church was born in slavery. His focus is on the pre-Civil War black church. This church, according to Cone, was related to a quest for social justice in this world. The slave preachers saw that slavery was inconsistent with Christianity. This recognition made early black churches the center of protest against the slave system. Cone dares to say:

> . . . white Christianity in America was born in heresy. Its very coming to be was an attempt to reconcile the impossible -- slavery and Christianity. And the existence of the black churches is a visible reminder of its apostasy. The black church is the only church in America which remained recognizably Christian during pre-Civil-War days. Its stand on freedom and equality through word and action is true to the spirit of Christ.[5]

The post-Civil War black church, according to Cone, soon became rather "a place of retreat from the dehumanizing forces of white power." It was a place where blacks were safe from the racist structures that replaced slavery. The black church gradually became an instrument of escape instead of, as formerly, an instrument of protest. Black ministers perpetuated the white system of black dehumanization. The white society recruited black leaders from the black churches who had bought into white theology and ethics. Blacks were told that they should live an upright life in preparation for heaven. But, on the other hand, they should not be concerned about white injustice -- this was a sign of a loss of faith. They were to be prepared for patience and long-suffering in preparation for the final judgment. Black ministers were duped by the reign of Jim Crow in the churches as well as the society and, as Uncle Toms, they led black churches into a state of apostasy. Cone says:

> The black church identified white words with God's Word and convinced its people that by listening in faithful obedience to the "great white father" they would surely enter the "pearly gates."[6]

Cone leaps historically from the pre-Civil War black church to Dr. King's ministry. King, according to Cone, saw clearly the meaning of the gospel with its social implications and sought to instill its true spirit in the hearts and minds of black and white in this land. He was a prophet with a dream grounded not in the hopes of white America but in God. His dream led him to take on responsibilities in the present. Cone sees black power as the only hope for the black church. He goes so far as to say that even though King did not endorse black power, he prepared the way for its coming.[7]

Major Jones, covering the same period, the post-Civil War church, argues that the black church "guided a people through a time of great danger." To preach the gospel with its fullness might well have invited genocide, Jones argues. I quote:

> Whether one is critical of the black church for its lack of aggressive protest, or rather praises it for its strategy of deception, which surely saved a people, may be determined by how one reads post-Civil War history.[8]

The years immediately following the Civil War, roughly 1867-1877, were troubled times. W.E.B. DuBois called these "mystic years." The North decided to try democracy. Many ministers turned to politics. Churches were meeting places. Ministers were often the only persons in a community sufficiently well developed to lead the people. They, therefore, had to devote themselves not just to church work, but to every matter of concern to the race. Whites had loosened black chains and were busy congratulating themselves for their selflessness and benevolence. Their sense of responsibility was at an end. Blacks who were landless, ignorant and penniless were left to deal with starvation, poverty and want. Blacks were free for a few years, but they became the political tools of the Republican party. When the southern whites decided to take matters into their hands again, the government merely turned its head and allowed blacks to endure a new type of enslavement. The white man was free to take the lives of blacks with impunity and to install sharecropping provided as a second form of enslavement.

We cannot gainsay the role which black ministers and churches played during these troubled times. Due to the oppression blacks experienced in the South they fled north and west into major urban centers. They were soon to discover in the cities that they could not compete with the opportunities offered to white ethnic emigrants from Europe who were racial cousins to those in power. It was then that the dark ghetto was born with its heinous crime and poverty. The black man's heaven turned into hell.

Black religion nurtured us through all these tragic experiences. Its African roots were transformed by the tragic soul life of both slaves and so-called freed men. The churches under the leadership of black ministers, laymen and women has weathered this storm and guided us through this long night of suffering. The black church has been not merely an ark of salvation, but a hospital for the sick, a haven for the lonely, an agent of social action and change. It has been a center of protest, and a place where blacks have found meaning and healing for bodies, minds and spirits. This is the role of the church in the history of black people.

Black Political and Social Theology 131

II. THE CHRISTIAN UNDERSTANDING OF THE CHURCH

The church is a fellowship or a community of believers. In the christian tradition, the church is a group of people who have accepted the discipleship of Jesus Christ. The fact that we are discussing the church rather than a mosque or a synagogue implies that we are addressing the Christian congregation.

This does not mean, however, that we are unaware that some blacks are Moslem, Jewish and secular. Indeed, some blacks are religious without belonging to any religious community. We need to take an ecumenical approach which will enable us to work for liberation across denominational and interreligious lines. In fact, our churches must assume an operational unity that will allow us to support even secular organizations like the NAACP and the Urban League which have a good track record in the cause of racial justice.

Our task here is to seek a deeper understanding of the nature of the black church. It is both an organism of the spirit and a historic organization or institution. It is invisible as well as visible. Here we do not refer to "invisible" in a sociological sense as E. Franklin Frazier does in his valuable study on the black church.[9] Frazier had in mind the unofficial and often secret religious gatherings of slaves unknown to their masters. Our reference is rather to the theological distinction the Protestant Reformers made between the earthly fellowship of believers in Christ and the communion of saints in heavenly places. This is the distinction the adherents of the social gospel made between the church militant and the church triumphant.

After the crucifixion and resurrection of Jesus Christ, some of his devotees waited in Jerusalem for the presence and power of the Holy Spirit. On the Day of Pentecost the spirit descended upon the faithful. Those disciples who had been downcast with doubt and despair were transfigured into forceful proclaimers of the good news that Jesus is both Lord and Christ. Many lives were changed to new moral and spiritual directions. A fellowship was born in which there was great sharing and caring. It was a community of love. It was a spirit-filled assembly. The apostle Paul was later to refer to it as the "household of faith" or the "family of God." We will return to the image of the church as family. This New Testament image of the church is essential to the self-understanding of the black church.

In I Cor. 12:14 the apostle Paul asserts that we are many members in one body. Here we may draw upon the meaning of an East African term *harambee* (unity). Africans tell us that all traditional cultures on that vast continent have a strong sense of unity within community. The statement "because I am we are" is often repeated to express this type of kinship.

The religious experience of our forebears contained this type of unity within community. Again, this is why black slaves understood the Bible and its message almost by instinct. Both the synagogue of the Old Testament and the church of the New Testament contextually belong to a non-Western social milieu. The relation of God to old Israel, the Hebrews and to New Israel, the church, could be readily understood by people aware of the presence and power of God in their midst. Africans understand religion as permeating the life of the entire life cycle and community. This is at the heart of the biblical message.

In saying that the church is the body of Christ, Paul is also pointing out that a body has many parts. Each organ or limb has a special function, but on the other hand, the body is a unity. It follows that the parts are inter-dependent. The health and wholeness of the one body depends upon how well each part functions and its harmonious working in concert with other parts. We now know, even better than Paul, the profundity of his insight. We can go even further and point to the delicate relationship between mind and body. A good neuro-surgeon will check out all the physical and nerve connections to the brain. If all is in order and the patient is still complaining, he or she will inquire about the patient's personal relations. Are you facing pressures on your job? Are you and your wife or husband having marital problems?

Paul, then, was on to something when he described the church as a body. A body is a unity-in-diversity. It allows for persons to fulfill themselves morally and spiritually, but it provides this self-fulfillment in the context of community. It is unity without conformity. There is room for self-expression, but this too is related to the well-being of others. We are a people needing to find a unity-in-diversity, but a unity-without-conformity. We need to know who we are as a people and forge our way to an operational unity if we would be free, but there must be an opportunity for each person to work through the identity crisis which racism has foisted upon us and realize our potential. We must have healthy individuals if our group life is to be healthy and whole.

Finally, the church is first and foremost a spiritual organism, a living body. Christ is the head of the church. The church exists under his lordship. It is anchored in faith. It is sustained by the spirit's presence and power.

All the affirmations of the Christian belief system converge in our understanding of the church--what we understand about God, sin, salvation, the redemption through Christ, the work of the spirit, preaching, sacraments and the life after death. All these are aspects of the faith of the church. It is through the life of its members committed to this faith, bound in a covenant with each other under the Lordship of Jesus Christ and through the guidance and power of the spirit, that the Christian mission is carried forth in the world.

In Ephesians 3:15, Paul refers to the "whole family in heaven and earth." African theologians are now concerned about the "communion of the saints" against the background of an extended family which has a built-in reverence for ancestors. This religious tradition holds a belief in kinship that connects the living with the living dead. Such a belief has concrete implications concerning respect for the elderly as well as for ancestors who have departed this life. All these concerns must be dealt with by African Christian theologians when they speak of the "communion of the saints."

While we can learn much from this disucussion that will help us to overcome the tension between the haves and have-nots in our pews and the relation between the young and the old, our focus will be limited to the family image in the African religious community, in the black church and, of course with the New Testament.

The word *ujamma* (familyhood) is considered by Julius Nyere, President of Tanzania, as the African way to socialism. As a socio-politico-economic program in that country, it is developed out of African and Christian components. But *ujamma* is African in a traditional sense. It refers primarily to the kinship ties within the extended family. This concept of family is at the heart of social organization and is permeated with religious beliefs and rituals. The life cycle of the individual as well as the destiny of the community is understood in the context of *ujamma*.

The black family and church have always been closely related in this country. In a real sense the church is a family when it is true to its purpose in the black community.

Black families were divided on the auction block. Not withstanding Gutmann's study,[10] slavery dealt a terrible blow to black family life. Those who were able to keep the family afloat did so through an almost invincible love and determination. After emancipation, economic necessity again separated the family. The flight to the urban North either divided the family or consigned it to the woes of the dark ghettos of the North. Unemployment and the welfare system almost finished the black family off. These are socio-historic realities. The black church, South and North, was the place where blacks came together in a fellowship of sharing and caring. The black church has been the place where the lonely could find friendship, where haves and have-nots could rejoice together and affirm faith in a common Lord. Let us not forget the healing ministry of the black church. Even when the black people have been other-worldly in its message it has enabled black people to assume dignity and maintain their sanity in an otherwise insane society.

In the present time the black church has been more than a haven for the lonely; it is a militant church -- a prophetic church. Our understanding of religion has always been holistic. Even the spirituals which capture the tragic soul life of slaves address themselves to freedom here as well as hereafter. Dr. Miles Mark Fisher, an authority on black spirituals and the history of the black church, writes in *Slave Songs in the United States* concerning the double meaning of the spirituals.

While white Christians divide up between those concerned about heaven and those concerned about life here and now, black Christians under the leadership of ministers and laypersons have always used their faith as a protest against injustices. Thus as the family of God we may now use our togetherness as a means for our deliverance. This is a tradition out of our historic black churches we need now to both celebrate and develop. We need to cultivate the presence of God as we come together for worship and service. Only thus will the worship and life of the black churches be prepared to fulfill their mission. The black church will not be able to function as an institutional agent of social change unless it brings the power and perspectives of its worship and life to bear upon its mission of liberation.

Major Jones has written a passage which I find helpful in making this point. He distinguishes between a static and dynamic concept of the church. The church, Jones argues, is not an *ecclesia* or community formed and founded once and for all that remains constant and unchanged. He speaks rather of the true church as "a congregating church." The people of God become an *ecclesia* only by the fact of a repeated concrete event when God meets them. Jesus said when two or three assemble in my name, I will be in their midst. Jones writes that the gathered church has the potential of becoming the "event church," if the people gathered lay hold of the entire promise of the gospel, become aware of the grace of the Father and are conscious of the abiding presence of Christ. The true church, then, is a group of people called of God to be the church of God in the world, accepting such a calling, and gathered as a people of God in his name. It is only then that the "event status" is conferred upon those gathered.[11]

If the impact of the black church is to continue we must take seriously the tradition to which we belong. It is a heritage with a deep spirituality which has brought healing to a long-suffering people. Its songs, sermons and ceremonies have bound up the wound inflicted upon us by an inhumane social order. Its priestly tradition has brought meaning and healing to us as persons, but the black church has produced prophets as well as priests. Therefore, black churches as institutions have been agents of social change for the liberation of black people.

III. THE WITNESS OF THE BLACK CHURCH

The black church remains as the strongest historic and nation-wide institution controlled by black people. In some sense the black church is an "ethnic" church which is capable of rallying issues which relate to black survival. White churches are mainly spiritual comfort stations. This is the reason why conservative evangelical churches are growing. A white church concerned about social change and ethical issues is usually small and ineffective. It sits on the fringe of church life. Many ethically concerned whites have had to leave their churches and form small cell groups to deal with what seems vital for them.

Because black churches are spiritually alive and socially concerned at the same time, there is a lot of promise for black churches to witness with great force in society. White preachers dare not preach on social evils from their pulpits less they face a dwindling membership and a shrinking budget. In some cases, they are disciplined by district superintendants and bishops, but in many instances black ministers must run to catch up with their people in social concern. We as a people need to hear a word of deliverance from our pulpits and we expect those who utter these words to be ahead of us in social involvements. The oppressed need and appreciate a word of deliverance. Only in this form is the gospel good news.

Before discussing further the witness of the black churches, I would like to draw your attention to a new form of racism. Nathan Galzer has written a book which sums up the new form of racism. The book is entitled *Ethnic Inequality and Public Policy*.[12] Glazer claims that "affirmative action" is "affirmative discrimination." William V. Shannon sums up the situation well:

> After two centuries of slavery and another century of Jim Crow second-class citizenship, the court decisions and civil rights legislation of the 1950's and 60's finally destroyed segregation and overt racial discrimination. . . .[13]

Shannon rightly conceives of these gains of the 50s and 60s as merely laying the foundation for further progress. He agrees with remarks made by President Lyndon Johnson in a commencement address at Howard University in June 1965. Johnson referred to the long period of deprivation of human rights blacks had endured and suggested that much needed to be done to upgrade these disabilities before all blacks would be able to compete. Johnson said:

> It is not enough just to open the gates of opportunity. All our citizens must have the ability to walk through those gates.

Johnson adds:

> This is the next and the more profound stage of the battle for civil rights. We seek not just freedom but opportunity. We seek not just legal equality as a right and a theory *but equality as a fact and equality as a result.*[14]

Harvard sociologist Glazer is saying "no" to Johnson. Galzer asserts that affirmative action has failed the black masses. It has helped those blacks who could have made it on their own -- the black middle class. His argument is an example of the new form of racism which exalts "merit" as the standard for progress.[15] Glazer does not understand what it means to be black in a society saturated with racism. There are scores of jobs which would be crowded out by white applicants if the Federal Government did not intervene to make sure that blacks obtained their share of such jobs. Also blacks who are doing well need to be reminded of their responsibility of reaching back to and aiding those who are still struggling to survive.

While continuing to be a soul-winning church, the black church must realize its awesome responsibility in dealing with collective evils. Many people are not even aware of their participation in a system that destroys black people. Joseph R. Washington, Jr. writes about racism as a pre-conscious and irrational fact in white America.[16] To be born white provides a white male with a ten-fold advantage and a white female with at least a five-fold advantage on either a black male or female. Most middle class people of my generation, with few exceptions, are the first affluent generation. Compare this with two hundred or more years of affluence in some white families. We are a people struggling to rise above mere survival.

Personal friendships with whites and even inter-racial marriages will not overcome this cleavage between the races. The problem is systemic, cultural and institutional. Whatever our personal preferences may be, we have a responsibility to free a whole people and our personal freedom is tied to their liberation. There is not place in this society where we can escape racism. There is no status we can achieve where racism does not haunt us or someone we love.

The black church as a powerful institution, made up of gifted and influential people from our race, has great potential as an agent of liberation for black people, but it is only partially mobilized. It needs to become conscious of its opportunity and its resources in this freedom struggle. We need a socially-conscious and well-trained staff in our large congregations. A single person at the helm of a 3,000 - 4,000 membership congregation is drained of all of his/her energy in dealing with emergency basket cases. We need to arouse, organize and activate the considerable lay leadership in our midst, including our youth. To this end we may no longer rely on the annual revival even though revivals are necessary to renew the faith of members as well as to call the unsaved to repentance. There must be persistent Christian nurture through teaching and counseling as well as preaching and worship. Our people must be educated in their new consciousness and responsibilities. They must understand the form and dimensions of the problems we face. They must understand the *this-worldly* message of the gospel of Jesus Christ who is lord of the church. The black church must be concerned with personal crises and do a good job in pastoral care. It must minister to the sick, the helpless, the dying and the bereaved. It must be engaged in social welfare. It must meet personal, family and community emergencies, but as an institution it must confront the unjust organizations and systems of power for the end of social transformation. The black church, following the example of Dr. King, must deal with political, social and economic causes which make life more human.

But the black church must be wise in its efforts. The church must always be true to its nature and mission in the world. It must bring to bear its understanding of the gospel upon all causes and movements. Its critical and objective frame of judgment must be anchored in the Bible and the confession of the Christian creed. Therefore, the black church is not just another agency, not just another organiztion. The power of the black church is not merely a material power. It is spiritual. It is anchroed in a community of believers who serve and work under the lordship of Jesus Christ.

The church may cooperate with secular institutions for humanizing the social order. It may give its support on issues which it endorses out of its commitment to the worth of each person under God, but the role of the church is not merely *functional*. Its task is to bring to its material resources a transcendent, spiritual perspective and moral insights which enrich and empower any effort for human fulfillment and social justice. Should our black churches deny their Lord and uproot themselves from a rich spiritual heritage, like Samson of old they would lose their spiritual power and hence their physical strength, and would be readily defeated by the evils we face. As a secular institution the black church, with its meager personnel and financial resources would be easily defeated. The strength of the black church is first of all in its power to motivate, to organize and to empower black people to face great odds in the moral struggle for human dignity. The black church will be and continue to be an awesome force for the liberation of black people, if it remains true to its faith and its lord, if it maintains its integrity and spirituality and is *unbossed* and *unbought* by the forces of injustice in our society.

Ask not for whom the bell tolls,
It tolls for thee.

*   An address presented to the Oklahoma Association of Black Personnel in Higher Education at its second bi-annual conference, April 28, 1978, in Oklahoma City, Oklahoma.

NOTES

1. Osadolor Imasogie, "African Traditional Religion and Christian Faith," Review and Expositor (Vol. LXX, no. 3, Sum., 1973), pp. 284.

2. Ibid., p. 288.

3. Ibid., pp. 289-290.

4. C. Eric Lincoln, "The Development of Black Religion in America," Ibid., p. 300.

5. James H. Cone, Black Theology and Black Power (New York: Seabury Press, 1969), p. 103.

6. Ibid., p. 107.

7. Ibid., pp. 108-109.

8. Major J. Jones, Black Awareness: A Theology of Hope (New York: Abingdon, 1971), p. 54.

9. Frazier's The Negro Church in America is reprinted in C. Eric Lincoln's, The Black Church Since Frazier (New York: Schocken Books, 1976).

10. Herbert E. Gutman, The Black Family in Slavery and Freedom 1750-1925 (Pantheon Books, 1976).

11. Jones, op cit., pp. 57-58.

12. Nathan Glazer, Ethnic Inequality and Public Policy (New York: Basic Books, 1976).

13. The New York Times Book Review, Feb. 8, 1976, sec. 7, p. 4.

14. Ibid.

15. Glazer, op. cit.

16. The Politics of God (Boston: Beacon, 1966), Ch. II.

*THE BLACK CAUCUS AND THE FAILURE OF CHRISTIAN THEOLOGY

I. IS THERE A THEOLOGICAL ALTERNATIVE TO BLACK POWER?

An attempt is made in this presentation to think theologically as a Christian about one of America's great social ills. To speak relevantly to the racial crisis, theology will need to become consciously anthropocentric, not in the humanistic sense, but in the Christian sense. This does not necessarily mean that Christology or God-talk will be abandoned. It does imply that human dignity, peoplehood, suffering, deprivation and injustice will be put in Christian perspective and treated theologically. The other side of the Barthian "God speaks, man listens" is "man cries, God hears." The theologian, to be relevant, must not detach himself from the mainstream of the life of those to whom his interpretation of the Christian faith is to be meaningful. This, I believe, is needful if the theological treatment of God, Christ, World, Kingdom are to be important.

Is there a theological alternative to Black Power? Is there a positive content in Black Power which may be converted into a constructive theological statement? Is there a place in theological discourse for such considerations? In other words, is there a problem-oriented approach to theology? Theology is "reasoning about God" (the *logos* of *Theos*) or as John MacQuarrie puts it, "God-talk." May we think about God in such a way as to include the unjust and inhuman conditions under which some humans live? How does theology meet the needs of "all sorts and conditions of men?" Not just WASPS (White Anglo-Saxon-Protestants), or in a more restricted sense, "White Middle-Class Protestants." Some two-thirds of the human race are among the disinherited. What has been written as Radical Theology, as secularity and God, i.e., about God in the "secular city," has left the Negro problem untouched. This may be the reason why Negroes have fled theology like the plague or abandoned it in favor of another opinion.

Speaking as a Black man, who happens to be a theologian by training and experience, it is my position that theology should and ought to speak to the human situation and should challenge men to life-and-death decisions in the racial crisis as in all areas of human misery and need. This implies a kind of existential social theology. If Christian theology cannot do this, it is either remiss or bankrupt. What I am considering is a "Black Theology" which makes just as much sense as a "Theology of Revolution" makes in Latin America or a "Crisis Theology" in Hitler's Germany. Let me make it quite clear that I do not personally envisage a "Theology of Violence," but I am suggesting that theology should undergird and support social change in the context of the Christian faith. My plea is for a "Situational Theology." The absence of a "social consciousness" in American theology is one of its greatest failures and especially at this time, its greatest shortcoming. It is literally fiddling while Rome burns. Given the crisis in our cities, the chaotic state of national politics and foreign diplomacy, it indulges in "faddism" while overlooking the great ills of our society. There is a real question whether anyone in theology can afford the luxury of a "Death-of-God Theology." Theology needs to be done with the *absence* and affirm the *presence* of God. Only a God who cares and who is living and present for redemptive ends can be meaningful to the disinherited. At this time in world history, we need a "Social, Ethical and Political Theology." This would be a "Theology of Hope" with hope for the hopeless, the helpless, the hapless.

II. THEOLOGY AND THE BLACK CAUCUS

This is an essay which examines the ideas behind the "Black Revolution" in America. I am here concerned with only one aspect of this very complex movement and from a specific point of view. The attempt is made to treat the "Black Caucus" trend in integrated religious bodies in which Negroes are a minority and to approach this movement theologically. My concern is to determine if theology has done its task in making the interpretation of the Christian faith relevant in the racial crisis. It is a point of view in which my own thoughts are informed by the thoughts of others, but it is in essence "how I am making up my mind" about a crucial problem of our time.

There is a need for a problem-oriented statement of the Christian faith in theological terms. More than a decade ago when I had just completed a doctorate in theology, there was an opportunity to work in up-state New York with an integrated group of college and university students, engaged in a migrant ministry. I remember a white seminarian's observation that it was an unusual pleasure for him to meet me and work with me because my being there had improved his appreciation for theology. He commented that the image created by the theologians who taught him was that a theologian was too good to soil his hands with migrants. Though I was working at this task at that time as much out of economic necessity as out of love for people, these insights have informed everything that I have attempted to do or say as a theologian ever since.

Theologians preoccupied with "secularity" might easily find an ethical way to make theology relevant without the loss of transcendence.

In a statement by the National Committee of Negro Churchmen, July 31, 1966, we read:

> ... too often the Negro church has stirred its members away from the reign of God in *this world* to a distorted and complacent view of *another worldly* conception of God's power. We commit ourselves as churchmen to make more meaningful in the life of our institution our conviction that Jesus Christ reigns in the "here" and "now" as well as in the future he brings in upon us. We shall, therefore, use more of the resources of our churches in working for human justice in the places of social change and upheaval where our master is already at work.[1]

Here it seems to me is an awareness that God matters in the "here" and "now" and that we must somehow make men aware of God in the upheavals of our times. This is to affirm God and secularity, but not to accept secularism. The Black Churchmen are aware that they and their people must still affirm the "Goodness" of God while they also affirm the "manhood" of man.

III. WHY THE BLACK CAUCUS?

The Reverend J. Metz Rolins, Executive Director of the National Committee of Black Churchmen, has informed me that every major white body, from Roman Catholics to Unitarians, have a "Black Caucus."[2] It is a rare phenomenon that such a movement in the Christian church should be so widespread. The cause of this is almost too obvious for discussion. It is a fact that the cry for "Black Power" has led to "Black Awareness" on the part of the Black community. This includes the Black churches.[3] The same type of "caucus" is found alike in integrated colleges and universities as in integrated denominations.[4] Many institutions have made concessions to Black students who have requested separate facilities in the larger community. Seminaries, well represented in marches and demonstrations, have also been beset by the "Black Caucus" movement.

The promise of America has not been fulfilled in the Negro's experience. Legal breakthroughs have been weakened by litigation and the slow pace of implementation. The classic example is the 1954 decision of desegregation in the schools and all similar legal determinations. The sit-ins and nonviolent demonstrations led to some radical changes. Negroes may now eat and sleep at many places across the country which were formerly closed to them. They may ride in the front of the bus and find a comfortable seat on the train in New York en route to Atlanta without the embarrassment of changing cars in Washington. Negroes may now go to some of the best schools on all levels. As a matter of fact, there is a very active recruitment program for qualified Negroes who are "highly visible" for a conspicuous exposure. But this has been primarily "tokenism" and for a pragmatic reason, viz. as "window dressing" to keep the wolf from the door. Other Negroes have received "political appointments" in Washington or from Washington as a kind of "peace prize" to the Black community. This Whites note as progress, as do the "black bourgeoisie" who have gained most by tokenism.

In the meantime the "dark ghetto" has deteriorated. The Black man in the mass has been the victim of rising prices, unemployment, poor housing and inadequate education. Whereas the socio-economic mobility of a few Negroes has increased considerably, the plight of the masses has degenerated to the point of entrapment. A climate of hopelessness, powerlessness and futility settles over the ghetto. Caught up in bitterness, these Blacks have expressed "Black Rage." This is something of the beginning of "Black Power."

The Black intellectual has also become aware that in America he cannot escape his "blackness." He now has a good job with an adequate income. He lives on the "Black gold coast" or in suburbia with White neighbors. He has been "brainwashed," as the Black students say, to think, believe, act and even worship as if he were White. But this is a fool's paradise, a world of make-believe. Every so often the *real* American with sharp rudeness makes him aware that he, too, is black.

This trauma may come through his being called "nigger" in a Southern town, or by some subtle denial of his privilege as a citizen in a Northern city. Though he works in an integrated office, there may be fewer opportunities for promotion for him than for his White colleagues with less training, ability or experience. He would like to keep up with his neighbors who are white. His neighbor who is white earns sufficient money to maintain a high standard of living which allows his wife to remain at home and fulfill the role as housewife and mother. But because, as a Black man, he is not elevated, his wife must be out of the home just to raise the note. Often the children must be "parentless" most of the time just in order that parents may try "to belong" to a we-group that has already rejected them by color. The cry of "Black Power" has made these people aware of their roots.

It is little wonder that race relations have moved from *demonstration* to *confrontation*. Lerone Bennett is correct, I believe:

> The Negro rebellion is a classic example of the confrontation of black and white. . . . This epochal event, which is beginning not ending, is unfolding on several levels. Black men and White men are standing now forehead to forehead, spiritually and physically. . . .[5]

We turn now to some explanation of why the "Black Caucus" movement has invaded the churches. Many Negroes have joined integrated denominations (those in which Negroes are in the minority and whites in the majority) for prestige. Some have been brainwashed into accepting their inferiority. They assume, therefore, that anything manned by Whites is automatically superior to the same thing in the Black community. Whites generally believe the same. This is the reason why it is difficult for Whites to understand why Negroes refuse to integrate on their terms. But others have joined White churches because they were sincere in the desire for true interracial fellowship or because through exposure to various educational and cultural opportunities their outlook has been altered. This fact persists notwithstanding the fact that in America the entire educational process has been oriented toward White superiority and Black inferiority. Not being aware of this in the past, many Negroes have assumed that White churches are bigger and better in every way. Even a Black sociologist of religion, Joseph Washington, took this line in his *Black Religion*. But to his credit, *The Politics of God* has been informed by "Black Pride" and "Black Awareness."

Stokely Carmichael's call for "Black Power" along with the reaction it has generated has made it almost impossible for any Negro to think the same and be satisfied with anything less than a revolution in the churches in reference to race relations. On the negative side, there has been the cry, "burn, baby, burn!" Some have taken it upon themselves to visit riots upon "racist America." Others have advocated a "Theology of Violence." On the positive side, there has arisen a pride in race, a self-respect, a renaissance of interest in the Negro's history and his contribution to American life and thought. The Negro child can now identify himself with great men who are black. This development is summed up in the statement "Black is beautiful."

In a word, what we have not found even in religious institutions is the *will* on the part of the White man to accept the Black man as his equal. We have found integrated congregations but not desegregated hearts. During the summer of 1968, a small group of young White Christians at Michigan State

University assured a group of "Black Power Students" that they would not work in the Black community but would go rather into the White community with a message. The White churches in their indifference to racial justice have created the occasion for the "Black Caucus."

To sum up, Metz Rollins says:

> Long segregated, separated, treated with scorn and disgrace, the black church and the black churchmen of the predominantly white churches are now coming into their own. No longer content to play second-fiddle, to be treated like step-children or wayward dependents by the white church and its leadership, the black church has nurtured an acute awareness of its own unique gifts, its own peculiar understanding of the Gospel of Jesus Christ, and a new appreciation for its own hallowed and tortured history. . . . In a period of black awareness and black consciousness in the larger black community, black churchmen are insisting that the witness of the black church is meaningful only as it becomes a militant advocate of the cause of justice and dignity for black people, regardless of their class or status.[6]

IV. THE FAILURE OF THEOLOGY TO CONSIDER THE CAUSE OF RACIAL JUSTICE

Two reasons for the indifference of American theology to race relations come immediately to focus: (1) There has not been in the history of this country a major contribution to theology by a Negro. (2) The serious character of the racial struggle has not made it "existentially feasible" for a Negro to indulge in protracted theological reflection as a vocation. In my first assertion, I am not denying that Negroes have made significant contributions to Christian thought. We are aware that even these contributions have not been given due attention. What we are asserting is that nothing like a systematic formulation of the Christian faith by a Negro writer has ever appeared. There has been no system of theology informed by a profound grasp of theology and Christian history projected by a Negro. The Negro in American has not produced a Ferré or a Niebuhr. American-born theologians have been few, but three hundred years of American history have not witnessed one major Black theologian. The second assertion is more of an explanation as to why this is so. Because of the serious character of racial conflict and injustice throughout American history, theological discourse, as I have previously intimated, is a luxury that the black religious thinker can seldom afford.

In order to appreciate the Negro's contribution to religious thought, even to theology in America, it would be necessary to re-define and re-structure the very province of theology. Theology, which means "God-talk" or "thinking about God," would need to become problem-oriented. Theology for the Negro will necessarily be ethical, social and political more than church-historical and philosophical. It must also be biblical-prophetic and anthropocentric as well as Christocentric. It must be more like theological ethics than systematic theology. In a word, it must be a real secular theology that is hyphenated to life. It must be God's word of grace and hope for those who have had too little of this world's goods. Radical theology and the ethic of the secular city speak to those who have too much -- White Middle-class Protestants and their rebellious offspring. A Black Theology must address the masses of Black-disinherited-ghetto-dwellers and their rebellious children.

There is an unexpressed assumption that theology is "off-limits" to the Negro scholar, even to those who dared to stick with it in spite of their graduate advisors in seminaries and graduate schools. Here it is possible for me to speak from the authority of experience as a Negro theologian. I recall a discussion a few years back at a great university in the East. The discussion was based upon Joseph Washington's *Black Religion*. Washington says emphatically that there are no Negro theologians. A Negro graduate student immediately introduced me as a Black theologian. After the session, a young White seminarian assessed the situation with a single question. He asked me: "How does it feel to be among the elite?" Another example will suffice to indicate the attitude of both races in reference to theology. Some months ago as I initiated a seminar in contemporary theology, I was in search of Professor MacIntosh's *Types of Modern Theology* as a kind of launching text for more recent departures in theology. As I approached a saleslady in a downtown religious book store with my request, she, a Negro, said, "We sell only religious books." I was shocked on two accounts: I was made aware that, as Negro churchmen, we have failed to study and teach theology to our people. They don't even know the meaning of the word. Furthermore, it illustrated the shallowness of this "so-called equal-opportunity-employer-under Christian-sponsorship." In the integration of the staff the necessary training process had been short-circuited. Almost at once I replied, "But theology has to do with religion." The matter was then turned over to the white owner-manager who, with a very paternalistic and superior air, informed me that this work was not in stock. With a passion to sell something, however, she suggested alternative books -- one of which had been "recommended by a bishop." I then informed the White saleslady that I was a theologian. Just as White churches have assigned its Negro members to the pew, White seminaries have confined Negroes to the student body. Negro scholars have usually been associated with certain stereotyped fields in which experience is more important than knowledge. In this as in many other ways, we may discern the failure of Christian theology and the necessity of the "Black Caucus" as a prophetic witness to this failure.

We begin to see reasons why the Christian churches in America, Black and White, have not made theology a live option for the Negro. A religious movement that cannot produce adequate interpreters of its own faith from all its members is close to bankruptcy. One of the real indications of the failure of Christian theology to be relevant is that Negroes have not perceived its importance. In a conference on the contemporary task of theology at Duke Divinity School in the Spring of 1968 not a single lecturer was black. As the sole "Black participant," who was accompanied by a lonely "Black auditor-student," we found it necessary to "make a case" for the role of theology in Negro thought and faith. If theology is essential to the Christian faith, how is it possible for White Christians to produce all the theology and claim all of the theologians? When theology does its work properly it will become "situational" to all sorts and conditions of men. Theology as centered in the person and work of Christ must have a word of grace from Him whom the common people heard with gladness.

V. TOWARD A BLACK THEOLOGY

Whatever theology the Negro embraces must be a "word of grace for action." No word for him can be redemptive unless it is a "word made flesh." Theology must be related to his daily experience. The Negro, engaged in theological discourse, must look at his experience of undeserved suffering in America.

His approach to theology must not be a detached, "ivory tower" theologizing. It must be problem-oriented and made up of the very stuff of life. The Black theologian will need to ask many hard and often embarrasing questions about the Christian faith. For example: Is racial justice related to the true unity of the Body of Christ? How may the Christian understanding of man be stated in a helpful manner for the oppressed, subjugated and excluded segments of humanity? What is the relation between the humanity of God and the true manhood of man? What does the suffering servant figure say to the Negro? Is post-resurrection man who knows Christ not only through the "fellowship of his suffering" but "the power of his resurrection" different from the idea of a man seeking to be crucified as an innocent, powerless sacrifice to the world and evil? What biblical images undergird the "Black Caucus" movement? The pilgrimage of Abraham? The Exodus? The Remnant? The Leaven?

How shall we interpret the doctrine of the Church? How shall we understand sacred individuality and the uniqueness of man as well as his belonging to a group which helps to define his peoplehood? Is it theologically valid to speak of a Black Christ or a White Christ? In what way may we understand the historical context of Christology -- as eternal, universal or normative? Can we trust the White interpretation of providence? Must the Black theologian reassess the meaning of God's acts in the history of his people? Is there a Christian theory of violence, and what would it say about the role of violence in effecting social change? Is there a possibility of developing a "soul" theology? Such a theology would bring together sociological and psychological insights into the nature and quality of the Black man's experience of segregation, suffering and victory in the American situation.[7] These are some of the questions which must be answered meaningfully by Black theologians if theology is to be viable for Black Christians.

It was no less a figure in theological history than Paul Tillich who described the role of theology as that of answering questions put to it by philosophy as it speaks situationally. The Black theologian's tools must be more psychological and sociological than philosophical. His problem-oriented approach to theological discourse will also provide answers for the human situation -- that of the Black man in America. But if Black Theology is seen to be Christian, it must bring the eternal message of the Gospel to bear upon issues of "Black Consciousness," "Black Pride" and "Black Power."

Black Theology must be radical and militant. It must move men to act upon the ethical imperatives of their faith. To the assertion that "Black is beautiful," it must answer *Amen*, but to the call for violence it must say *No*. Black Theology must be informed by biblical exegesis and historical theology. It must unite faith with ethics and answer the cry of theology of involvement and vigorous action in a real world of sin, suffering, injustice, evil and death. The Black man's theology must also be a theology of deliverance. The easy identification of the Negro theologian with all races and classes will lead him to a universal theological position. He can include in his reflections all dimensions of life -- even the experiences of the disinherited of the earth; for he has known the depths of suffering. He is a "member of a fellowship of those who bear the mark of pain." His theological task is to interpret this experience in the Christian context.

The experience of the Negro in America could be the "stuff" of a vital theological renewal. His "suffering-victory" experiences are normative for the proper understanding of the Christian faith. There is a sense in which the Black Christian "dies daily." His is a constant movement from cross to resurrection. It is not needful that conditions remain as they are that grace may abound, but given a theological interpretation of his experience, there is the possibility that all theology may be enriched. Whereas many theologians are indulging in journalism and faddism, the Black theologian may in a vital sense speak of the *kerygma* in life-and-death terms. Richard Baxter, a great English divine, once spoke of the business of preaching the Gospel as "speaking as a dying man to dying men." When theology becomes situational, it too may become a message of a dying man to dying men.

Paul Lehmann in a recent article has spoken of "what God is doing in the world to give human shape to human life." He suggests:

> In this world, the measure which Christian Theology and ethics take of the integrity of the church and the Christian life becomes concrete at exactly those points at which the dynamics of social change call into question the integrity of the church and Christian life. Christian Theology can and must risk socio-political judgments whenever boundaries of social differentiation -- social or otherwise -- cut so deeply into the fabric of the humanity of man that men literally cry out for justice. When that cry goes up, God's patience has run short; the days of men and structures deaf to that cry are numbered.[8]

This very relevant statement is not as meaningful as it should be, at least to the Black Christian. It is amazing that Lehmann is able to refer so eloquently to the situation in South Africa and Latin America while living and teaching near the world's largest "black ghetto" -- Harlem. In the words of Voltaire, Lehmann should "cultivate his own garden." The theology to make human life human for the American Negro has not been written. This will be the task of a Black Theology.

---

*   This essay was presented as a lecture in the ethics section of the American Academy of Religion during October, 1968, in Dallas, Texas. It was also given in May, 1969 at the Annual Institute of Religion at Howard University's School of Religion. It has appeared as an article in The Journal of Religious Thought, Vol. XXVI, Summer Supplement, 1969, No. 2. The date of the essay explains its capitalization of "Black" and its sexist language.

NOTES

1. "Black Power," *New York Times*, Sunday, July 31, 1966. The NCNC is known as the NCBC (National Committee of Black Churchmen). Either may be used according to date of reference.

2. Letter, Sept. 13, 1968. A representative list of caucuses may be found in the NCNC *Newsletter*, June 1968, p.6.

3. *Ebony*, Sept. 1968.

4. *Michigan State News*, June 27, 1968 (See a statement by Professor George Johnson).

5. *Confrontation* (Chicago: Johnson Publishing Company.), 1965, p.3.

6. NCNC Newsletter, June 1968, p.5. See also A.F. Poussaint and Joyce Ladner, "Helping Hands were out of Touch," *The National Observer*, August 12, 1968.

7. These are questions put by the NCNC's Commission on Theological Concern, August 21, 1968.

8. Paul Lehmann, "A Theological Defense of Revolution," *Worldview* (117-8, Jul.-Aug., 1968), pp. 18-19.

A BLACK THEOLOGIAN LOOKS AT BLACK POWER

Black power is like the weather; everybody is talking about it. It has become in the United States a household slogan. Black power is accepted by blacks as a summing up of "the mood ebony", the black experience, or the black presence. Blacks instinctively understand its message. Whites, on the other hand, do not readily understand it. They equate it most often with the demand for white blood. The appropriate response is, as whites understand it, white power in terms of law and order or repressive police power. Thus black power confronts the white blacklash. Blacks do not, *en masse*, equate black power with violence as manifested in the riots of the recent "Hot Summers." Being wary of oppression and victimization based upon race, blacks find that black power expresses their new mood better than any slogan thus far uttered. It captures the feeling of powerlessness and lack of freedom of a long-suffering people. Black power is capable of a constructive moral and religious interpretation. This essay attempts a theological understanding of black power.

Every theologian has a faith-claim. I stand as a black Christian within a circle of faith. I am aware of the difficulty, especially at this time, of being both black and Christian. As a black man, as a Christian, and as an interpreter of the Christian faith, it is my task to present a Christian theological understanding of black power. This being so, I must be guided by biblical faith, church history, and the best theological interpretations of the Christian faith. As one who has approached theology ecumenically for many years, I have sought to use, as instruments for understanding Christian doctrines, the best qualitative sources. The denominational ties of particular authors have not been of real concern, but the quality of their writing has been of primary interest. The skin color of theologians will not concern me in this present task. My only concern will be the quality of their understanding of the Christian faith. Whatever I use from others will be transformed through my understanding of black consciousness and black power.

II. BLACK POWER IN HISTORIC PERSPECTIVE

Black religious experience does contain some relics of an African past. This is especially true of its emotive and experiential character. There is such a thing as an African temperament in Afro-American life, thought and faith, which has survived all the black people's tragic experience of repression in America. Some of us are seeking to articulate this factor that may enrich all people when fully expressed. Lerone Bennett has described it as "sensitivity."[1] Vincent Harding refers to it as "agonizing sorrow-joy."[2] This black experience conceived in religious perspective is Afro-American in the sense that whatever remains of the Afro-American past has been transformed in the American environment. W.E.B. DuBois speaks of the black man's longing to attain a "self-conscious manhood" through the merger of his "double self" into a better and truer self.[3]

The goal of the "stride toward freedom" expressed in the integration movement from 1954 to 1966 was the rapid assimilation of blacks into the white mainstream. In religion, as in social, economic and political matters, the assumption was that "whiteanity" (the Euro-American version of Christianity) was superior to the culture that had been nurtured and preserved in the Afro-American religious tradition. Blacks seeking membership in a white church fellowship were required to assume "cultural nudity" in order to be acceptable and fully belong to the white fellowship. In other words, they were inflicted with what black awareness would describe as a spiritual as well as a cultural amnesia in reference to their Afro-American religious heritage. Their acceptance of "whiteanity" was an indication that they were far removed from the heathenism associated with African traditional religion and culture. The result has been a singificant number of "Christian half-breeds": blacks who have rejected their Afro-American religious past, but who have never been fully accepted, nor do they really belong in the majority white religious bodies. Having become conscious and proud of their blackness and having discovered their powerlessness, these blacks are now forming a caucus. The black caucus and blck ecumenism stem from this situation.

Integration, even among Christians, was not understood as a give-and-take exchange of insights and values, between equals, for mutual enrichment. It was rather an all-or-none embracing of the white understanding and expression of the Christian faith. Race relations during this civil rights period generally moved in one direction. The relation between black and white people was that of inferior to superior. Black, on the one hand, was understood as evil, impure, ugly, false and unrighteous; Christianity was not the coming together of equals, but an extension of the slave-master, servant-boss mentality characteristic of American race relations from the beginning. By joining an integrated WASP fellowship, blacks exchanged their freedom of cultural and spiritual expression in Afro-American Christianity for a cultural and spiritual colonialism.

In some ways membership in the Roman Catholic church was even worse. The Roman leadership was ultra-authoritarian and almost completely white. In addition, Roman teaching, ritual and practice was completely foreign to black experience.

Whereas the black church had provided blacks with a psychological, sociological and spiritual outlet for oppression, the white church robbed them of all these. As members of a black church, through worship and fellowship, blacks, at least once during each week, were free to be themselves as human beings and be accepted by others as such. This reprieve from mistreatment, this emotional release, this awareness of dignity and belonging, gave them strength, courage and endurance as they faced another week of hardship. White congregations cannot give blacks what they need for they do not have it to give. Is it surprising that blacks who are an insignificant minority in a vast white majority situation are saying that they want some power? The black caucus is an expression of black power in the churches.

Black power is an idea whose time has come. It is another instance in which an idea has consequences. Perhaps the undefined or indefinable character of black power is its strength rather than its weakness. An ideology rather than a clearly defined doctrine, black power has literally transformed the complexion of race relations. It is not merely a slogan; it is a summons to radical social change and a reappraisal of racial values. According to this ideology, blacks are "black and proud," and "black is beautiful." This is the basis not only of a new pride, but of a new self-image, self-understanding and self-identity that enables blacks to affirm both their past and their present and to accept their dignity as children of God.

This is the point of departure for a theology of black power. Black power has enabled black people who once saw through "a glass whitely" to be deculturated to the extent that they now see through "a glass blackly." Black power has provided black people with the courage to be black, to affirm their African heritage and their Afro-American past as part of their mature peoplehood and as part of their affirmation of the Christian creed.

The constructive and affirmative implications of black power, as I view them, are perfectly acceptable to the Christian faith. They are certainly open to meaningful Christian interpretation. Black power thus understood is the best antidote to all the phoniness, escapism and nihilism so characteristic of blacks, Christian and non-Christian alike, who have tried so hard to belong to white society. Some blacks have given up on America altogether. Because they have equated Christianity with "whiteanity", they have rejected Christianity as well. Black nationalism, back-to-Africa movements, the passage into white society through light skin, some interracial marriages (often practiced by successful blacks who discover that success is inadequate to admit them to white society), and even membership in certain churches (e.g., Episcopalian, United Church of Christ, Roman Catholic) have all been used as status symbols. In addition, black writers and intellectuals with means (e.g., Richard Wright, James Baldwin, W.E.B. DuBois) often travel from country to country seeking identity and a true home.

The more excellent way is "Black Power." Through black power, black people affirm their blackness in a white racist society. They discover who they are. They are proud of their past and present. They get themselves together. They no longer need to be alienated, to escape, hate or reject themselves or their people. Self-affirmation is the basis of self-determination, meaning and fulfillment for black people where they are. Black people can now confront whites as equals. They now know that they can give as well as receive. Black people now recognize their own humanity for what it is. Their humanity and peoplehood can now be accepted.

But acceptance regardless of skin colour or ethnic origin is the birthright of every human being. Thus the "by any means necessary" doctrine of some theological advocates of black power must be rejected.[5] We as blacks cannot, on a Christian basis, affirm our humanity while denying others their humanity. Reconciliation between equals beyond confrontation and liberation must always be kept in view.

II. BLACK THEOLOGY AS EXISTENTIAL AND POLITICAL

Because community control is its social aim, the social, political, economic, and cultural aspects of a powerless people must be included in any worthy treatment of black power. A theological understanding of the black individual is existential while the theological understanding of the black community is political. When the National Committee of Black Churchmen, a black ecumenical body of Christians united in their blackness, spoke out against racism in church and society, they spoke rightly of "powerless conscience" confronting "conscienceless power." A theological understanding of black power is, at once, personal and social.

Those whose faces are black discover that nobody knows their name. This is their identity crisis. Through black power they cry "I am." They affirm their being as dignified human persons. As social persons, they affirm community through black power. They enter the policy-making arena of politics, economics and welfare, overcoming the helplessness and powerlessness of the dark ghetto. The outsiders -- the slumlords, politicians and social engineers who have been manipulators of black peoples -- discover that the new blacks, poor, uneducated and exploited, have now asserted their right to self-determination and community control in those matters concerning their well-being. Black theology in its anthropology and its ecclesiology must provide an adequate Christian understanding of personhood and peoplehood, of divine sonship and of the beloved community, to undergird the humanizing of life for black people. The black church has as its mission the task of empowering its members to become "light", "salt" and "leaven" in the dark ghetto and among all black people.

Black power may thus liberate the black church to be truly the church in its witness both to whites and to blacks. The affinity of the black religious experience to the biblical experiences of the redemptive suffering of both Israel and primitive Christianity may yet lead the church in America to be the church. The ministry of black power through faith and ethics is not only to the oppressed, but to the oppressors as well. Black power demands not only that we free the slaves, but that we destroy the slave system. It requires a root-and-branch job in race relations. Black power insists upon the death of Jim Crow in all the experiences of blacks in America. Christian theology, in its understanding of human sin, attacks the human condition at the depth level where finite creatures exalt themselves to the status of the infinite. It can contribute much to the removal of preconscious racism as well as its manifest expression.

III. REVELATION AND COMMUNICATION IN BLACK THEOLOGY

What is the medium and the message of a theological understanding of black power? Here we are raising the problem of communication. This is to ask about revelation and hermeneutics at once. How seriously must black theology take God's self-disclosure? How does a theologian communicate to the oppressor the meaning of revelation appropriated under conditions of oppression? Is it possible to be true to the givenness of revelation and address one's attention to revolution, culture and racial injustices?

Karl Barth often writes that God's word is for man. Emil Brunner insists that God's revelation is addressed to man. There is some disagreement between Barth and Brunner regarding the extent of this revelation and our ability to understand fully what God is making known. On this point, Brunner is more liberal than Barth. John Baillie reminds us that God does not reveal himself in propositions, but he gives himself to us in personal self-communication.[6] Baillie takes the blight of sin seriously, however, and cautions us that due to human sinfulness there is inherent human inability to know fully what God reveals. Rudolf Bultmann would agree with these that in revelation we are being addressed by God and that our proper response is to listen in faith to what God is saying. Bultmann understands revelation as that which leads to self-understanding. Paul Tillich is concerned with divine revelation as answering questions raised by the human situation. All of these theological insights on the meaning and understanding of divine revelation are helpful to the black theologian. They must be applied, however, in a special manner to the concept of black power.

The language of black power is emotive. It is aimed at awakening black Christians and arousing white Christians. Black Christians are to be awakened to a sense of dignity and action that will enlist them in the cause against racial injustice. White Christians are to be aroused and activated in the struggle against racism in the church and in the power structure controlled by other white people.

Liberal white Christians are likely to refer most glibly and self-righteously to "all we have done for those people." They are likely to be mere spectators in the push for racial justice. They are often well educated and comfortable from a socio-economic point of view. Their white skin is their assurance against black competition. They may even render service in the black community as an act of conscience. The ungrateful rhetoric of black power appears to them as too extreme; for, as they see it, things are better than they were and are getting better all the time. White liberals often hold that blacks have a persecution complex and always misunderstand the intention behind all so-called racial incidents. According to liberal whites, they have had all the same experiences. This rationalization of racism prevents white liberals from really seeing racism for what it is. If they did more listening and less explaining away, they would be more helpful to black people. The truth of the matter is that blacks are undersensitive rather than oversensitive. If this were not the case, all black people would be insane, truly insane.

Spectators of racial injustice find it difficult to understand the radical character of racism simply because they are spectators and not participants. Since they are not of the oppressed, they are not committed. It is hard for them to fully understand the cry from the depths uttered by the oppressed. Jim Crow has given rise to an oratory of protest. A hermeneutic of oppression is used by those who long for relief from unjust and inhuman treatment. Outsiders, as spectators, however empathetic, have difficulty decoding the message delivered by those who bear the mark of oppression. However shocking or fearsome the language, the message is born of long suffering on the edge of despair. Anger and rage are inherent in the cry for black power. Black power is closely associated, in the minds of its black spokespersons, with black deliverance. "Victory or Death" for black people should be understood in the spirit, at least, of Patrick Henry's "Liberty or Death" approach to the American Revolution. In a similar manner, black people are determined to be free and equal.

IV. BLACK THEOLOGY: EMPOWERMENT AND MEANING

The *Black Manifesto* was the most celebrated document to be treated by the U.S. religious press in 1969. This explosive message was addressed to racist religious institutions; it demanded reparations for black people for injustices suffered during slavery and subsequent discrimination. Unfortunately, more attention was given to the language used by its author, James Forman, than to the message. Beneath this Marxist language were several proposals that Christians would do well to examine with some seriousness. A few perceptive Christian thinkers discerned that through Forman, as a strange prophet, God was saying something urgent to religious institutions in America about making life more human in a tangible way. There are indications that the message is beginning to move some white religious bodies. "Black empowerment" is the result. Through grants to black-controlled community organizations, with no strings attached, some development and self-determination is being made possible. A few whites are withholding funds from their national religious organizations because it is believed that too much is being given to blacks. Blacks, on the other hand, are insisting that what is being given is too little and perhaps too late.

Black power is empowerment for social betterment, but it is also a search for meaning. Christian faith, as we have seen, has a personal dimension. Each individual is addressed by God. God's love for us is personal; it is an individualized love. God asks each Adam and every Eve, "Where are you?" God confronts each of us on the plane of personal existence and in the divine presence each of us is free to cry, "I am."

Black power, conceived theologically and applied to individual existence, is a search for meaning. Those who describe black religion as an opiate for escape from the brutal realities of black existence are partly right. In many instances the escapist relief of religious enjoyment, festivity and celebration has preserved the sanity of black people under the lash of unjust and inhuman treatment. But it is a mistake to consider the black encounter with the Christian faith as only an opiate. In Christian faith and worship the black Christian has found *meaning* for an otherwise senseless existence, best described as "a living death." In *Fire Next Time*, James Baldwin describes his discovery that the church is just as good for escape as sex, liquor and drugs. What he did not discover, if I read him correctly, is that the Christian faith is better, that it gives meaning to an otherwise meaningless existence. A vital dose of the Christian faith, properly understood, can be an antidote for the rage and anger that, at present, is leading so many black youths to suicide. Such a faith would not eliminate succor and comfort, for Christianity remains a priestly religion, but Christianity is also a prophetic religion that incites to revolution against injustice.

Black theology must interpret the elements of black self-respect, pride, awareness, self-worth, dignity and identity inherent in the slogan, black power. Black power has brought a new worldview into the socio-psychological environment of black people, enabling them to affirm their being and have the courage to be black. This new deposit of purpose in their black lives has given them the vigor and determination to move forward. They now know the dignity of divine sonship; they are *really somebody*. Freedom and transformation of human personality are now theirs. Surely these positive values are valid raw materials for a new theology of blackness. The true humanity of blacks has entered into their self-awareness and self-understanding. Against this background a valid Christian anthropology for black people is now possible in America.

According to the inspiration of black power, human beings stand within the concern of God's love. Black people are enfolded, as are all others, in God's creative and redemptive purpose. Whereas others may emphasize human nature and destiny, it is urgent for black theology to stress the dignity of blacks that has been denied them so long. Black power has created the climate for dignity. The black people's dignity has been restored because they are able to understand and accept it. Having affirmed their dignity, blacks may then understand their nature and destiny. Blacks are natural children of God by creation. They are spiritual children of God by adoption, sharing with all people in the benefits of God's saving work in Christ.

Black power, in affirming the empowerment of blacks, also speaks to the need for revolutionary social transformation. For black people to accept injustice and inhuman treatment passively is to partake in the system that enslaves them. The Christian faith is revolutionary in its very nature. It is the responsibility of Christians, aware of their stake in blackness in a white racist society, to keep the pressure on. To opt for violence is to seek an impossible solution. Oddly enough it may turn out to be not only unethical but impotent. It should be observed that the richest and most powerful military-industrial complex was impotent in Vietnam against peasants. The Christian understanding of black power requires us to confront white power and use every constructive means available to win our freedom and maintain our dignity. If we take the cross by the other end and make a sword out of it, if we try to win our humanity by attempting to rob others of theirs, then injustice will merely change hands. We must use every social, political, cultural, economic, moral and religious means to win our liberation that our Christian understanding of God and humanity allows. But we must, at the same time, work for reconciliation beyond confrontation and liberation.

This means that the Word must become flesh in the experience of black Christians. A sentimental Jesusology is inadequate for people who have affirmed their Christian adulthood. They now have the freedom and the responsibility of children of God. As those created and redeemed by a God of love, justice and power they are called forth to make human life more human. In the light of the Christian faith what appears to people as impotent is power laden. It is no accident that the cross is the symbol of the Christian faith. What James W. Douglass says of the oppressed of the Third World may be also said concerning black power in Christian theological perspective:

> Wisdom and power come not from the privileged, but from those who know life from having found it in death, and light from having perceived it in darkness. For those on the margin of the earth . . . need has given birth to power, but a power virtually unrealized and unexplored.[7]

Black power as understood by those blacks who have given up on the Christian faith and its understanding of God, humanity, world and salvation may require victory or death. This attitude must be understood against the background of oppression under which blacks have suffered. To opt for liberation using the threat of violence may appear to some to be courageous and the only course available. But when some black militant speakers went to a high school in Washington, D.C., recently urging young blacks to take to the streets and "take care of business," the students walked out on the speakers and returned to their classes. Their common sense had reinforced my faith that young blacks are capable of planning their own future. Aristotle is correct, I believe, in placing courage midway between cowardice and foolhardiness. A Christian theological understanding of black power is realistic concerning human beings as sinners and racism as an expression of sin. But the Christian faith has not given up on people or on life. We have not given up on people *because* we have faith in a God of grace and power who cooperates in the destiny of those with a believing trust. In the Christian understanding of black power, we vote for victory *and* life, for liberation and reconciliation.

NOTES

1.   Lerone Bennett, The Negro Mood, (Chicago: Johnson Publishing Company, 1964), p. 61.

2.   "The Afro-American Past," New Theology, M.E. Marty and D.G. Peerman, eds. New York: Macmillan, 1969), p. 177.

3.   The Souls of Black Folk, (Greenwich, Conn.: Fawcett, 1961), p. 17. More definitive still is C.G. Woodson's study of African survivals in Afro-American religion. See The African Background Outlined, (New York: Negro Universities Press, (reprinted, 1968), pp. 358-391, passim.

4.   Alex Poinsett, "Think Tank for Black Scholars," Ebony, February 1970, p. 48.

5.   James Cone, Black Theology and Black Power, (New York: Seabury Press, 1969), p. 6.

6.   Emil Brunner, Natural Theology, trans. Peter Fraenkel, intro. John Baillie (London: G. Bless, 1946). This work contains ideas of Brunner, Barth, and Baillie on revelation. Cf. E. Brunner, Natur und Gnade (Zurich: Zwingle-Verlag 1935), pp. 7-9.

7.   James W. Douglass, The Non-Violent Cross, (New York: Macmillan, 1968), p. 12.

CIVIL RIGHTS: THE UNFINISHED AGENDA

As an ethicist and theologian, I would like to address myself to the unfinished agenda of civil rights. My views, as will be evident, have been influenced by the recent black movement. Civil rights have usually been cast in the mold of equal rights through legislation provided by Congress and the Courts. These decisions have been related most frequently to desegregation of schools and public facilities for all Americans. Voting rights and discrimination in employment likewise have been subsumed under civil rights.

I. THE PERSPECTIVE

Civil rights sponsored in the context of integration, was the order of the day in the decade ending with the mid-sixties. The word "integration" is perfectly acceptable when, properly defined, it is used to denote the possibility of meaningful dialogue between the races in the pluralism of American life. The word, however, has been so woefully abused in practice that it is not very useful for our purpose. Integration in fact turned out to be a one-way street. Its advocates among both races did not question white superiority in values and life style. Racism was considered a social and ethical problem, but for the most part it was not given proper attention as a theological problem as well. The norm in all things was assumed to be white, and it was thought that blacks needed only to embrace the "given" of the majority culture. Few people heard, and fewer still listened, as James Baldwin warned: "Who wants to enter a burning house?"

Now some of us have participated in both the civil rights and the black movements and have derived benefit from both. My attitude has been one of maintaining a critical distance from each of these important breakthroughs in the Afro-American's quest for freedom in this country. To my way of thinking there is discontinuity as well as continuity between these movements as represented on the one hand by such persons as Martin Luther King, Jr., Thurgood Marshall and Roy Wilkins; and, on the other hand, by Stokely Carmichael, Amir Barraka and Ron Korenga. The black movement has the potential of broadening and deepening the former movement while absorbing its most important components.

Black religious nationalism is fortified by drinking deep from the entire cultural milieu of all peoples of African descent. This movement wipes out the amnesia of Afro-Americans, gives them a sense of history, and takes some of the sharpness out of the disruption caused by slavery and discrimination of their cohesive communal life. Black religious nationalism restores personhood and a sense of peoplehood as the basis for self-respect and community. This new consciousness of the riches of black culture brings with it a mood of legitimate pride. Thus, there is the possibility of overcoming the self-hatred which throughout history has caused the black community to self-destruct. This has real potential for a discovery of meaning in life as well as for effective protest.

Consciousness of the worth of self and one's people is inadequate to win human rights unless supported by sufficient power to win goods and services. Consciousness without power is like a fuse to set off explosives among the oppressed. In the black movement we have not only discovered our own self-worth, we have also discovered our strengths for our own liberation. Psychological liberation has supported a protest toward economic and political liberation. While some interpret this new grasp for power as a threat of violence, there are others who see this combination of consciousness and power as the only alternative to violence for a people who find intolerable the victimization of racism. I would argue that the tragedy of the late 60's in our cities would have been in the nature of a nationwide holocaust had not this new movement emerged to sustain black hope.

Throughout this discussion, I will attempt to reveal how American history is viewed from the bottom up rather than from the top down. It will be evident that the myth of the American dream explodes when considered in the context of civil religion. The critique of black religious history, ethics and theology will be focused upon the broken promises of white America in reference to black and other non-white groups. The women's movement and the problems of white ethnics seem to be more in the nature of a family dispute. These problems, though real, are not to be fused with racism and the more systemic forms of oppression of non-white peoples in this society.

II. A BICENTENNIAL BROADSIDE

On July 4, 1852, Frederick Douglass said:

What to the American Slave is the Fourth of July? I answer a day that reveals to him more than all other days of the year the gross injustice and cruelty of which he is the constant victim. To him

> your celebration is a shame; your boasted liberty,
> an unholy license; your national greatness, swelling
> vanity; your denunciation of tyrants; brass-fronted
> impudence; your shouts of liberty and equality,
> hollow mockery; your prayers and your hymns, your
> sermons and your thanksgivings, with all your re-
> ligious parade and solemnity are to him mere bom-
> bast, fraud, deception, impiety and hypocrisy --
> a thin veil to cover up crimes which would disgrace
> a nation of savages.[1]

One and a quarter centuries later, black Americans are still haunted by Douglass's probing question, "What is America to us?" As Congressman Mitchell of Maryland reminded his peers on Capital Hill, this is still, in the black experience: "A sweet land of bigotry."

Gayraud S. Wilmore puts the issues clearly before us. White Americans, in the Constitution and in all major foundational political documents, speak in universal and absolutist terms concerning liberty, but they are slow to concretize and partic-ularize these principles and values in the life of the oppressed. When the question of the universality of liberty, "liberty and justice for all," was raised by blacks, it was spiritualized. "Most Americans," says Wilmore

> adopted a position that separated what Christ does
> for a person from what a Christian state is obliged
> to do. The slave was indeed a brother in Christ,
> but the liberation effected by conversion, baptism,
> and regeneration was a liberation from sin, not
> from political and economic oppression.[2]

Oddly enough white Christians used the same texts to claim liberty for themselves as they used to deny liberty to blacks. Following the examples of the great reformers, white Christians, after independence, made the spiritual and other-worldly interpretation of liberty normative.

The theology of the Second Great Awakening presented Christ's work primarily as liberation from the sins and vices of worldly life, quite apart from the issues of politics and ec-onomics. Not until the pronouncements of the abolitionists and Northern black preachers were American Christians to hear again that Christianity had to do with physical as well as spiritual liberation.

According to Wilmore, the difference between black and white ideas about liberty went a step further. The liberty for which black Christians petitioned was based upon a concept of legality contained in the founding documents and interpreted by an enlightened Christian conscience. Whatever the intentions of men like Jefferson and Hamilton might have been, "liberty and justice for all" neither included all the people, nor provided a legal shelter which could control the exploitive interests of men of property. For this reason, blacks early insisted upon maintaining a connection between the liberating work of Christ and positive law. For blacks, liberty meant an order of justice inaugurated by the Declaration of Independence and the Constitution, and implemented by specific legal measures.

Rosemary R. Ruether writes about "America as Babylon." She begins:

> "America, America, God shed his grace on thee and crowned thy good with brotherhood from sea to shining sea." In this favorite hymn, America appears as Utopia: sunlit purple hills, wind rustling through the golden grain, the cornucopia of fruited plains: the whole, encircled by smiling seas, kissed from above with divine blessing. America is Zion.[3]

She continues:

> In America, the messianic vision becomes an idyllic dream superimposed upon reality, making reality itself impossible to see . . . . The American dream is an ideology which distorts reality, dulling the power to see and judge truthfully.[4]

Ruether warns that the church in America has sided with the dream which is opposed to the prophetic vision of the biblical faith she confesses. The church is political on the side of the status quo but apolitical toward the real evils of the world.

> All too swiftly the American Dream began to become the American nightmare: the place of black slavery, the genocide of the American Indian; obliteration of their reverence for the land; befouled streams and jungle cities; corrupt bureaucracy and military might sucking dry the resources of the earth impoverishing still further the peoples of colonized regions to feed its technology; supporting regimes around the globe to contain a rumbling dissent with police-state methods which, more and more, is coming home to roost.[5]

This Dream is held by many denominations which view the nation as a church and have institutionalized piety on the Potomac. The Mormons, who believe in a white man's heaven, have dramatized this outlook by building a multi-million dollar mausoleum to God and country near the nation's capital. Sherwood Eddy wrote years ago that many Americans have identified the Kingdon of God with the American Dream. Many devout Christians believe that if the Kingdom comes it will be in America.

III. AWAKENING FROM THE AMERICAN DREAM

In writing about the period in the U.S. from 1960-1970, Paul E. Kraemer perceives that the civil rights trend developed into a human rights movement which challenged the overall basic ideas, values and institutions of American society. He was from abroad and observed a pervasive mood of disquiet and dissent in society, manifested in the student protest, the peace movement and the civil rights movement. But he noted that the black struggle was central to the entire situation.

Dr. Benjamin Spock, at a 1967 New Politics Convention observed:

> The disadvantages which black people suffer in health, education, job competence, employment, have been imposed by the white community through 300 years of abuse and humiliation. The Founding Fathers declared that people who are oppressed and can find no other redress must rebel. . . . Black people have long taken oppression ten times as cruel as what the colonists suffered in the 18th century. Whites have practiced a thousand acts of physical and psychological violence on blacks for every act of black violence. . . .[6]

In a work by Heffey and Plowman, Congressman John Anderson speaks out against the liberals of the 60's and for the Evangelicals of the 70's. This justifies somewhat the conclusions of the Kraemer study which observed that the American protest movement was from civil rights to human rights to radicalism. By 1970 the life cycle had run out and the movement ended in disarray. The weakness of the study is that it does not account for the persistence of the black struggle nor does it assess the impact of repressive forces upon any and all non-conformist activist groups.

But let's look more closely at Anderson's assertions. He sees the National Prayer Breakfast as the religious-political event of the year in Washington. So prestigious is this affair that thousands of Americans covet the engraved invitations. The excitement over this event marks the decline of liberals in religion as well as in politics. As an advocate of the "God movement" in Washington, he does not see much difference. As Anderson sees it:

> . . . Things have changed. Now they (the liberals) are the "kooks" and we are the beautiful people. *Our* prayer breakfasts are so popular that only those with engraved invitations are allowed to attend. Our evangelists have the ready ear of those in positions of highest authority. Our churches are growing, and theirs are withering. They are tired, worn-out 19th century liberals trying to repair the pieces of an optimism shattered by world wars, race riots, the population explosion, and the spectre of worldwide famine. We always knew that things would get worse before the Lord came again.[7]

This is a good dose of triumphalism.

Civil Christianity is said to produce good character and mellow people, open to compromise and able to bridge partisan differences. But who is asking whether there is a sensitivity to oppression? The God-movement exalts absolutes, but gives no clues as to how to apply these to politics and decisions. Congress persons (perhaps) are being called to preach and Watergate offenders are being converted, but where are the advocates of social justice? Here is a religion of retreat from controversy and support for one's own kind. One wonders how this civil Christianity differs from T-M groups or Hari Krishna. This God-movement has been constant in Washington. It is still alive and well.

The Hartford appeal seems to provide a kind of theological underpinning for the Evangelical God-movement in Washington and civil religion throughout the nation. Its mood is privatized. It is apolitical in reference to liberation from oppression in the social, economic and political realms.

Graham knows only personal sins of the flesh. Salvation for him is personal and for the next life. He proclaims a soul and saviour gospel. He gives inadequate attention to systemic evils -- the abuses of wealth and power which cause millions to weep and moan at home and abroad. Under the leadership of Nixon, we as a nation were on the eve of Fascism which could have meant the lapse of our nation into the most barbaric type of inhumanity, but the Evangelist who served as a priest at the King's court was silent on these matters. And yet Graham is the ideal spokesman of God for thousands of Americans who either see religion as personal piety or desire to use it to maintain the *status quo*. Billy Graham is a world capitalist using the full benefits of big business and mass communication to execute every evangelist campaign. While preaching a gospel of spiritual and future salvation he has a total stake in the political economy of the rich and the powerful here and now. One notes a direction in Graham similar to that of the notorious black religious exploiter, Reverend Ike. The difference is that Ike's Gospel is consistent with his life-style.

Sam Hill, Jr. describes the Southern church's short-run term of evangelism. This seems to be akin to the nation-wide movement, and largely accounts for the growth of conservative churches. The disciple bears his verbal witness with a view to getting a verdict from the lost person. But this short-term evangelism does not square with the rhythm of life. We need, according to Hill, to turn from a crusade --

> Free the children immediately Lord, immediately-- into a mission that might involve the rest of our days . . . as did Moses and Aaron . . . . We will have to stay at it, and at it, and at it. Pharaoh has to be shown. [8]

Our ministry is to be never-ending; for it is a mission for the whole person, in the setting of a whole society, and for all of life.

Yvonne Delk puts the mission of the black church at the time of the bicentennial celebration clearly in focus as it faces its task:

> The Bicentennial is a time when the black church can mobilize its resources and organize a . . . movement for human liberation, a movement which will act for the eradication of hunger, disease, poverty, ignorance and other afflictions which cripple the spirit and denigrate human dignity.[9]

IV. WE STILL ARE NOT FREE *

The civil rights agenda is unfinished. We still remain in the period of a Second Reconstruction. The "Benign Neglect" spirit that informed Nixon's White House and the Burger Court is still in effect. Blacks did not need to be reminded by Gerald Ford that he is a Ford and not a Lincoln. His policies, his insensitivity, his vetoes -- all make it clear that for all his piety and claims to moral rectitude he had sided with the rich and powerful against the black and the poor.

The Carter Administration won primarily because of a coalition of disaffected groups: minorities, women, labor and the poor. The problems are still immense and Jimmy Carter was a man and not a Messiah. He did, however, appear to bring an ethical consciousness and sensitivity to the Oval Office which has been absent since the assassination of John Kennedy. This in itself was a great gain that should bear some fruit.

We still are not free! Dr. King in his last address at Howard University had as his constant refrain: "We have come a long, long way, but we still have a long way to go." Furthermore, he noted that "all Africa will be free and we still will not be free!" He could not have known the accuracy of his prediction. Pockets of colonialism and racism still exist in Africa, but much of that continent is now free from colonial rule and is intensely engaged in nation-building. Racism, revolution, economic and psychological neo-colonialism still grip much of the continent (the struggle for Rhodesia is a gruesome reminder), but liberation in Africa of one country after another has outstripped our wildest dreams.

Blacks of African descent who were brought to this country in chains, their blood leaving a trail in the Middle Passage, still are not free. The irony is that this country prides itself on being the bastion of democracy -- "the home of the free." Pride and hypocrisy are large as the hallmarks of our history. Yet for some "this is the nation with the soul of a church." This is a "righteous kingdom," and yet it is a place where priests grow fat and prophets are stoned.

Lerone Bennett, in answer to the question, "Should blacks celebrate the bicentennial?" related the following incident. He was in Nairobi when the reins of government were handed over to Kenya by the British. The British flag was lowered and the liberation flag of Kenya was hoisted. There was great rejoicing in the huge crowd in celebration of this happening. A white American turned to Bennett, taking him to be a Kenyan, congratulated him, and recalling the freedom of his fellow countrymen 200 years ago, remarked how wonderful it is to be free. Whereupon Bennett replied to his fellow American: "I, too, am an American, but we still are not free." As his friend disappeared into the crowd distraught and bewildered by this stark reminder of America's unfulfilled promises, Bennett asked himself: "What is it that makes white Americans love freedom so much abroad, while at the same time refusing to grant that freedom to fellow citizens at home? Americans will fight and die for freedom abroad, but will not live up to it at home." Thus it is and has been throughout the dark night of suffering of our people in this land. We, together with the native Americans, are perhaps the starkest reminders that America is not "a righteous kingdom" as many romantic visionaries of this bicentennial season would have us believe. There is an unfinished civil rights agenda. We still are not free!

Charles H. Long writing about "the ambiguities of innocence" has this to say:

> ... America must come to terms with its own depth of reality before it can move authentically into the future. It is not a coincidence that the basic problems which confront us as a nation today result from the fact that we have not taken the integrity of nature seriously. The exploitation of our natural resources and of Negroes and other racial minorities stem from this fact.[10]

Without self-discovery, according to Long, our future will be "an escapism sustained only by physical and psychological repression." Already we see signs of this in the revelations being made almost daily from investigation into the activities of the FBI and CIA. As I viewed the political section of the capitol city from the balcony of a hotel, during a break in a professional meeting, a Jamaican friend spoke approvingly of the sheer physical beauty of the city on this starlit night. There was a momentary silence, and then he added: "But this is a city of great corruption."

Laurence Leamer writes in the *Washingtonian:*

> In Washington, power has become the ultimate reality. The civil religion provided a neat handle for the action, a God to pray to in the private moments of private sentiment, and during those periodic election rituals of public obeisance to the citizenry, but the God of the Eternal City was power.[11]

Nathan Hare warns blacks that they must not allow black nationalism or pan-Africanism to make them unaware of the American reality. He feels that we are often in danger of over-universalizing our situation so that we are taken out of the struggle. Hare writes:

> ... We live in the heart of the octopus that is America, while our kindred around the world are gripped by its tentacles. They can help by cutting off one or the other tentacle, especially when the tentacle grasps resources, but the greatest damage can be done by those of us in the heart of the octopus. Black people all over the world are looking to us while we go on failing our challenge and our mission.[12]

Most constructive black thought and action may be said to be reformist and not revolutionary. Blacks are not Marxist in a wholesale or doctrinaire manner. The Marxist analysis is useful, but Marxists are often very insensitive to the difference between classism and racism. Therefore, racism often runs unabated within Marxist movements. African socialism, based upon traditional communalism, is more attractive. Blacks are devoutly religious in sentiment and will not accept a purely economic anthropology which does not allow for the spiritual dimensions of life.

Martin Luther King, Jr., a symbolic figure, was a believer in the principles upon which this nation was founded. He affirmed much of the political and legal theory he read in the foundation documents. His "I have a Dream" address at the foot of the Lincoln Memorial, during the famous March-on-Washington, attests to this affirmation.[13]

King, however, was not an unrealistic dreamer. Like Vernon Jordan, he saw the need for a grass-roots movement to influence the social, economic, and political institutions of this country in order to make them more responsive and humane in the service of the black and the poor. Jordan observed recently:

> Black people have the numbers and the know-how to help bring about the political "browning of America" that will at long last result in the total inclusion of blacks in the democratic political process."[14]

Congressman Charles Diggs observes that the black movement for freedom, justice and equality has, at one and the same time, become more political and less a purely protest movement operating outside the system. He continues:

> This development should be viewed as a positive step in our political evolution . . . . While black nationalism has passed its peak of intensity, it has nevertheless instituted a degree of racial consciousness among a growing number of black elected officials which is helping us achieve a greater degree of balance as we fulfill our responsibilities to black and non-black Americans."[15]

Whatever the station or achievement of any black American, we as a people are free. None are truly free until all are free. We have common cause with our brothers and sisters everywhere. Those who have a measure of success and who have some leverage should use it to make life more humane for all. This suggests an examination of values and principles.

V. LOVE, JUSTICE, AND POWER

In order to provide a perspective from the vantage point of theological ethics, it is essential to look briefly at how we understand love, justice, and power separately and interdependently.

There must be a place for human responsibility and self-respect in the way we understand Christian love. Any interpretation of love which makes sense for human liberation must be centered in God's grace, as symbolized by the Cross, but the human dimension must reach inwards, outwards, and upwards. Self-love, neighbor-love, and love of God are interrelated and interdependent.

Justice is rendering to each one his or her due. But we must make sure that basic human rights are included in the way we understand justice. It is too easy, to succumb to an understanding of justice in which the rich and the powerful determine what is due to the powerless -- the black, brown, yellow, and red citizens in our nation. This is the reason non-white persons in this society often find common cause in their liberation struggle. Justice must be based upon *equity* -- mutual respect and equal sharing in the benefits of freedom. In a separate and unequal society like ours, where generation after generation of oppressed peoples have suffered injustice, there must be a *compensatory* element built into the appropriate expression of justice. From the very beginning, our circumstances are unequal because of the oppression that has prevented the realization of the human potential among minorities. Therefore, it is not just to expect these victims to be equally qualified with the beneficiaries of the society.

Justice like love is a moral attribute of the Judeo-Christian God. God's justice assures the fact that love is undergirded by moral rectitude and not by sentiment or "cheap grace." In God, justice and love are well-balanced. Compassion and mercy are always expressed by God in the framework of justice and equity. Thus, Christians as they relate to God must do so out of a love that includes a loving concern for the self and other selves, but this love is related to justice. God is lovingly just.

The "pushing and shoving justice" must cut across merely personal and interpersonal relations on a one to one basis and reach into the public sector of human society. Justice has to do with the manner in which laws are enacted, the ways bills are passed, the administration of justice, the criminal code, and all aspects of positive law -- life in all its dimensions, whether personal, social, or systemic. The systemic aspects of human life include the cultural and the institutional realms. The liberation motif in all human concerns is a basis for the expression of justice. Only if all people are treated with respect as whole persons may love be expressed and justice done. This includes the underprivileged, the powerless, and the weak, whether black, brown, yellow, red, or white.

It is power in God that affirms the actuality of God in being and goodness. God is a perfect ontological and ethical being. Omnipotence makes it so. God is able to support his goodness with ability to realize that goodness in creation, through providence and in his salvific purpose. Power serves goodness in the way God works out his purpose in creation, history, and human life.

In human affairs, power is instrumental rather than intuitive in the implementation of goals and the realization of values. This is due to human imperfection. A powerless people find themselves at the mercy of the high and mighty of the earth. Only a visionary optimist expects the powerful to take due care of the best interests of the weak and the powerless. One would have to wink at human sin and overlook human selfishness to expect this to happen. Human oppression, and the misery which accompanies it will not be overcome unless the oppressed take their liberation into their own hands. They must seize the power available to them as a means of their own deliverance from social, economic, and political oppression. They must write their own agenda, provide their own timetable and use all the resources at hand to win their freedom. But power, though associated with love and justice, unlike them needs to be carefully directed. Power must be used to serve love and fulfill justice. It is a means to the end that love may be expressed and justice done. Power must never become an end in itself; for it is easily abused. It corrupts the one who abuses it, and harms those towards whom it is directed. What we are advocating is a humane and moralized use of power for the realization of the highest human values -- personal, social, and institutional. The oppressed know that God is a God of the oppressed, as James H. Cone has said. But they, by relating to this God, join him in the struggle for thier own liberation. In the oft-quoted expression by Harvey Cox, they seek to find out what God is doing in the world and join him. One way to do this is to meet God as he comes to us through the Incarnation in Jesus as the Christ. Jesus was born in a stable; he preached to the poor; he ministered to the outcasts and he died accursed in the marketplace between two criminals. Where else need we look for a Saviour who is a liberator?

VI. A NOTE ON LIBERATION AND RECONCILIATION

J. H. Cone writes that I am naive in bringing up reconciliation. He sees this as pre-mature and a type of betrayal of the struggle. Oppressors should take little comfort in this disagreement among black brothers in a common struggle.

While I do not hold the dream of Martin L. King, Jr., I do see the need for interracial fellowship and cooperation in the pluralistic society in which we "live, move, and have our being." The goal for what King called "The Beloved Community" includes the humanizing in American society of all power for human liberation. That is to say, we all have a stake in better human relations. This is so in a pragmatic as well as a Christian sense. We all will be ill-at-ease in a society in which millions of fellow citizens have been stripped to naked existence and pushed to the edge of survival. We all live at the mercy of those victims of our society who have been dehumanized by racism and/or poverty.

As Christians our understanding of the Gospel cannot preclude liberation. Here we see the Gospel as addressing not merely the sins of the flesh but likewise the estrangements between one person and another. We must go even beyond a concern for a humanization of wholesale institutional, cultural, and corporate movements that make teeming millions suffer at home and abroad. The politics which control the national life of Americans must be transfigured. And this transfiguration of politics -- of the whole system is the only basis for genuine Christian reconciliation between equals.

To expect blacks to accept an inferior status and the victims to be reconciled with the beneficiaries of American society is not to be loving, just, or reconciling. It is to accept that sentimentality and "cheap grace" which has rendered our churches morally powerless to right the wrongs in our society.

The unfinished agenda of the oppressed in America includes economic, social, political, and cultural components. Some groups may specialize in dealing with one aspect alone. For example, Jesse Jackson has taken up what he calls "silver rights," the economic dimension. The Black Caucus and black politicians across the country are majoring in political affairs. According to Andrew Young, "politics is feeding the hungry." Black theologians and churchmen are examining the theological and ethical aspects of the human liberation struggle. But we all are seeking cooperation on the human rights issues together with operational unity in working for their fulfillment. Our national goals present a challenge to us to win these rights which are God-given and not merely man-bestowed.

* AUTHOR'S NOTE

This chapter was obviously my reflections upon the Bicentennial of the United States. It should be read with this date in mind. These reflections, however, inspire me to provide a brief updating.

The Carter Administration did prove to be true to much that blacks expected by way of social reform. Most blacks were encouraged by Carter's moral leadership and his good intentions. He was not successful, however, in delivering many of his promises for a more just society. He faced financial problems, a reluctant Congress and did not have a strong personality. But his performance was sufficiently effective on the social justice issues that most black voters were willing to offer him a second term.

Ronald Reagan did not interest many black voters. He has spotlighted a few blacks who have been willing to sell their birthrights for temporary gain. Reaganomics, or the political economy of the Reagan Administration, has meant bad news for blacks as for most poor and middle class Americans. While disclaiming any personal racism, he has been more insensitive to black suffering than any president of recent history. He has been tone-deaf to the cries of the oppressed at home and abroad. He is anti-Communist to such a degree that he is antagonistic towards the Soviets to the greatest degree possible.

Reagan has selected militarism over social reformation. His philosophy and his programs support this trend. His domestic and foreign policies follow this leaning. His absence of leadership in race relations and social justice issues have left a vacuum for racism. This void is being filled even by violent forms of expression. For example, his New Federalism is likely to set race relations back to the pre-1954 period, legally, economically, socially, and morally.

Conservative religion had a great deal to do with making Reagan's ascendency possible. But the religion of the New Right is different from the Quietism in Evangelical circles in the past. It is militantly political. It is just as focused on America as God's country as the traditional approach. It is characterized by one-issue proposals, by half-truths and by enlarged support by persons of means. Jerry Falwell is the priest in the king's court, rather than Billy Graham. While Graham insisted upon the separation of church and state, Falwell claims the right to speak for God, as it were, on political issues. With this close association between Reagan and Falwell, we have moved dangerously close to the Worship of the God of Success and the Moloch of War while injustice and suffering run rampant in the land. It is urgent that Americans exercise their political power to turn this situation from its destructive course before time runs out.

NOTES

1. Cited by Yvonne Delk in "Black Churches and the Bicentennial," Bicentennial Broadside (New York: NCC, 1976), p. 23.

2. Gayraud S. Wilmore, "Black Christian Perspectives on Liberty," Broadside, p. 26.

3. Rosemary R. Ruether, "America as Babylon," Broadside, p. 19.

4. Ibid.

5. Ibid.

6. Cited by P.E. Kraemer in Awakening From the American Dream (Chicago: CSSR, 1973), p. 11.

7. See M. Marty, "God Movement in Washington," Christian Century, p. 1008.

8. Religion and the Solid South (Nashville: Abingdon Press, 1971), p. 38.

9. Broadside, p. 23.

10. America and the Future of Theology, edited by W.A. Beardslee, (Philadelphia: Westminister, 1967), pp. 49-50.

11. "God and Man in Washington," The Washingtonian (Jan., 1975), p. 38.

12. Black World (Jan., 1976), pp. 28-29.

13. See Leigh Jordahl, "Civil Religion and Gospel," Dialog, 14 (Fall, 1975), p. 281.

14. "Black Ballot Power," Political Action Workshop (Nov. 5, 1971), Howard University.

15. "The Afro-American Stake in Africa," Black World (Jan., 1976), pp. 5-6.

PART IV

BLACK MINISTRY:
SPIRITUALITY AND LIBERATION

THE PRIESTLY AND PROPHETIC DIMENSIONS
OF BLACK SPIRITUALITY

Herbert H. Farmer, a theologian at Cambridge University, always saw the vital core of religion as succor and demand.[1] He had in mind the comfort and consolation of a profound religious faith and the disturbing dimension of religion in the presence of injustice and inhumanity. Indeed, this twosome -- succor and demand -- may be traced to the nature of God, as Creator, Provider and Redeemer. Love, mercy, grace, lovingkindness are attributes of the divine nature. But there is wrath, pathos and a thirst for righteousness also at the heart of God.

Whenever religion addresses the whole person, the complimentary aspects of religion are present in dynamic tension. The comfort and challenge of religion are essential to meet the needs of the total person-in-community. Religion in its deepest expression is individual and social with a *vertical* reach to God and a *horizontal* reach to other persons. Persons-in-relation or a "corporate personality" is crucial for vital religion. Religion is at once personal-priestly and corporate-prophetic. If deep spirituality and social-ethical involvement are not interrelated in religious experience, there is the absence of a significant part of a holistic relgous experience. Not only are the personal aspects of religion combined in vital religion, the this-worldly and the other-worldly greet each other.

I. BLACK RELIGIOUS EXPERIENCE

Whether in Africa or the New World, black religion is a whole experience for the total person. W.E.B. DuBois was correct when he indicated that black spirituality came from Africa. He was also on target when he used the imagery of the extended family in referring to the black church. African as well as the Afro-American religious experience is personal faith and the faith of the community at one and the same time. It is not a one-hour, once per week affirmation. It permeates the whole person and radiates throughout our communal relations. It is personal, but it is also familial, social, political and even economic.

In this regard one notes the similarity between black religious experience and the faith of the people of the covenant in the Old Testament. A Malaysian doctoral student of mine wondered why people converted to Christianity in his home country neglected the Old Testament. He based his research upon this problem because he believed in the unity of the Bible. After much investigation in biblical sources in the West, he still was no closer to an answer. It occurred to me that his vision would be enlarged and his understanding improved if he studied his own people and their culture. He read Asian theologians, studied the ethno-history of the Malaysians and then the Bible in this new perspective. He was now able to compare the people of the Old Testament with the culture of a people influenced by the Chinese family-system. This cast significant light upon the meaning of the Old Testament for Chinese Christians. This stimulated the creative reflection of this student to the point that he went beyond the requirement and ventured out on his own.

He discovered presently the manner in which Western missionaries had preached a one-sided gospel. Even the New Testament had been interpreted in an other-worldly manner. The voice of the prophets of social justice had been silenced. The life of the covenant people under divine direction had not been preached. There was a privatized, spiritualized and personalized version of the gospel presented to his people. He discovered a holistic gospel in a unified Bible. Furthermore, a new self-image emerged. He began to appreciate the writings of Third World theologians and biblical scholars. He could now define his existence and the culture of his people in an affirming way.

Charles H. Long, in an important essay, indicates that we need to study the specifically "religious" elements in black religion.[2] He searches for "symbolic images" and "methodological principles." He treats such matters as: Africa as a historical reality and religious image of the involuntary presence of the black community and the experience and symbol of God. He presses the point that sociological and/or apologetic treatment of black religion misses a purely descriptive encounter with black religion as a phenomena.

First, the image of Africa as it appears in black religion is unique; for the black community in America is landless. This, by the way, is becoming literally true. On June 9, 1978, a reporter on NBC News quoted statistics released by the National Association of Land Owners. According to this report, in 1910, blacks owned 15 million acres of land. Blacks now own only 5 million. It is being lost at a rate of 6,000 acres per week. This picture is dismal because so much of the land is owned by rural, poor and uneducated blacks who, by fraud or taxation are liable to continue to be stripped of their possession of land. It is predicted that by 1990, blacks will own few if any acres of farm property. Long is correct; it is not land per se, but the religious meaning of land that has great importance to blacks. The black man's image of land emerges as an image which is always invested with historical and religious possibilities.

Second, blacks came to the country in chains. Our lot has been oppression in many forms. The nature of our existence here has been that of "an involuntary presence." Long writes:

> The slave had to come to terms with the opaqueness of his conditions. . . . He had to experience the truth of his negativity and at the same time transform and create another reality. Given the limitations imposed upon him;, he created on the level of his religious consciousness.[3]

Finally, Long discusses the experience and symbol of God. He searches the oral tradition for clues to the meaning of this symbol. The Bible was used by slaves, but it was adopted to and invested with their experience. For example, the deliverance of the children of Israel from the Egyptians became an archetype which enabled him to live with promise.

God is viewed as being all-powerful and a moral deity. A fundamental distinction is made between God and Jesus. The trinitarian distinctions are for experiential rather than dogmatic reasons. The experience of God is placed within the context of the other images and experiences of black religion. God is a powerful Creator and supreme reality. There are aspects of both Hebraic and Christian perspectives on history, but black religion is unique. The history of blacks in America is one of crisis. The intervention of the deity in the black situation has not been identical with the confirmation of the reality of their being within the structures of America.[4]

Jesus in black religion takes the form of a demi-deity by which Long means, a deity as companion and creator, a deity related more to the human condition than deities of the sky, and the subjection of this deity to death at the hands of men. Long writes:

> Christ as fellow sufferer, as the little child, as the companion, as the man who understands -- these symbols of Christ have been dominant.
>
> "Poor little Jesus boy, made him to be
> born in a manger.
> World treated him so mean
> Treats me mean too. . . .[5]

There are other black contributions to our understanding of black spirituality. One is reminded of W.E.B. DuBois, Howard Thurman and James D. Tyms, among others.[6] Thurman's Ingrosoll Lectures on Immortality at Harvard is a must for those who would plumb the depths of black spirituality in the spirituals.[7] Much of recent scholarship by black scholars in religion has centered around the "radicalism" of black religion to the omission of the essentially "religious" content of black religion. This radicalism often takes a functional focus. The emphasis is upon what black religion *does* rather than upon what black religion *is*. It is unfortunate to dichotomize black religious experience in this way.

Among writers on black theology, Cecil Cone is rather unique in lifting upon black religious experience as the basis for a black theology.[8] Cecil Cone urges black theologians to transcend their "black power" frame of reference and search for the almighty sovereign God in the black religious heritage. The God he discovers, however, does not necessarily resemble the biblical God with a well-rounded moral character. Cecil Cone asks us to celebrate this God, but I would like to know more about this divinity. I am, therefore, disturbed about the "radical" aspect of black theology being sacrificed in favor of spirituality and celebration.

It is the genius of Thurman that he writes out of black religious experience and not about it. Thurman also brings a profound black spirituality together with a powerful social consciousness. One might almost conceive the latter as the religious foundation of "black power." Mysticism supports social change in Thurman. Long describes and Cecil Cone would celebrate, but in Thurman one is moved to live and act out black religious experience. This view of Thurman may not be as forceful on the political side as we would like. But without it we have neither the motivation or the sustaining power for social transformation. Among more youthful writers, Henry Young represents the holistic view.[9] Young's historical-theological study of black religious experience is a major contribution to a holistic perspective. It is essential that the *priestly* and *prophetic* dimensions of black religious experience be seen as interdependent.

II. BLACK SPIRITUALITY

Black theology builds upon the foundation of black religious experience in both its priestly and prophetic dimensions. Black religion is a religion of freedom according to Joseph Washington. Survival in a situation of racist oppression has made it so. But there is a balance in black religious experience between an existential search for meaning and a protest against injustice. To see it only as emotion and celebration is to short-circuit its full content. The "compensatory" character of black religious experience in Benjamin E. Mays is complimented by the "radicalism" in Gayraud Wilmore. Vincent Harding finds both characteristics in black religious history. As we have seen, Henry Young notes a unity-in-diversity among major black religious leaders. Young writes that on the whole, they are holistic in their perspective:

> They all speak from an organismic conception of reality. . . . They do not separate spiritual liberation from physical liberation.[10]

It has been essential to give another image of black religion than a passive, quietistic, other-worldly one. On this score black theologians have helped to turn the situation around. Black religion has been caricatured to the extent of burlesque by black novelists and playwriters because of extreme emotionalism as well as gross immortality on the part of some black religionists. Some contemporary black churchmen have over-indulged in celebration to the neglect of the social imperatives of the gospel. But unless they provide a solid foundation in personal faith and social ethics for their congregations, I predict that they will reap a lean harvest in the near future.

Thus black theology must lay its foundations deep in biblical faith as well as in the black religious heritage. Black theology should be temporally and specially Pan-African. We should excavate our rich spiritual heritage flowing from Africa into the New World and we should be in touch with contemporary efforts to contextualize Christian theology in the post-colonial period in Africa and the West Indies. But the *context* of theology is not identical with its *content*. Ethnicity is the medium for the message, and determines the hermeneutics of a theological program. But in theology the medium is not synonymous with the message. The method and language for communication may be determined by the culture in which the faith is to be understood and lived out, but behind this expression is the Universal World which is not captive to any culture. The gospel is never culture-bound, it is culture-transforming. The task of black theology, then, is to bring the spiritual riches of black spirituality in relation to the gospel which transforms everything it touches.

Black theology has rediscovered the God of the Exodus -- the God of Moses who led a whole people from bondage to freedom. But Dr. King had already uncovered the prophetic tradition. He clearly saw the biblical challenge for social justice in the Bible. For King the God of Amos was the God of Jesus. Even prior to King's *Letter from a Birmingham Jail*, Howard

Thurman had laid a solid perspective for younger colleagues in *Jesus and the Disinherited*. Majoring in his treatment of the depths of black spirituality, Thurman paused to indicate the emphathy Jesus has for the disinherited in his birth, ministry and death. Thurman observes that Jesus is a friend and fellow-sufferer with the oppressed.

This is not the direction white Christianity and its theology is moving. White Christians are worshipping a god of success. A white friend of mine is concerned about what he calls a "religion of hedonism." The faith in such a god/religion has no support for persons who confront failure and the contradictions of life. It is not suprising that there is a trend in white churches toward an unbridled otherworldliness with an intense emotionalism. Blacks retain their evangelical zeal, but this is necessarily balanced by a deep commitment to liberation from earthly as well as spiritual forms of oppression.

A people who know the meaning of suffering from a long stretch of history, need a faith that brings comfort and assurance. The tears of Jeremiah, the anguish of Habakkuk and the patience of Job have tested and challenged our faith through the long night of black suffering. The manner in which the Judeo-Christian faith has been filtered through the faith of blacks has developed it into a tower of strength for survival and meaning. Our understanding of God and the affirmation of faith has steeled black believers against the adversities of life heaped upon them by an unjust and inhuman system of oppression based upon racism. A lot of the emotionalism in black worship is healing-therapeutic. It releases the tension which oppression forces upon a whole people. It is an aid to psychological health in a racially pathological situation in which black people struggle for sanity.

Black religion also brings meaning. Our task, therefore, is to provide theological underpinning for meaning in black life. We must not be so enchanted by gospel music that we are unaware that the young people who are singing are struggling to find purpose, value and meaning in their lives. They are seeking bread! Are we giving them stones? Even worse, are we seeking to understand what their quest is all about. Gospel music is emotional, otherworldly. It has little if anything to do with finding meaning for life in a hostile world. Unless we are able to anchor the celebration of our youth in biblical faith and personal and social ethics, our success story will have a short history.

The spirituals came out of our slavery experience. They had the advantage of gospel music of being both this-worldly as well as other-worldly. This has been well-establshed by John Lovell, Miles Mark Fisher as well as Howard Thurman.

Fisher argues convincingly that slaves sang about freedom now as well as about freedom after death.[11] Perhaps it would be useful for us to sing spirituals along with gospels and seek to interpret for our young the religious and theological foundations of both forms of music. In addition much black "secular" music has a dual feature: social criticism and religious fervor. James Cone, for example, has treated the "blues" as secular spirituals.

Samuel Carter has treated the black prayer tradition. Carter writes:

> . . .The Black prayer tradition has given birth to churches, developed church leaders, provided a pathway for female leadership, and proved itself a healing ground for physical, mental, and spiritual diseases. . . .Were the Black prayer tradition not intimately associated with the liberation struggles of Black people, the critics of prayer could rightly accuse it of being a pious flight from reality. Indeed, the liberation march of Black people in education, publication, and civil rights owes its strength to the genius of Black prayers. . . .[12]

In these words the writer has brought together the priestly and prophetic stands of black religion through prayer. The understanding of faith which blacks have expressed in spontaneous prayer is the stuff out of which a priestly theology for blacks must be forged. Prayer is the "soul's sincere desire." It reaches the depths of the human spirit -- even its unconscious level. But prayer has also given utterance and courage to black prophets of liberation. Dr. M.L. King often initiated his freedom marches in a prayer meeting. Black theologians have yet to unlock and interpret the raw materials for theology in the prayer life of blacks. Along with our study of slave conversion narratives and confessions of faith, we need to know what the unexpressed longings of blacks in the secret places of the heart have uttered before God.

We turn now to emphasize the prophetic dimension of black theology. We have discovered the pathos or the passibility of God anew. So much emphasis upon the transcendence and otherness of God has eclipsed the loving-kindness and the righteousness of God in the face of human sinfulness, both personal and social. God is compassionate and God's anger is kindled in the face of injustice and inhumanity. God's mercy and justice greet each other on the plane of humanity. God is benevolent and provident. The creator is the sustainer as well as the redeemer and sanctifier. God cares for us and suffers with us. He is not an absolute alone at the top of some Tower of Babel. He is the "beyond within." Aristotle's god was not moved by the suffering of humans -- it was an unmoved mover. But the God who reveals his mind, will and purpose through Jesus, is a self-moving, loving God. God is with us in Christ. His love and his justice are outpoured toward our liberation.

God is lovingly just. We are to be both in relation to our fellows. Our loyalty to God must be manifest horizontally in relation to others as well as vertically in relation to God. Love for God is demonstrated in love for fellow humans. The same is true of justice. Being just in human relations is the highest expression of love. The whole person (body and soul) and the community (persons-in-relation) are within the scope of our theological concern. What happens in personal transgressions must be faced and overcome. But at the same time, we must confront our collective sin and guilt and be redeemed from the latter also. Whatever oppresses other humans who bear the image of God, whether sins of the flesh or will, whether sexism, racism or classism, must be blotted out. All these sins separate us from God, self and our fellow humans. Evangelical theology must be supported by a holistic perspective. In a word, our understanding of salvation must be for the whole person in all relations, human and divine.

What we meet in the theology of James Cone or Martin Luther King, Jr. is the prophetic note of black religion/theology. As different as they appear, the quest for social justice through a profound understanding of biblical faith informs both. They both draw deep upon the Old Testament and the revelation of Jesus Christ, but say in no uncertain terms: "Let my people go!"

III. CONCLUSION

Black spirituality is a reflection upon black religious experience as it encounters biblical faith. Black religious experience has its roots in Africa and was developed in Afro-American religious history. It is holistic -- it is concerned with the whole person and the liberation of a whole people. It indicates that redemption is both personal and social, spiritual and physical. It is a theology of a living black community of faith determined to be free.

NOTES

1. H.H. Farmer, Revelation and Religion.

2. Charles H. Long, "Perspectives for A Study of Afro-American Religion in the United States," History of Religions, Vol. II, No. 1 (August 1971).

3. Ibid., p. 59.

4. Ibid., pp. 61-62.

5. Ibid., p. 64.

6. See W.E.B. Dubois, Souls of Black Folk (Chicago: A.C. McClurg, 1908); Howard Thurman, Deep River (New York:Harper, 1955); and James D. Tyms, Spiritual Values in the Black Poet (Washington, D.C.: University Press of America, 1977).

7. The Negro Spiritual Speaks of Life and Death (New York: Harper, 1947).

8. Cecil W. Cone, The Identity Crisis in Black Theology (Nashville: American Methodist Episcopal Conference, 1975).

9. Henry J. Young, Major Black Religious Leaders -- 1755-1940 (Nashville: Abingdon, 1977).

10. Ibid., p. 13.

11. Miles Mark Fisher, Negro Slave Songs in the United States (Ithaca, Cornell University Press, 1953).

12. Harold A. Carter, The Prayer Tradition of Black People (Valley Forge: Judson Press, 1976), p. 129.

THE BLACK CHURCH'S MINISTRY TO FAMILIES: PRIESTLY MINISTRY

The black church is obligated to provide a priestly ministry to black families. In our next chapter we will be concerned with a prophetic ministry. This separate discussion of the two aspects of ministry in no way denies the holistic character of the black church's ministry to black persons. The distinction, for discussion sake, is based upon the need for clarity and depth of reflection. The priestly ministry of black churches refers to their healing, comforting and succoring work. The prophetic aspect of ministry is its social justice and socially transforming aspects. The bridge between these is the relation between love and justice. The interdependence of persons and their liberating and reconciling relationship with each other is the means for the black church's holistic ministry to persons and to a people. In an oppressed community, the priestly and prophetic aspects of ministry are but two sides of the same coin. Personal concerns relate to social concerns and social realities determine the limits of personal freedom.

I. THE PURPOSE OF THE BLACK CHURCH AND ITS MINISTRY TO FAMILIES

The informed reader will note that I have in mind H. Richard Niebuhr's classic study, *The Purpose of the Church and Its Ministry*.[1] In reference to this study by Niebuhr, I wish to lay a foundation for the black church's ministry to families. What racism has done and is still doing against blacks means most of the ministry of black families will remain under the sponsorship of predominantly black churches. With this latter fact in view, we may now adopt some of Niebuhr's insights for our purpose.

According to Neibuhr, the church lives and defines itself in action vis-a-vis the world. The relation between the world and the church is variable but dynamic and important. Niebuhr views the world as a companion of the church. The world is sometimes enemy of the church and sometimes partner. On the one hand, the world is the community of those who are occupied with temporal things. On the other hand, it is the community to which Christ sends his disciples. The world can reject the church and become idolatrous or it can view temporal things as gifts of God and enter into a partnership with the church. Ministry in the church is to the world. It is a conversation of church and world filled with humility and self-assurance.[2]

Having described the relation of the church to the world, Richard Niebuhr goes on to discuss the purpose of the church. The purpose of the church is "to increase the love of God and neighbour." Churches are divided, theologically, Niebuhr states, over whether the last end of the church is the individual salvation of souls or the realization of the redeemed society. He sees this conflict as based upon inadequate Christology. In Protestant circles, at least, the problem is enlarged by a blind devotion to the Bible. Catholics have the problem, on the other hand, of too much loyalty to the church. The love of the church becomes the first commandment. Neither love of the Bible nor love of the church should overshadow the love of God.

The Christological problem, however, is present in all Christian circles if there is a division between the "Christ of faith" and the "Jesus of history." Some proclaim the lordship of Jesus Christ; others advocate a Christian humanism. The Son of God party is founded in strong ecclesiastical institutions as well as among fundamentalists. The Son of Man group shows considerable interest in the social involvement of the church. The way to overcome this division between Christians on Christology is to hold a corrective trinitarian conviction, which does not allow the separation of the Son of Man and Son of God, from the Father and the Spirit. Niebuhr writes:

> Devotion directed toward Jesus Christ is at least partly redirected by him to the One he loves and who loves him, and to the world created and redeemed by the love of God. Nothing less than God -- albeit in the mystery of his being as Father, Son and Holy Spirit -- is the object toward which Scriptures, Church and Jesus Christ himself direct those who begin by loving them.[3]

It is essential, according to Niebuhr, that the whole church community confess the faith expressed above. Inherent in the love of God and neighbor is both "law" and "gospel;" both the requirements laid upon humans and the gift of grace bestowed. Love of God and neighbor is the gift given through Jesus Christ by the demonstration in incarnation, words, deeds, death and resurrection that God is love. The purpose of the gospel is not simply that we should believe in the love of God; it is that we should love him and neighbour. Niebuhr observes:

> Faith in God's love toward man is perfected in man's love to God and neighbour. We love in

incompleteness, not as redeemed but in the time of redemption, not in attainment but in hope.

What he desires to state is that it is through Jesus Christ that we receive sufficient faith in God's love to exercise responsive love toward others. We long for perfection, but we see it as a possibility and not as an attainment.

Niebuhr goes on to insist that the law and the gospel are inseparably related in the love of God and the love of the neighbor. He advocates neither a solitary union with God nor a nontheistic humanitarianism:

> . . . The neighbor cannot exist or be known or be valued without the existence, knowledge and love of God, so also God does not exist as God-for-us or become known or loved as God except in his and our relation to the neighbor.[4]

We now look briefly at Niebuhr's description of love. By love is meant rejoicing in the presence of the beloved, gratitude, reverence and loyalty. One rejoices over the existence of the beloved. One desires the presence of the one loved. One experiences happiness in that presence and rejoices in everything that makes the beloved great or glorious. Love is gratitude for the existence of the other. It is reverence in the acceptance of the other for what he or she is. It is a respect for the otherness and a profound unwillingness to violate the integrity of the other. Love is loyalty; it is the willingness to enter into self-sacrifice rather than to allow the other to cease to be. One enters into commitment of self to make the other great.

What do we have in mind when we speak of God whom we are to love? God, according to Niebuhr, is

> the Source and center of all being; the Determiner of destiny, the Universal One -- God the Father Almighty, Maker of Heaven and Earth.

Reconciliation to God is the greatest challenge of life. It is coming to terms with life itself. Love of the creator is love of being, rejoicing in existence, in its source, totality and particularity. Niebuhr writes:

> There is in such love of God a will-to-believe as the will-to-be-loyal to everything God and his Kingdom stand for. Love to God is conviction that there is faithfulness at the heart of things: unity, reason, form and meaning. . . .

All of this seems to by-pass the day-by-day experiences of the oppressed -- those who live on the edge of survival. Has Niebuhr forgotten those who are the victims of man's inhumanity? He comes closest to these God's "little ones" as he writes:

> The problem of man is how to love the One on whom he is completely, absolutely dependent; who is the Mystery behind the mystery of human existence in the fatefulness of its self-hood, of being this man among these men, in this time and all time, in the thus and so-ness of the strange actual world. It is the problem of reconciliation to the One from whom death proceeds as well as life, who makes demands too hard to bear, who sets us in a world where our beloved neighbors are the objects of seeming animosity, who appears as God of wrath as well as God of love. It is the problem that arises in its acutest form when life itself becomes a problem, when the goodness of existence is questionable, as it has been for most men at most times; when the ancient and universal suspicion arises that he is happiest who was never born and he next fortunate who died young.⁵

Lest we think Niebuhr pessimistic, we should be mindful of the plight of blacks in the history of this nation. We could easily illustrate the harshness of existence, even today, by observing the conditon of the black masses in any major urban center in this country. How then can we be reconciled to God -- love him and our neighbor -- when life itself is so unlovely? We cannot say, "God is in his heaven and all is right with the world." It is the fact of wholesale unmerited suffering of the entire black race which led William R. Jones to write his serious treatise *Is God a White Racist?* While I am theologically closer to Niebuhr, I am existentially closer to Jones. I do not believe that the theodicy question can be raised as poignantly as Jones raises it unless one has been victimized by a form of oppression like racism. Sexism is closest to racism but both are evils against creation. I like the way Jones states the problem, but I prefer Niebuhr's theological perspectives.

Who is my neighbor? The neighbour, according to Niebuhr, is a friend who has shown compassion and the enemy who fights against me. The neighbor is one who is in need -- one who is hungry, naked, imprisoned or ill. My neighbor is the one who is oppressed and the one who has accepted my oppression without revulsion. My neighbor is one who has rewarded me for being a member of an exploiting group. My neighbor is also a person of compassion who ministers to my needs -- the stranger who befriends me. The neighbor is in all times and places. Our focus must not be upon humankind in its totality, but, rather, upon individuals in community. Niebuhr's conclusion is noteworthy. He warns us against a universal love which is distant and abstract and points us to a love of neighbor which is particular and concrete. Only thus may an oppressed individual or group lay claim to their own humanity while accepting the humanity of others.

By way of summary, Niebuhr writes:

> . . . This love of God and neighbor remains the purpose and the hope of our preaching of the gospel, of all our church organization and activity, of all our ministry, of all our efforts to train men for the ministry, of Christianity itself.[6]

I have spent a lot of effort to set forth Niebuhr's perspectives for constructive reasons. This author of many great books (e.g.,*Christ and Culture* and *The Meaning of Revelation*) has brought his rich theological and ethical insights to bear upon the purpose of the church and its ministry. He has a deep and balanced theological perspective which is essentially ecumenical. He grounds his ecclesiology in Christology and his Christology in turn in the Trinity. How we understand the church is related to how one understands Christ in the internal relations of the Godhead. The love of God and neighbor is reflected in how one understands his/her God relationship and how one enters into Christian discipleship against the church's confession of this faith. Law and gospel are inseparable -- human effort and the gift of grace are essentials for love of God and neighbor. The neighbor is many things. But among the neighbor is the oppressed. Niebuhr could not have known the pangs of either sexism or racism and could not describe these. He does, however, keep us close to the concrete, particular aspects of neighborliness as related to individuals in community as well as the community of individuals. The contribution he has made to our understanding of the purpose of the black church and its ministry is profound. My exceptions to his study are important to black church theology. He does not give adequate attention to the need for "self-love" defined as self-respect and the relationship between love and justice as black church theology requires.

II. BLACK MINISTRY TO THE INTERNAL PROBLEMS OF BLACK FAMILIES

1. THE NEED FOR A THEOLOGY FOR MINISTRY

It is just not true that activism is sufficient in itself. The black church needs a theology both for its self-understanding and its sense of mission. We need to know not merely how and when we should act, but why we should act. Theology and ministry in the black church are inseparable.

This theology for the black church must be more than a lay version of theology. It must take seriously the black experience of religion. There are several books written by black writers which help us to describe the nature of the black religious experience. Among these are Howard Thurman's *The Negro Spiritual Speaks of Life and Death*, Benjamin E. Mays' *The Negro's God*, Joseph A. Johnson, Jr., *The Soul of the Black Preacher*, W.E. DuBois' *The Souls of Black Folk*, Cecil W. Cone's *The Identity Crisis in Black Theology* and Henry J. Young's *Major Black Religious Leaders*.[7] There are other valuable studies which attempt to explore the black religious experience from some angle of vision or some particular means of investigation -- as mysticism, as literature, as matter for preaching or as a basis for theological discourse. These studies and others like them provide the vital raw material for the development of a black church theology.

Here C. Eric Lincoln states clearly what needs to be said. According to him we cannot depend upon white theologians to provide theology for the black church. The black church must do its own theological reflection:

> The black church has traditionally relied upon a "preached" theology. . . . Now that era may be past. The Blacks of this generation, and possibly for generations to come, are going to write their own theology in the light of their circumstances and their needs. A white Jesus, whether preached, taught or implied by cultural habits, simply won't do. In a society like ours, *he can't do anything for black folk!*
>
> A white church that is painfully adjunctive to instituionalized racism -- the consequences of which are devastating the whole society -- can't do anything for black people. It can't do anything for itself.
>
> White theology suffers mortally from the sin of omission. It has sent its theologians to study in Europe where the problem isn't, or imported the best European theologians to bring us the light, but not for *our* darkness.
>
> In consequence, American theology has had few words to speak to *our* condition. White theology has not done anything for black people except ignore them.[8]

Lincoln's statement is consistent with his overview of the black condition based upon his study of the history and sociology of the black experience. Blacks did not come to America minus any culture. Due to oppression based on race, they have had their destiny defined for them by the over-culture, but they have carved out for themselves adequate space to develop a survival culture. According to Lincoln, black churches and families have been vital instruments in the development of a healthy and viable people, but unlike some other black religious scholars, influenced heavily by the social sciences, Lincoln sees a very great need for developing a black church theology.

2. THEOLOGY AND MINISTRY TO BLACKS

Many black activists, including many ministers, see black theology as excess or useless baggage. People have said to me that Leon Sullivan and Jesse Jackson have no use for a black theology. They don't need a theology, these observers argue, for they are doing an effective job without it. Black theology has made its case whether any particular church leader accepts or rejects it. We do know that some powerful black church leaders have taken a forthright stance against theology. A case in point is Joseph H. Jackson, president of the multi-million membership National Baptist Convention,[9] but on the other side of the spectrum, we have Joseph A. Johnson, Jr., a bishop and biblical scholar in the C.M.E. church who has produced his own version of what he calls a black Christian theology. Johnson writes:

> A new understanding of the Christian faith emerged out of the black Christian witnessing community . . . . One's experience of the life of faith comes from participation in the community of faith and the form of this experience will vary widely depending on what the racial group brings to the faith.[10]

The value of the work of Bishop Johnson is very encouraging. He is dedicated to a version of black theology which underscores effective preaching and ministry in black communities. His knowledge of scripture is considerable and he has been an effective church leader for many years. He has presented a challenge to all black theologians to provide a theology of ministry in black churches. Joseph R. Washington, Jr., a religious ethicist and social scientist, puts the matter this way:

> It is incumbent upon the black church to discover what its ministry, indeed, its special ministry has

to be. When this discovery has been made then it is incumbent upon the black church to see that that ministry takes place wherever black people are.[11]

All movements for social change require thought related to action. When churches are involved in social transformation, we must be concerned wtih an adequate theology for that purpose. Dr. Martin Luther King, Jr. spent many years reflecting upon a theological ethic for the movement he later was called upon to spearhead. Many activists in the black church today are still indebted to King's thought as a basis for action. I do not believe that black churches need to be totally dependent upon others to provide them with a theology. To do our thinking, we need to mine our own African/Afro-American heritage incessantly for alternatives to our dependency upon others. Our beliefs, thoughts and actions require the same agenda. Church leaders and religious activists need theological foundations for ministry. Black theologians and church leaders must no longer work at cross-purposes. They need to reinforce each other. We must move from action to reflection and from reflection to action.

3. THE BLACK CHURCH CONFRONTS BLACK SUFFERING

A people who know the meaning of suffering from a long stretch of history need a faith that brings comfort and assurance. The tears of Jeremiah, the anguish of Habakkuk and the patience of Job have tested and challenged our faith through the long night of black suffering. The manner in which the Judeo-Christian faith has been filtered through the faith of blacks has developed into a tower of strength for survival and meaning. Our understanding of God and the affirmation of faith has steeled black believers against the adversities of life heaped upon them by an unjust and inhuman system of oppression based upon racism. The emotionalism in black worship is therapeutic. It releases the tension which oppression forces upon black people. It is often an aid to psychological health in a racially pathological situation in which black people struggle for sanity. Yet it is obvious that a theologically grounded form of worship should be more than a release of tensions built up by oppression.

Much of the priestly content for black church theology is hidden in the black prayer tradition. Prayer in the black church unearths the tragic soul life of a black suffering race. Prayer reaches into the depths of the human spirit — even its pre-conscious level. But prayer is also conscious and powerful with meaning for the oppressed. Strength from black prayer is shared by members in black fellowship. Many black Christians are sustained and nurtured by prayers of fellow pilgrims delivered at the mid-week prayer meetings. Some traditional worship services begin with a prayer meeting. Black church theology has yet to unlock and interpret the raw materials for theology in the prayer life of blacks. Along with our study of slave conversion narratives and confessions of faith, we need to know what the unexpressed longings in the secret places of the heart that blacks have uttered before God. While we arouse black Christians to action against social evils, we need to know what spiritual resources have held the pieces of life together and sustained a suffering race through its dark night of suffering. Prayer is the bridge between the black church and family. There is a direct connection between the church-altar and the family-altar in the black tradition.[12]

Black church theology must not give all of its attention to social transformation. The existential tap-roots of religious experience provide the fountainhead for morale and meaning. Without healing in our personal lives we will not be prepared for liberation. Strong families as well as warm fellowships provide the matrix for the comfort, healing and belongingness which makes life whole.

It has been the faith we have in a God who enters into our joys and sorrows that has brought us to this day. We have believed that God suffers but is not weak. The crucified God of the black tradition is an able God. We do not ask "Is God a white racist?" We believe that God is loving and just. We attribute our suffering based upon racism to the injustice and cruelty of other human beings. Edward P. Wimberly states the case well:

> God is able to enter into our pain and suffering caused by the devastating powers of evil. But God can do more than this. He can help us find resources to help us live meaningful and triumphant lives in spite of the threatening hand of suffering . . . . Our God may suffer, but like all suffering, it is only temporary. God is able.[13]

All humans suffer because life has its moments of pain and disruption -- sometimes physical, psychological or spiritual. But victims of structural oppression bear a double portion of suffering. Much of their anguish is caused by pain inflicted upon them individually or as a group, by other human beings. Oppressed people need an adequate faith to sustain them as they face the reality of their lives, as persons, as families and as people -- hence the peculiar mission of black families and churches.

4. MINISTRY TO A BLACK FAMILY FACING A PERSONAL CRISIS

Much pastoral care in the black church tradition is done through preaching, teaching and pastoral remarks. The informal worship in many traditional black churches provides opportunity for group counselling and therapy to occur. Furthermore, the black church is often much like an extended family of care, sharing and fellowship. It is a place where one belongs, is affirmed and finds acceptance. The pastor is regarded, in many instances, as a father or mother. Members relate to them much as they do to parents. Even a young pastor may be thus regarded by older people. The relation between pastor and people in the black church needs careful attention. It may promote or stunt growth in people. If the relation of pastor to people becomes "paternalistic" it can cripple people so that they will not be able to face reality. On the other hand, the close kinship ties which the black pastor has with his/her people provides a real opportunity for nurturing persons toward spiritual maturity as a wise parent does for his/her offsprings.

Henry Mitchell describes the process of evangelism in the black church with the image of the extended family in view. He believes that new members should be attracted to membership in a black church by the family atmosphere of the fellowship. Mitchell writes:

> When a church has become the family of God, the next step is to lead its new members by adoption to an awareness that they are literally God's children, with all that entails. The purpose of new Christians is not statistical and financial, nor is it to gain support for a written creed. The purpose is to help them to a sense that they are children of God and to act as befits His children, living out that commitment in the context of the very family of God.[14]

What Mitchell is saying about evangelism is related to what we are saying here about the nature of pastoral care. We must bear in mind what can be done and what cannot be done in keeping with the resources of many black churches. This means that the pastor needs to be perceptive in transferring some responsibility for pastoral care to other capable persons in the "extended family," as well as referring parishioners to professional persons or agencies.

Edward P. Wimberly has written a definitive study entitled *Pastoral Care in the Black Church*.[15] I have been greatly assisted in my perspectives by this book as well as through personal conversation with the author. According to Wimberly, pastoral care has four functions: healing, sustaining, guiding and reconciling. He emphasizes the black church's ministry to families. Wimberly is realistic regarding the obstruction to pastoral care based upon racism. He sets limits to what may be expected as far as healing and reconciling are concerned. The strong emphasis, he believes, has been the black church/pastor's approach to sustaining and guiding. Healing and reconciling may result, but these are not predominant in pastoral care in the black tradition.

As we keep this in mind, let us consider another assertion by Wimberly. He notes that a family has a network of sub-systems: the relationship between spouses, siblings, in-laws, etc. When a crisis develops in the family, the pastor needs to get to the cause of the trouble. The root-cause could be in any one of the several sub-systems. This root-cause could result in the breakdown of the entire family situation. If one ministers to the family considering only the secondary causes, his/her ministry will not be effective. Furthermore, he believes that role-playing in counselling is native to the black heritage and can be used effectvely in leading persons/families out of crises.

We must be prepared to minister to the human situation as it is -- not as we would like for it to be or as it used to be. I was reminded recently, as I conducted a family life conference in a local church, that I would alienate many people who needed to attend the sessions if I limited my concerns to "a healthy marriage." This mother wanted me to include her daughter, recently separated from her husband. The daughter had moved in with her mother and had two children. This mother reminded me of the single parent families who are increasing in number in white churches, but have long been a concern for black pastors. We need therefore to prepare for ministry to many different kinds of families.

NOTES

1. H. Richard Niebuhr, *The Purpose of the Church and Its Ministry* (New York: Harper, 1956).

2. Ibid., pp. 26-27.

3. Ibid., p. 31.

4. Ibid., p. 33-34.

5. Ibid., pp. 36-37.

6. Ibid., p. 39.

7. H. Thurman, *The Negro Spiritual Speaks of Life and Death* (New York: Harper, 1947);

   B.E. Mays, *The Negro's God* (New York: Atheneum, 1968);

   Joseph A. Johnson, Jr., *The Soul of the Black Preacher* (Memphis: C.M.E. Publishing House, 1970);

   W.E.B. DuBois, *The Souls of Black Folk* (New York: Fawcett, 1978), and *The Gift of Black Folk* (New York: Washington Square Press, 1970);

   Cecil W. Cone, *The Identity Crisis in Black Theology* (Nashville: African Methodist Episcopal Church Press, 1975).

   Henry J. Young, *Major Black Religious Leaders——1755-1940* (Nashville: Abingdon, 1977).

8. "Black Church," *Christianity and Crisis* (XXX/18, Nov. 16, 1970).

9. Joseph H. Johnson, *Nairobi: A Joke, a Junket or a Journey* (Nashville: Townsend, 1976), p. 69. His criticisms are aimed primarily at James Cone's program, but he in fact rejects all black theology as we know it.

10. *Proclamation Theology* (Shreveport, Louisiana: Fourth Episcopal District C.M.E. Press, 1977), p. 126.

11. "How Black is Black Religion?" in J.J. Gardiner and J. Deotis Roberts, eds. *Quest for a Black Theology* (Philadelphia: Pilgirm Press, 1970), p. 28.

12. See Harold A. Carter, *The Prayer Tradition of Black People* (Valley Forge: Judson Press, 1976).

13. "The Suffering God," in Henry J. Young, ed., Preaching on Suffering and a God of Love (Philadelphia: Fortress, 1978), pp. 61-62.

14. Henry H. Mitchell, "Towards a Black Evangelism," The Journal of Religious Thought (Vol. 35, No. 1, 1978), p. 65.

15. For those interested in pastoral care, Wimberly's book is a necessary manual for ministry in the black church: Pastoral Care in the Black Church (Nashville: Abingdon, 1979).

THE BLACK CHURCH/FAMILY AND THE POWER STRUCTURE

> The Spirit of the Lord is upon me; He has appointed me to preach Good News to the poor. . .that the downtrodden shall be freed from their oppressors, and that God is ready to give blessings to all who come to Him. (Luke 4:18,19).

This is an often quoted text in black theology. It seems to set the stage for the external concerns of the black community in its quest for social justice. It is this central theme of "liberation" which relates black theology to other similar theological movements. Before we make a brief comparison, however, between black and other liberation theologies, we need to set forth what we will be primarily concerned about in this final chapter.

The ministry to black families has to take under review the external social, political and economic factors which relate to black family crises. For an oppressed community, most personal problems cannot be isolated from social causes. The black church has to see its ministry as related to the whole person in all of his/her relationships. Black slaves brought with them a holistic concept and practice of religion from Africa. Biblical faith, as understood by blacks, undergirds and deepens this understanding of religion. Therefore, the Christian faith as understood in the black church tradition is rightly concerned about the whole person and all of life. Some will say correctly that this is not what they observe in all black churches. My rejoinder is that these churches are not true to their heritage and it would be well if they would consider that heritage. They will find in it much that would lead them to a profound understanding of the Christian faith itself.

I. BLACK FAMILIES FACE SINFUL SOCIAL STRUCTURES

Here is a case history in sinful social structures:

I am a minority. I am a single parent of two young children who are *not* on welfare. My children go to one of the eighty-seven pre-school/after-school child-care centers in the Los Angeles area. My son, who is four years old, attends the center full time and my daughter, eight years old, goes before and after school, thus enabling me to go to work for eight hours, five days a week in the Hollywood area.

Now I learn that the child-care center that I depend on so much is to be closed down next year. Not just the one my children go to but all of them. The Board of Education, in its infinite wisdom, has decided that the day-care centers would be a good place to make a budget cut for Proposition 13.

To say that I disagree with that cut is putting it very mildly. Where are people in my type of situation supposed to turn? Although I earn more (not much more) than the minimum wage, I am still living at what the federal government considers the "poverty level."

So far, my landlord has not made me any offer of a rebate or rent cut, and I'm not going to hold my breath with anticipation of any offer in the future. My utility bill arrives like clockwork. My children have to eat every day and I have to pay my rent. I don't drive the car that's broken in the driveway (not enough money to fix the brakes), but instead ride a small motorcycle to save on gas. I don't squander my earnings!

If I have to go out and find new day-care facilities for my children, which there is no great abundance of, I don't know where I'll get the money to pay. At the very minimum, private day care in someone's home (which is less expensive than private centers) is a dollar an hour per child. That would amount to $55 a week. That's $225 a month out of a monthly income of about $560 take-home pay after taxes. Yes, I pay them too. After paying rent of $260 a month, I don't have a heck of a lot left over. And I'm better off financially than a lot of working mothers. What are we to do?

The saddest part of this whole mess is that the children are the ones that are hurt the most. I imagine that some children will be left at home alone to fend for themselves while mother is at work. You think no mother would leave small kids by themselves? Don't bet on it. Ask at any social service office. I won't leave my children by themselves, but come next year I won't be able to leave them at the childcare center either. Quite a dilemma, huh?

To the school board, et al, I say, "Keep cutting, gang! Those of us who are making an honest effort to stay off the welfare roles, feed and educate our children, really don't need your kind of support.[1]

                        Marcie Hall
                        North Hollywood

This letter is ideal for a look at black families confronting the structures of our society. Ms. Hall is a minority in Los Angeles, probably black, since she does not appear to be Spanish-speaking. She has two children. No mention is made of the father(s) or any support from him/them. She is a working mother and is not presently on welfare. She expresses a real concern for the welfare of her two children. She speaks as a responsible parent. The famous Proposition 13, a property tax-cut bill, is viewed as responsible for the promise to cut out day-care centers. The school board of the city, charged with the responsibility of allocating funds for education, decided that day-care centers were expendable. There was no apparent sensitivity to families like Ms. Hall's where the mother's income is indispensable. In Ms. Hall's view, there was no real human concern in Proposition 13 and the L.A. School Board decision. A minority parent and two small children were face-to-face with sinful social structures.

Whatever the race of this family, there is an obvious economic and social problem related to the system. Both state law and the local school board had created a problem for this family and many like it. The issue really goes deeper -- it was as the result of the "haves" aganst the "have-nots." In Southern California, this is spelled out to mean a revolt of mainly affluent white people against poor black and Spanish-speaking people. Even middle class blacks were threatened by the consequences of Proposition 13. Their jobs, possessions and life-style were all at the mercy of this bill. Having just moved into good paying jobs, they were vulnerable to seniority provisions in many employment situations. One black churchman, a successful businessman, viewed the effects of Proposition 13 upon fellow church members and made this decisive statement:

> If I had known the consequences of Proposition 13 upon most black people, I would have willingly paid more taxes.

A word needs to be said concerning the Los Angeles School Board also. The letter by Ms. Hall is dated July 11, 1978. In January 1979 I joined a group of black ministers and other black citizens at a school board meeting to protest the fact that a vacancy on the school board was not being filled. The board did not, at that time, have a black member. In the presence of the obvious groundswell of support the black leaders represented, the school board met and simply entertained a motion to adjourn. I remained with the black ministers in an after-rally and shared the agony of this experience. A group of the most affluent and prominent citizen-leaders had met in good faith to ask for a spokesperson from the black community to be considered to fill a vacancy related to the education of black youth, but they were ignored. It was, as it were, a demonstration of powerlessness in the face of a situation of institutionalized racism in the vital area of education. At that very moment Los Angeles County was under pressure to seriously consider improving the quality of education for minorities. Any careful observer can see why the welfare of black families cannot be isolated from a study of the problems in the larger society as they affect the black family unit.

In July of 1979, it was my good fortune to be in Los Angeles and attend the ceremony in which Rita Walters, a black woman, was sworn in as a member of the Los Angeles School Board. The most significant statement of the public session was Mrs. Walter's speech in which she expressed a compassionate concern about the humanity of all the parents and children. It dawned upon me that she had a deep grasp of the Christian ethic as it has been expressed by Martin Luther King, Jr. and others coming out of the black church tradition.

II. BLACK FAMILY LIBERATION

The black church has as one of its greatest tasks the "liberation" of the family. It will be unfortunate if blacks begin to participate in male-female conflicts in imitation of others on issues not crucial to the welfare of the black family. The problems which confront the relationship between black men and women are serious, but they must be seen for what they are and dealt with in that context. Most black families abide solidly within the black subculture essential to black survival. We will be defeated if we give our attention solely to mainstream problems and by-pass those concerns peculiar to the black condition. In the following brief sections I will describe some of the problems faced by black women, men and children and the family unit as a whole.

1. BLACK MOTHERHOOD

The choice of "motherhood" as a topic under which to discuss the black woman does not imply that the sole purpose of black women is to be mothers. My concern here is with black families. Black women are often single parents as well as partners with black men in a family unit.

Michele Wallace has exploded the "myth of the black superwoman," but at the same time she has levelled a broadside at all black men.[2] Her treatment of the myth that black women are self-sufficient and can live a full life without the love and companionship of a man is an important contribution. She has courageously related the woman's point of view concerning a subject that needs in-depth discussion. She has indicated that what has been accepted as a given in the black women's make-up may well be an adjustment to the harsh reality confronting them. She may have given too much attention to the white woman as the black man's alternative to black women. The fact is that most black men who have turned to white women were first in love with one or more black women and often married to at least one black woman. The other fact is that there was serious trouble between black men and women long before white women were readily available. A further fact needs mentioning. Many black men who have left their families for a white companion have not made it with white women either. What we really ought to deal with is the root-cause of the male-female conflict within the black situation. Both men and women may share some of the blame.

Wallace views most black women as Amazons or as an imitation of "a lady" in white society. In either case they are not true to their own feelings and desires. She does not spare her black sisters and criticizes some of the best known black women. Angela Davis, according to Wallace, built her life in the Black Movement around the black male as "political prisoner." She even fell in love with one who considered black women as enslaving. Wallace writes:

> Angela Davis, a brilliant, middle-class black woman, with a European education, a Ph.D. in philosophy, and a university appointment, was willing to die for a poor, uneducated black male inmate.

Nikki Giovanni receives an even more harsh treatment by Wallace. Giovanni was the reigning poetess of the Black Movement during the sixties. According to Wallace, she mainly supported black men, suggesting that they return to their roots and partake in the revolution for black liberation. In consequence of the message of her poems, Giovanni is said to have shut herself off from black women while black male poets had a tendency to ignore her. She became an unstable poetess, an opportunist. Wallace writes:

> She began to speak positively of the church and to focus more on having babies and loving the black man. . . . She herself had a baby and refused to disclose the name of the father. Early in the seventies she told young black women to become mothers because they needed something to love. She also told young black people that school was useless and a waste of time -- despite her own years of education at Fisk University. Soon after, she backed away from these positions, amending her original statement about having babies to you-

should-only-have-one-if-you-could-afford-to-take-care-of-it like she could, and actually encouraging Blacks to go back to school.³

Wallace views Davis and Giovanni as representing the best black women were allowed to achieve. Davis suggested that you support the black man in the Black Movement -- if need be go to prison with him. Giovanni said "have-a-baby." According to Wallace, her visit to Riker's Island prison revealed the bitter consequences of Davis' advice. She met black female prisoners who where there because of black men they loved. The "mass" black woman was there because she supported a pimp, a dope supplier or a robber, but the political black women were there for the same reason -- support of a black man. The results of Giovanni's advice, according to Wallace, is also evident.

> By the time she advised [black women] later to first make sure they had enough income to support the child, a lot of women were already on welfare.

As we examine what Wallace has to say about the motherhood of black women, the more one wonders concerning the future of the black family. Motherhood outside of marriage and often independent of marriage vows is nothing new. This is to state a fact and not make a judgment. E. Franklin Frazier wrote about what he called "unfettered motherhood" toward the end of the last century. Frazier stated that many black women refused to be married to the father of an unborn child, "because she did not want to be bothered with a husband." Frazier goes on to say:

> She was not ashamed of her pregnancy, she was proud of the fact that she was to become a mother and had been congratulated by the women in the neighbourhood on her fertility.⁴

Now, according to Frazier, motherhood and marriage were two different things. Motherhood was usually accepted with seriousness. Frazier writes:

> The unmarried mother is as sensitive as the legally married mother to what is expected of the woman as a mother.

The following conclusion by Frazier is very instructive:

> Motherhood signifies maturity and the fulfillment of one's function as a woman. But marriage holds no such place in the esteem of many of these women.

There is a direct line from the past to the present. The government's National Center for Health Statistics reported that in 1976 the number of black children born out of wedlock exceeded 50% of all black births. This is said to be a 50% increase over a 13 year period. I am aware that this report is controversial and that these figures need to be carefully interpreted and examined. Even if the statistics are partly wrong, the black family is still in serious trouble. June Brown, a black columnist of the *Detroit News* raised the crucial issue:

> If the strength of a race depends upon the strength of its families, then the black race is getting weaker every year.[5]

If motherhood is sacred and independent of marriage and if black women, past and present, view the black man only as a means to childbirth, then we need to ask why. This, I believe, is related to the black man's lack of sense of obligation beyond begetting children. If men are allowed to freely beget children without any sense of love or responsibility, it is not good for the woman, man or child and it will eventually be the undoing of the black family and the black race.

While some of us may have assumed that black women have babies out of wedlock because they desire to have this fulfillment under impossible circumstances, the real problem may be elsewhere. Is the separation of motherhood and wifehood indeed a real problem? Do black women, even in marriage, separate the roles to such an extent that the spouse aspect of marriage is expendable when children are born? Again Ms. Wallace is on target when she points to the escalation of the baby-out-of-wedlock phenomenon among black women. She desires to know why so many black women choose this type of motherhood. Many say that if they do not marry by thirty, they will have a baby anyway. She observes that this is an old trend but there is a disturbing difference, and it does not seem to be out of love for children. Wallace observes:

> Whereas [in former times] unmarried black women with babies have usually lived with extended families, these women tend to brave it alone. Whereas the black women of previous generations have generally married soon after the baby was born, these women may not and often say they do not wish to. Whereas the practice of having babies out of wedlock was generally confined to the poorer classes of black women, it is now not uncommon among middle-class, moderately successful black women. A woman may pick a man she barely knows. She may not even tell him he is going to be a father or permit him to ever see the child.[6]

While there is much in Wallace's book that I would take exception to, I can appreciate fully the issues raised here. As one concerned about the liberation of black families, motherhood, both outside of wedlock and within marriage, which is isolated from a total family relationship, is problematic. The concern is intensified if one has real interest in the future of the young in a pluralistic society hostile to the well-being of black people. We need to ask, "How do we make 'motherhood' a part of a healthy and whole family relationship?" Not only does the black woman need someone to love, the black man has the same need and the black child needs the love of mother and father. Circumstances will lead to some single parent black families. Some of these single parent families may be headed by fathers who will love and care for the young. But as far as possible these should be exceptions based upon necessity and not the norm for black families.

What we have discussed here is not a blanket attack upon black women. It is a call for self-examination in light of history and in face of great odds which a racist society has imposed upon all blacks. There are so many problems which are a part of the black woman's experience. Some of these are loneliness, scarcity of eligible black men, involuntary sterilization, lack of opportunities for abortion, inadequate sex education, the unfaithfulness and brutality of some black men and a larger society insensitive in its welfare services. The miracle is that there are so many lovable and caring black women who have found a way to cope with the harsh realities of life -- who suffer without bitterness.

Inez Smith Reid, in a study for the Black Women's Community Development Foundation, interviewed black women nationwide. The entire study is worth careful examination, but she provides us with a look at some adaptations black women are making in face of the desire to be liberated. She warns that "liberation can be a trick bag."[7] She provides this crucial observation:

> While some in the black community may decry traditional marriage and opt instead for mutual understanding or simply living together in lieu of a formal marriage ceremony, all in the name of freedom, the question remains -- as posed by many women-- will this represent freedom or liberation from responsibility? That is, will men with increased freedom feel no compunction about walking out on women and/or ignoring the needs of children they have helped create? Moreover, while some view the pill as a liberating force, in the sense that freedom from a constant process of nine month pregnancies may mean more time for "revolutionary" activities,

others look upon it as an oppressive mechanism which through evil side effects not only can incapacitate one in terms of performing activities for the black struggle, but also effectively preclude the production of additional troops for the "revolution." Furthermore, polygamy may indeed allow more freedom to experiment and experience different lifestyles. Yet it is equally apparent that the introduction of polygamy . . . into Black American society may also cause personal and psychological conflict as well as augment the economic strains on black men . . . [8]

With this statement by Inez Smith Read, we conclude our purview of black women as mothers and turn to black men as fathers.

2. THE BLACK MAN: FATHERING

Black men have a bad reputation as fathers. This statement is not intended as an absolute condemnation of all black fathers. Many black men are serious about their fatherly responsibilities. Indeed, some have worked themselves to death early in order to fulfill their obligations to a family. Black fathers have also shown deep affection for their children and have spent considerable time caring for the young. There are enough of the caring fathers to provide hope that more men may be encouraged to assume this important role. I have personally been blessed with such a father -- we continue to share precious moments together. His fathering has challenged me to assume responsibility for my family.

Edward V. Stein notes that there are two aspects to fathering -- the biological and the psychological. The biological aspect is brief, easy and satisfying. The psychological part is a lifetime endeavour -- it has "peaks and valleys of anguish that would try a god." [9]

Stein points out that science has reduced the biological aspect of fathering to a peripheral dimension. Through artificial means, a few males could supply enough sperm to repopulate the whole earth. Psychological fathering, on the other hand, is greatly needed. It is an individual responsibility and is needed now more than ever. Stein illustrates his concern for psychological fathering by referring to a study of suicidally depressed patients in San Francisco General Hospital. The patients ranged in age from adolescence to 59. All seven indicated that she or he had lost a father in childhood, either through divorce, desertion, or death. Stein did not conclude, therefore, that all suicidal patients result from the absence of the father in the family. He does draw, however, the reasonable conclusion that fathering is psychologically important.

A student of mine in a doctoral program admitted that I had become for him a surrogate father. Here was a brilliant and able student who had fought his way through all types of difficulties, personally and socially. He had been into the underworld in a major urban center. He had experienced drugs and promiscuous sex and had known life at its worst. He was reared by a mother, along with several sisters. Before his drunkard father deserted the family he had promised to kill him. After a radical experience of conversion he was able to accept his father and visit him. Though he is extremely close to his mother and sisters, he indicated that he often needed a father, especially in his early adult life. When I met him, he opened up his life to me as if I were his own father. A few weeks before I met him, I had lost my son in an automobile accident. The feeling was mutual -- I needed a surrogate son and he needed a surrogate father. A sense of kinship developed between us and continues today. There is nothing unusual about this in the black tradition. This case illustrates concretely the importance of the fatherly role.

Nathan Hare writes about "the frustrated masculinity" of the black male. Black men, according to Hare, are preoccupied with the effort to be masculine. Traditionally, they were not even able to protect their wives and daughters from white men. Moreover, black males are often unable to be good providers. Even if they are hard workers and gainfully employed, their wives often make more income than they do. The tension between a non-professional husband and a professional wife may be severe. Sports do not necessarily compensate for the need for masculinity felt by black men. White racists have used the myth of the black man's sexual power to fan the flames of race hate. The black male, according to Hare, has been an object of curiosity to many white women. The society has tried "to stifle or minimize the masculinity of the Negro male in actuality, sometimes even by outright castration."[10] Some black males are so frustrated by the social pressures under which they live that they reject work altogether "and turn to pimping as a compensatory exploitation of the female." Dr. Alvin F. Poussaint, a noted black psychiatrist, asserts:

> . . . Whites' reactions to the sexual mythology which they have created have wreaked havoc on the black man's psyche -- distorting his self-image and creating his anxieties. Because whites have feared black male sexuality, they have made every effort to make the black man impotent.[11]

Black men should never confuse sexual liberation with political liberation. In fact the pursuit of the white woman in some cases could be a compensatory action. This is true if the black man defines his worth, values and virility only in terms of his association with white women. On the other hand, it is disturbing that many of the "high achievers" among black males turn to the white woman for companionship. Part of the answer may lie in Robert Staples' observation:

> Some middle-class men turn to white women who fit even better the model of femininity as set forth in this country.

Staples is on target as he continues:

> (Black) women, to a large extent, are victimized by the fact that the very same characteristics they need to obtain career mobility (aggressive, strong achievement drive) are the ones which make it difficult to attract and hold a man. Thus, they are often placed in the position of a forced choice between career and marriage. And men place them in this position by their insistence on women playing supportive, noncompetitive roles.[12]

The issue of the scarcity of available black men is crucial. Between the ages of 15 and 30 the mortality rate of black males is higher than that of black females. War, homicide and suicide are high on the list of the shortage of black males. Almost a half million black males are behind bars, an estimated one-third of black men in the inner city have a drug problem, and 25 to 50 per cent are unemployed.

It appears that what slavery did not do to remove the father from the black family, urbanization did. Staples continues:

> In the South . . . men helped to provide for their families. As they came to the urban North, materialistic values gained ascendancy. The symbols of manhood, sexual conquest, dominance of women etc., became important to black men because they lacked the real symbols -- political and economic power.

Thus we come to the real issue -- the manner in which the powerlessness of the black male in the structures of society has had a negative influence upon black male-female relationships and as a result upon the black family. What we have written here is a reminder of the awesome task before those who desire to minister to the father or fathers-to-be in black families. The work of Jesse Jackson of PUSH is essential. He has correctly challenged the black males to responsibility in the black family. But we must see this challenge in the context of the oppressive racial structures of the larger society. Black men and women must see their roles and rights in relation to each other as they seek to save the family.

3. THE BLACK CHILD

It is difficult to grow up today. Any child has extreme temptations and conflicts to confront. The black child faces unusual obstacles beyond the usual concerns of childhood. The remarkable fact is that we have such a large number of wonderful black youngsters.

Any problem affecting children in general can be greatly enlarged when seen in relation to the black child. The manner in which divorce relates to the welfare of children is a good example. All children are disturbed by the disruption of a stable family. When divorce is seen in relation to child custody and support, the black child receives a crushing blow. The increase in divorces means that more children live in single-parent households during their formative years both psychologically and socially.

A study released by the U.S. Census Bureau entitled "Divorce, Child Custody and Child Support" suggests that the nation's divorce rate has climbed from two per cent per 1,000 in 1940 to 5.1 per cent per 1,000 in 1976.[13] By 1978 some 19 per cent of families with children were maintained by one parent -- 17 per cent by the mother and two per cent by the father, up from 7.5 per cent by mothers and 1.1 per cent by fathers in 1960.

Black families were hit severely by this trend. The proportion of mother-only families grew from 21 per cent to 45 per cent between 1960 and 1978; among whites the increase was from six per cent to 13 per cent. Families maintained by father only in the same period grew from one per cent to 1.7 per cent among whites and from 2.3 per cent to 2.7 per cent among blacks.

The support issue is just as upsetting. Black women constituted 28 per cent of women eligible for child support, but only 12 per cent of these black women were actually receiving child support payments. The study showed that 45 per cent of divorced mothers who had finished college received child support; 29 per cent for high school graduates and 11 per cent for non-high school graduates. Given this account of the relationship of education to increased child support, it is logical to conclude that black women and their children were severely hit by this discrepancy.

This study gives a dismal pciture of the plight of the black child of divorced parents, but it is extremely limited. It does not treat the situation of unwed parents and their offspring. It does not take a look at the black child in foster homes or institutions. It does not deal with the black child in criminal institutions. The poor black child does not have the benefit of the best opportunities for reform and is often punished to the full extent of the law. The black child, especially males, are victims of police brutality and even killings. Others are exploited by their own people as dope peddlers and prostitutes. The plight of many black children is hard. The black child is in need of all the support that parents, relatives and churches can possibly give.

Two black psychiatrists, James P. Comer and Alvin F. Poussaint, have provided some useful perspectives on the black child in white America. The first problem discussed is how black children have had to cope with white oppression. They write:

> In the past, black children were taught the rituals of servitude and docility from the time they could talk. . . . Today the black child is still made to feel inferior to whites. From his earliest days he senses that his life is viewed cheaply by white society and that he enjoys little protection at its hands.[14]

Secondly, the black child must learn how to adapt to society in a manner to gain self-esteem. Comer and Poussaint continue:

> The black child has been forced to live in two cultures -- his own minority culture and the majority one. He has had to teach himself to contain his aggression around whites while freely expressing it among Blacks. Some people call this a survival technique.

Finally, the black child has had to resort to those tactics which are necessary for self-preservation. Comer and Poussaint observe:

> Over the years black children have become skilled in the use of a variety of techniques in their struggle for survival and well-being in a hostile and unjust society. They have had to learn to be practical as well as cunning. They have had to learn how to win some acceptance from belligerent

whites. Black children as a result have often assumed the responsibilities and burdens of adulthood at a far too early age. Many have had little of what we call a childhood. In the black world adolescence starts early in life, and unlike most white youngsters, many black children do not enjoy the luxury of a period of playtime and learning which extends into their late teens.[15]

4. FAMILY LIBERATION

What we are attempting to say here is related to how all the problems triggered by instituionalized racism affect the black child and the entire black family. Books and essays by white scholars are helpful as problems are expressed in individuals and families,[16] but they do not deal adequately with the structural evils in society. We do not have time to treat how neo-racism is crushing the life out of some of our best and brightest black youth in schools and colleges as well as in professional life. Our continuing concern will be to tell it like it is for black family members for a lifetime. While many white theologians are preoccupied with the unborn and the dying, the black theologian must be concerned about the abundant life for black folk between birth and death. Eternal life is a quality of life which the Christian begins in the new birth. It grows and continues into everlasting life. Black church theology provides a foundation for ministry to black men, women and children *now*.

We are convinced by our study and the assessment of the empirical reality of black life that the black church has as a primary task the strengthening of black families. While the liberation of black men, women and children, separately, must move forward, priority must be given to black families. Families are the "moral schools" for children. Our future as a people will be determined by how well we meet the needs of healthy black families. The relation of black families and churches is mutual. If the black church does not minister appropriately and urgently to black families, it will hasten its own death.

III. THE BLACK CHURCH AND FAMILY LIBERATION

Our entire study comes to its conclusion in this section. We have attempted in these pages to show how the black church's theological self-understanding can lay a foundation for ministry to black families. American families are in trouble. Black families, as part of a racially oppressed community, face an acute crisis. Black families face internal problems, but the external situation often outweighs the inner tensions.

Black Ministry

Another way of stating the case is to argue that sinful social structures aggravate the inner tensions to unmanageable proportions.

Since black families are the source of black church life and growth, the measure of its ministry to black families will determine the quality of its own mission. When the black church is viewed as a family in the proper understanding, all persons, whether married, single or divorced, will come to a sense of kinship in the church as the family of God. The church is the family under the lordship of Jesus Christ to whom all families in heaven and earth owe their substance and health. Let us hasten the day when the church will be a family and the family a domestic church. Then will God's kingdom be nearer than we have believed.

NOTES

1. <u>Los Angeles Times</u> (July 11, 1978). The account is among "Letters to the Times" and is titled: "Plans to Close Child Care Centers."

2. Michele Wallace, <u>Black Macho and the Myth of the Super-Woman</u> (New York: Dial, 1979). See especially Chapter 3 for her views on black women and "the myth of the superwoman."

3. <u>Ibid</u>., p. 167

4. <u>The Negro Family</u> (Chicago: University Press, 1969) pp. 93-94.

5. As reported by Bill Drummon in <u>Los Angeles Times</u> (May 22, 1978).

6. Wallace, Ibid.

7. Inez Smith Reid, "<u>Together</u>" Black Women (New York: Emerson Hall, 1972) Ch. II. Cf. R.G. Weisbard, <u>Genocide: Birth Control and the Black American</u> (New York: Greenwood Press, 1975).

8. <u>Ibid</u>, pp. 120-121.

9. Edward V. Stein, ed., <u>Fathering</u> (Nashville: Abingdon, 1977) p. 11 CF. William Raspberry, "Their Father Made the Difference," <u>Washington Post</u> (June 15, 1979). According to Raspberry, Lee Junious, a black father, uneducated, unemployed, divorced, manages to inspire four kids to excel in school.

10. Nathan Hare, "The Frustrated Masculinity of the Negro Male" in Robert Staples, ed., <u>The Black Family</u> (Belmont, California: Wadsworth, 1971) pp. 131-134.

11. "Sex and the Black Male," <u>Ebony</u> (August 1972) p. 115. This entire article is worth reading. Cf. Gwendolyn Cook, "Socialization of the Black Male" in Lawrence E. Gary, editor, <u>Social Research and the Black Community</u> (Washington, D.C.: Institute for Urban Affairs and Research, 1974) pp. 76-87.

12. Robert Staples, "The Myth of Black Macho: A Response to Angry Black Feminists," <u>Black Scholar</u> (March/April, 1979) p. 28. Brenda Daniels-Eichelberger, "Myths About Feminism," <u>Essence</u> (November 1978) pp. 74 f. Cf. Marguerete Ross Barnett, "Black Male-Female Relationship," <u>Washington Star</u> (July 1, 1979), a review of Michele Wallace, ibid. See also, Marcia Ann Gillespie, "Macho, Myths and Michele Wallace, "<u>Essence</u> (August 1979) pp. 76-102.

13. "Number of Children in Divorces Triples" in Los Angeles Times (Monday, July 2, 1979, Pt. I-19).

14. Black Child Care (New York: Simon and Schuster, 1975) p. 11.

15. Ibid., p. 12.

16. Cf. Howard J. and Charlotte Clinebell, Crisis and Growth: Helping Your Troubled Child (Philadelphia: Fortress, 1971). Some sources on black children and youth worth reading are: George B. Thomas, Young Black Adults (New York: Friendship, 1974); Andrew Billingsley and Jeanne M. Giovannoni, Children of the Storm (New York: Harcourt Brace Javonovich, 1972); Phyllis Harrison-Ross and Barbara Wyden, The Black Child (New York; Peter H. Wyden, 1974) and E. Franklin Frazier, Negro Youth at the Crossways (New York: Schocken, 1969).

TORONTO STUDIES IN THEOLOGY

1. Robert Ross, **The Non-Existence of God: Linguistic Paradox in Tillich's Thought**
2. Gustaf Wingren, **Creation and Gospel: The New Situation in European Theology**
3. John Meagher, **Clumsy Construction in Mark's Gospel: A Critique of** *Form-* **and** *Redaktionsgeschichte*
4. Patrick Primeaux, **Richard R. Niebuhr on Christ and Religion: The Four-Stage Development of His Theology**
5. Bernard Lonergan, **Understanding and Being: An Introduction and Companion to** *Insight*
Edited by Elizabeth Morelli and Mark D. Morelli
6. Geffrey Kelly and John Godsey, editors, **Ethical Responsibility: Bonhoeffer's Legacy to the Churches**
7. Darrell J. Fasching, **The Thought of Jacques Ellul: A Systematic Exposition**
8. Joseph T. Culliton, editor, **Non-Violence — Central to Christian Spirituality: Perspectives from Scripture to the Present**
9. Aaron Milavec, **To Empower as Jesus Did: Acquiring Spiritual Power Through Apprenticeship**
10. John Kirby and William Thompson, editors, **Voeglin and the Theologian: Ten Studies in Interpretation**
11. Thomas Day, **Dietrich Bonhoeffer on Christian Community and Common Sense**
12. James Deotis Roberts, **Black Theology Today: Liberation and Contextualization**
13. Walter G. Muelder, **The Ethical Edge of Christian Theology: Forty Years of Communitarian Personalism**
14. David Novak, **The Image of the Non-Jew in Judaism: An Historical and Constructive Study of the Noahide Laws**
15. Dan Liderbach, **The Theology of Grace and the American Mind: A Representation of Catholic Doctrine**

3 6877 00044 4132

DATE DUE

APR 21 '86			
AP 19 '90			
DE 06			

BT   107377
82.7
.R58   Roberts, J. Deotis.
1983   Black theology today

HIEBERT LIBRARY
Fresno Pacific College - M. B. Seminary
Fresno, Calif. 93702